World Economics As

I0069888

Book Series

Volume 1

The Economics Curriculum:
Towards a Radical Reformulation

Titles produced by the World Economics Association & College Publications

Piketty's *Capital in the Twenty-First Century*
Edward Fullbrook and Jamie Morgan, eds.

Volume 1
The Economics Curriculum: Towards a Radical reformulation
Maria Alejandra Maki and Jack Reardon, eds.

The **World Economics Association (WEA)** was launched on May 16, 2011. Already over 13,000 economists and related scholars have joined. This phenomenal success has come about because the WEA fills a huge gap in the international community of economists – the absence of a professional organization which is truly international and pluralist.

The World Economics Association seeks to increase the relevance, breadth and depth of economic thought. Its key qualities are worldwide membership and governance, and inclusiveness with respect to: (a) the variety of theoretical perspectives; (b) the range of human activities and issues which fall within the broad domain of economics; and (c) the study of the world's diverse economies.

The Association's activities centre on the development, promotion and diffusion of economic research and knowledge and on illuminating their social character.

The WEA publishes books, three journals (*Economic Thought, World Economic Review and Real-World Economics Review*), a bi-monthly newsletter, blogs, holds global online conferences, and is about to launch its Textbook Commentaries Project.

The Economics Curriculum:
Towards a Radical Reformulation

Edited by

Maria Alejandra Madi

and

Jack Reardon

ISBN 978-1-84890-165-0

Published by College Publications on behalf of the World Economics
Association
College Publications
Scientific Director: Dov Gabbay
Managing Director: Jane Spurr

http://www.collegepublications.co.uk

Cover design by Laraine Welch
Printed by Lightning Source, Milton Keynes, UK

The current volume is one of the outcomes from a conference on *The economics curriculum: towards a radical reformation*. It was led by Maria Alejandra Madi and Jack Reardon, David Wheat and Halyun Zhao and took place in May-June 2013. The volume is, appropriately, the first in our series. The problems and issues around the economics curriculum are among the most pressing ones in the profession. Moreover, their ramification spread throughout economies and societies.

We hope that the volume will make a contribution to the debate towards changing the curriculum and towards changing attitudes in mainstream economics. We are very grateful to Maria and Jack for developing this volume under particularly difficult circumstances.

Edward Fullbrook and Grazia Ietto-Gillies
October 2014

Website http://www.worldeconomicsassociation.org/

Executive committee

Juan Carlos Moreno Brid, Mexico, UN Economic Com. for
  Latin America and the Caribbean
C. P. Chandrasekhar, India, Jawaharlal Nehru University
Ping Chen, China, Peking University and Fudan University
Edward Fullbrook, UK, University of the West of England
James K. Galbraith, USA, University of Texas at Austin
Grazia Ietto-Gillies, Italy / UK, London South Bank University
Steve Keen, Australia, University of Western Sydney
Richard C. Koo, Japan, Nomura Research Institute
Tony Lawson, UK, Cambridge University
Peter Radford, USA, Radford Free Press
Dani Rodrik, USA, Harvard University

Acknowledgements

We are grateful to the World Economics Association for giving us the opportunity to lead an online conference on the economics curriculum (curriculumconference2013.worldeconomicsassociation.org) and to develop this book from it. We benefitted from many of the open comments that the conference attracted and we would like to thank the contributors to the debate: Paul Davidson, Grazia Ietto-Gillies, Roy Langston, Rahul Deodhar, Haiyun Zhao, Anieta Lewis, Sean Pascoe, Warwick Smith, John de Chadenedes, Olaf Schilgen, R. Kowalski, A. Barzey, Yeshitela Seifu, Anthony Barzey, Edward K. Ross, Dragoljub Stojanov, Andrea Micocci and Asad Zaman.

We gratefully acknowledge permission from the journal *Economic Thought* to reprint the paper "Should the History of Economic Thought be Included in Undergraduate Curricula?" written by Alessandro Roncaglia.

A special thanks to Grazia Ietto-Gillies, the Chair of the WEA Conference Programme. She has given us encouragement and support throughout the conference and the development of this book. She has commented and advised extensively on the structure of the book and on the Introduction and Conclusions chapters. This book would not have been possible without her friendly support.

The economics curriculum: towards a radical reformulation

Contents

Part One

Setting the scene

Introduction
Jack Reardon and Maria Alejandra Madi

1 Rethinking economics education

Alfred Marshall, in the eighth edition of his *Principles of Economics,* wrote that "economic conditions are constantly changing, and each generation looks at its own problems in its own way" (Marshall 1946 [1920]: v). Of course, all generations assume their problems are uniquely formidable, but a good case can be made that our problems, especially the cataclysmic consequences of global warming, intractable poverty and a growing disparity between the rich and poor – are formidably complex. It is hard, at least for us, to disagree that "we are living in a period of dramatic change – a period of chaos – where conventional structures, business and development outlooks, and even the human role on Earth are going through a period of controversy, questioning and change" (Kras, 2007: 47).

We add, with urgency, the failure of economics education to the list of our current problems. Economics education has failed to explain the existing economy; it has failed to help students understand capitalism and how it evolves; it has failed to solve long-standing problems such as poverty; it has failed to prepare students to solve the problems of the future especially global warming, which has become an outstanding problem of the present; it has failed to teach our students to listen, to dialogue, and to work with others. And economics education has failed to incorporate most of the intellectual developments in other disciplines, parrying them for the comfortable confines of 19th century Newtonian physics, "Think of the many revolutions in our understanding of the physical world which have occurred in the twentieth century: from Newtonian to Einsteinian physics; from Mendelian genetics to DNA and the human genome; from determinism to chaos theory. Any scientist from the nineteenth century would be bewildered by what is commonplace today in his discipline – save an economist" (Keen, 2001:169). Economics remains ensconced in the 19th century, providing students with a 19th century map for 21st century problems.

The failure of economics education explains the appearance of two ostensibly puzzling books – at least to outsiders – but very damning to the existing modus operandi of current economics education: Hill and Myatt's, *The Economics Anti-Textbook–A Critical Thinker's Guide to Microeconomics*, and Komlos', *What Every Economics Student Needs to Know and Doesn't Get in the Usual Principles Text."* Just their very titles suggest something deeply astray with economics education. Hill and Myatt write:

> "Our fundamental aim in writing the *Anti-Textbook* has been to provide economics students with the basic ideas with which they can begin to think critically about what they read in their textbooks . . . One needs to read with a critical eye, and to note what is omitted and what is unsupported" (2010: 254).

And Komlos:

> "The ideological commitment to market fundamentalism which led to excessive reliance on markets in the making of public policy, has brought us, in turn, to our current, precarious situation. I hope the present volume can help rectify this misconception and improve the teaching of economics by completing a more complete perspective" (2014: 3).

Imagine a textbook written for medical students that omits and misleads, and is hopelessly out of date causing a new anti-textbook to be written, correcting for errors? Wouldn't there be outrage, cause for alarm and even a revolution in medicine? That these two books needed to be written (and yes, they needed to be written) speaks volumes of what is wrong with economics education.

A longstanding problem with economics education is its goal to make students think like economists (as if we think alike) rather than enable students to think like global citizens to help solve our generation's problems. Rather than expose students to different viewpoints, neoclassical economics bullies students to accepting only one view as legitimate while disparaging other views as not economics (Fullbrook, 2009), while concomitantly "bullying, harassing, and threatening heterodox professors" (Lee, 2009: 222).

The monism intrinsic to neoclassical economics is antithetical to learning, and stifles curiosity. Monism ossifies its tenets and makes economics (and economists) obdurate to change. It is monism that has prevented economists from going back to the drawing board, so to speak, to revise and reconceptualize. It is monism that compelled Gregory Mankiw, shortly after the nadir of the recent financial crisis, to write, "We still have to teach the bread and butter issues, the gains from trade, supply and demand, the efficient properties of markets and so on. These topics will remain the bread and butter of introductory courses" (Mankiw, 2009). Ironically teaching these 'bread and butter issues' prevented us from seeing the crisis in the first place.

The failure of economics and economics education has led to clarion calls around the globe to reconceptualize and rethink economics. In 2001 French economics students petitioned their professors for a more realistic and pluralist teaching of economics:

> "Too often the lectures leave no place for reflection. Out of all the approaches to economic questions that exist, generally only one is presented to us. This approach is supposed to explain everything by means of a purely axiomatic process, as if this were THE economic truth. We do not accept this dogmatism. We want a pluralism of approaches, adapted to the complexity of the objects and to the uncertainty surrounding most of the big questions in economics (unemployment, inequalities, the place of financial markets, the advantages and disadvantages of free-trade, globalization, economic development, etc.)".

This call led to the development of the Post-Autistic Economics Network and eventually the World Economics Association.

In 2011 a student-led global movement to reconceptualize economics – Rethinking Economics (RT) – was formed. It is an umbrella organization of student groups from over thirty countries spread across six continents. The students of RT share dissatisfaction with the existing economics curriculum, not only how we teach but what we teach. They criticize neoclassical economics as monist, deductively abstract, not rooted in evidence, and unrelated to the world in which we live. According to the RT web page:

> "Economics as it is taught currently is **disconnected** from **real-world events** and policies. In many departments, much of the curricula in the last few decades have slowly lost all mention of contemporary events or facts. This means that students are not being equipped to engage in real-world debates. We believe economics graduates should be prepared to consider and react to the economic problems that the world faces, because societies are shaped by economic events and policies, which are in turn shaped by people's understandings of economics" (Rethinking Economics, 2014).

Central to RT's mission is their call for pluralism:

> "In most courses 'economics' is shorthand for "neoclassical economics". There is no recognition of the variety of schools of thought within economics, across history or across the world. Academic integrity requires that alternative economic theories be introduced to students, alongside those currently taught. Economic questions cannot necessarily be answered adequately from a single theoretical standpoint or solely from a mathematical approach" (Rethinking Economics, 2014).

It isn't our goal to replace the monism of neoclassical economics with the monism of heterodoxy, which is often no different from the adamancy, recalcitrance and arrogance of neoclassical economics, especially in their treatment of outsiders. Indeed it is well-known that "disciplines are like tribes, they have a specific culture and specific habits, norms and rules, and they do not easily accept outsiders" (Weehuizen, 2007: 165). Rather our goal is to fundamentally reconceptualize economics education, so that it is pluralist, enables understanding of our world, and actively engages with other disciplines. The closed borders hermetically sealing economics from other disciplines is no longer acceptable.

In rethinking economics and economics education it is important not just to map out goals and strategies but also to ascertain any obstacles along the way, as well as the vested interests in propping up and perpetuating such obstacles. Edward Fullbrook noted a formidable and intricately interconnected nexus of obstacles consisting of "the basic institutions of neoclassical economics: university departments, associations, journals, classification systems, economics 101 textbooks, and its basic narrative [which] collectively and interactively block any effort at meaningful reform (Fullbrook, 2010: 95). He explained that "this intransigence and insuperability stems from the fact that as institutions, although independently constituted, they are interlocking and their characteristics inter-determined" (Fullbrook, 2010: 95).

A common interwoven element in this nexus of obstacles is economics education: we can't understand the call for pluralism if existing economics education is monist; we can't understand the call for reformation if current textbooks exhort that economics is as good as it gets, and that only tinkering around the edges is necessary – a little less chalk and more talk. We can't understand the call for reformation if economics isolates itself from other disciplines and parries developments in other fields.

Call it a reconceptualization, a rethinking, a revolution, but whatever it is, it must be a global concerted effort. None of us can change economics education on our own; on the contrary solitary efforts are doomed to failure: to be quickly sniffed out and summarily extirpated. We need to engage on multiple fronts with simultaneous entry points with as many people as possible from all parts of the globe, as the RT exhorts, "individual departments are not the cause of the problem. It is difficult for any individual economist or department to act independently of others. We need to take the lead by pushing for reform together, within and across countries" (Rethinking Economics, 2014).

It is within this spirit of global effort at fundamental change in economics education that we offer this volume. We hope that not only will this book directly contribute to rethinking economics but also lead to direct change in the economics curriculum. The call for reform has been eloquently and persuasively made; this volume represents one small step in the call to action.

2 An overview of papers in this volume

After the *Introduction* that lays the background and conceptual foundation for the rest of the book, Part Two – *Challenging the current economics curriculum* – includes contributions related to the evidence on what is wrong with the existing economics education. The objective is to discuss issues such as: What are the some of the main critiques of current practices on theory, methods and structures?

The first chapter, by Lars Palsson Syll, highlights that many of the standard assumptions made in neoclassical economic theory are not possible to make more realistic by de-idealization or successive approximations without altering the theory and its models fundamentally. The author presents three examples from neoclassical economics textbooks – on wage rigidities, the law of demand and revealed preferences – to warrant the assertion that some of the model assumptions made by neoclassical economics are restrictive – rather than harmless – and a *fortiori* cannot in any sensible meaning be considered approximations at all.

In Chapter 2, Asad Zasman explores the disastrous consequence that resulted from this deification of science and emphasizes that before talking about curriculum change, we must redeem our souls. How can this be done? The first step in curriculum change requires the creation of teachers who have a clear understanding of the challenge that we face in order to rethink the nature of human beings and of human knowledge. In this attempt, there is the need to overcome the market mentality and rethink morality in economics.

Part Three – *Current gaps in economics curriculum* – includes contributions related to what is missing in the current economics curriculum. The aim is to identify and suggest solutions for current gaps in the curriculum. This chapter will address specific areas: varieties of methodologies, history of economic thought, modern economies and firms, finance and economic policy.

In Chapter 3, Sheila Dow argues that methodology should be in the core of the economics curriculum since methodology allows students to understand why different approaches to economics exist and how we might analyse and foster constructive communication between them. Dow addresses that changes in economics curriculum are particularly challenging for teachers. As a result, to achieve any reform, some transitional programme would be required to raise the methodological awareness and knowledge of teaching staff.

Chapter 4, by Alessandro Roncaglia, aims to emphasise the importance of history of economic thought when existence of different approaches to economics is recognized. As an illustration, classical and marginalist conceptualizations of the economy are briefly discussed. The relevance of HET (History of Economic Thought) is mainly founded on the openness to confrontation with different points of view, absence of definitive truths but consciousness of degrees of superior or inferior quality in economic analysis.

In Chapter 5, Grazia Ietto-Gillies begins with the provocative assertion that TNCs have very little impact on today's economics curriculum. Ietto-Gillies also highlights that an understanding of modern economies cannot be arrived at without an understanding of how TNCs operate and argues for the relevance of inclusion of such a study for both the micro and macro curriculum.

Chapter 6, by Maria Alejandra Madi, addresses that economics education in the 21st century presupposes the recognition of the subject – the economic systems in transformation. Madi aims to show that an understanding of modern economies cannot be obtained without a real world approach to financial issues and their outcomes in terms of market regulation. Her proposal includes four main topics to be considered in any economics curriculum reform- financial instability, financial dynamics and the labor market, banking dynamics, financial regulation.

In Chapter 7, Nicola Acocella explores the evolution and challenges of teaching economic policy in Italy and highlights the differences with that part of Continental Europe, in particular in Scandinavian countries, the Netherlands and Austria. Indeed, in his opinion Economic Policy in Italy was mainly built as a discipline by collecting innovations produced abroad in various areas, but with scarce additional personal research. After discussing the developments of the discipline in Italy, Acocella analyzes why developments of Economic Policy in Italy and other countries had a limited impact on teaching in Europe (and elsewhere) and discusses some factors that could facilitate its diffusion in the next years.

Part Four – *Laying the foundations for a future economics curriculum* – emphasizes what economics major should know and the need for trans-disciplinary and interdisciplinary work. Chapter 8, written by David Hemenway, discusses five ideas that are usually not well-covered in economic textbooks: 1. People are not solitary creatures, but social animals; 2. Tastes are malleable and particularly so for children and adolescents; 3. There are lots of children and adolescents in the world (though few in economic textbooks); 4. Retail purchasers rarely have detailed information about the products they buy; 5. Large corporations (and other economic institutions) often have a substantial social and political power. These ideas are discussed generally and illustrated with respect to the market for cigarettes.

In Chapter 9, Arturo Hermann's contribution analyses how, within a pluralistic and interdisciplinary perspective, a number of heterodox theories can help us to identify significant aspects of the concepts of market and capitalism. In his work, the author highlights the importance of an interdisciplinary approach for reaching out the manifold aspects of these concepts and, on this basis, to identify suitable policies for our most urgent economic and social problems. Hermann mainly focuses on the psychoanalytic perspective in elucidating many aspects of the person-society dynamics, with particular attention on how it can improve the process of policy action.

In Chapter 10, Paul Ormerod proposes a fairly root and branch reform of the curriculum. Inevitably, quite a lot of things from the standard curriculum would have to give. Among the main reforms that Ormerod would make, he explores the teaching of macroeconomics through the perspective of important episodes in economic history; the teaching of modern simulation software which enables behaviour out of equilibrium to be explored; the teaching of alternative models of agent decision making and the teaching of network theory.

Chapter 11, by Constantine Passaris, points out the pedagogical fault lines on the contemporary economic neoclassical landscape and proposes a new model for economic pedagogy and for the professional preparation of future economists. After describing the errors and omissions in the academic training of contemporary economists, Passaris suggests specific remedies and solutions towards enhancing the efficacy of the economics curriculum. In her opinion, the process of modernizing the economics curriculum requires building intellectual bridges with the new global economy, enhancing historical content, acknowledging the academic value of interdisciplinarity, embracing academic mentorship, internationalizing the curriculum and redefining the role of quantitative economics.

At the end of Part Four, Jack Reardon's contribution in Chapter 12 discusses the problems of current economics education and explores solutions founded on a pluralist approach. Reardon establishes the prerequisites for a radical reformation in the economics major and presents the main guidelines of a curriculum proposal: 1. Year One: exclusively devoted to prerequisites; no economics course taken. 2. Year Two: Political Economy, Money and Credit. 3. Year Three: Focus on Poverty 4. Year Four: Focus on Environmental Sustainability and Global Warming. In his opinion, we need a holistic pluralism that goes beyond the traditional disciplines.

References

Fullbrook, E. (2009) 'The Meltdown and Economics Textbooks', In: Reardon, J. (ed.), *The Handbook of Pluralist Economics Education*, Routledge: London, pp.17–23.

Fullbrook, E. (2010) "How to Bring Economics into the 3rd millennium by 2020", *Real-World Economics Review*, issue no. 54, http://www.paecon.net/PAEReview/issue54/Kessler54.pdf

Hill, R. and Myatt, T. (2010) *The Economics Anti-Textbook–A Critical Thinker's Guide to Microeconomics*, London: Zed Books.

Keen, S. (2011) *Debunking Economics*, London: Zed Books.

Komlos, J. (2004) *What Every Economics Student Needs to Know and Doesn't Get in the Usual Principles Text,* Armonk, New York: M.E. Sharpe.

Kras, E. (2007) *The Blockage: Rethinking Organizational Principles for the 21st Century*, Baltimore, Maryland: American Literary Press.

Lee, F. (2009) *A History of Heterodox Economics - Challenging the Mainstream in the Twentieth Century*, London, Routledge.

Mankiw, N. G. (2009) 'That Freshman Course Won't Be the Same', *New York Times*, http://www.nytimes.com/2009/05/24/business/economy/24view.html. May 24, Accessed May 24, 2009.

Rethinking Economics (2014) *Our vision: A direction for the reform of economics education,* http://www.rethinkeconomics.org/#!our-vision/colf

Weehuizen, R. (2007) 'Interdisciplinarity and Problem-based Learning in Economics Education, The Case of Infonomics' In: Groenewgen, John (ed.) *Teaching Pluralism in Economics*, Cheltenham, UK: Edward Elgar, pp. 155-188.

Part Two

Challenging the current economics curriculum

CHAPTER 1

Economics textbooks – anomalies and transmogrification of truth

Lars Pålsson Syll

1   Introduction

Models describe or depict specific parts of a target system, usually the real world. All theories and models have to use sign vehicles to convey some kind of content that may be used for saying something about the target system. But purpose-built assumptions – like "rational expectations" or "representative actors" – made solely to enable reaching deductively validated results in mathematical models, are of little value if they cannot be validated outside of the model.

All empirical sciences use simplifying or unrealistic assumptions in their models, which is acceptable, as long as the assumptions made are not unrealistic in the wrong way or for the wrong reasons. Being able to model a "credible world" – a world somewhat similar to the real world, is not equivalent to actually investigating the real world. Even though all theories and models are false, since they simplify, they may still possibly serve our pursuit of truth. But then they cannot be unrealistic or false in any way; the falsehood has to be qualified.

Some of the standard assumptions made in neoclassical economic theory – rationality, information handling and types of uncertainty – cannot be made more realistic by de-idealization or successive approximations without altering the theory and its models fundamentally. Economic theory cannot just provide an economic model that mimics the economy. Theory is important, but we can't start to question data when there is a discrepancy. This would presuppose an almost religious faith in the validity of the preferred theory. When the relation between map and reality is poor, we have to redraw the map.

15

If we cannot show that the mechanisms or causes we isolate and handle in our models are stable, i.e., when we export them from models to target systems they do not change from one situation to another, then they only hold under *ceteris paribus* conditions and *a fortiori* are of limited value for our understanding, explanation and prediction of our real world target system.

The obvious shortcoming of the basically epistemic − rather than ontological − neoclassical modeling is that similarity or resemblance *tout court* does not guarantee that the correspondence between model and target is interesting, relevant, revealing or adequate in terms of mechanisms, causal powers, capacities or tendencies. No matter how many convoluted refinements of concepts made in the model, if the successive approximations do not result in models similar to reality in terms of structure, isomorphism, etc. − the surrogate system becomes a substitute system that does not bridge to the world but rather misses its target.

Constructing "minimal macroeconomic models" or using economic models as "stylized facts" or "stylized pictures" somehow successively approximating economic reality, is a rather unimpressive attempt at legitimizing using fictitious idealizations for reasons more to do with model tractability than with a genuine interest of understanding and explaining features of real economies. Many of the model assumptions made by neoclassical economics are *restrictive* rather than *harmless* and could *a fortiori* not be considered approximations at all.

Below I will give three examples from neoclassical principles of economics textbooks − revealed preferences, the law of demand, and wage rigidities − amply justifying this rather harsh judgment. In doing this, I also hope to contribute to the ongoing and necessary work on constructing a deprogramming manual for survivors of undergraduate courses in neoclassical economics.

2   Revealed preferences and the revolution that was called off

In 1938 Paul Samuelson offered a replacement for the then accepted cardinal theory of utility, "The discrediting of utility as a psychological concept robbed it of its possible virtue as an explanation of human behaviour in other than a circular sense, revealing its emptiness as even a construction" (1938: 61). According to Samuelson, the ordinalist revision of utility theory was, however, not drastic enough. The introduction of the concept of a marginal rate of substitution was considered "an artificial convention in the explanation of price behavior" (1938: 62). One ought to analyze the consumer's behaviour without having recourse to the concept of utility at all, since this did not correspond to directly observable phenomena. The old theory was criticized mainly from a methodological point of view, in that it used non-observable concepts and propositions.

The new theory should avoid this and thereby shed "the last vestiges of utility analysis" (1938: 62). Its main feature was a consistency postulate which said "if an individual selects batch one over batch two, he does not at the same time select two over one" (1938: 65). From this "perfectly clear" postulate and the assumptions of given demand functions and that all income is spent, Samuelson in (1938) and (1938a), could derive all the main results of ordinal utility theory (single-valuedness and homogeneity of degree zero of demand functions, and negative semi-definiteness of the substitution matrix).

In 1948 Samuelson no longer considered his "revealed preference" new. It was then seen as a means of revealing consistent preferences and enhancing the acceptability of the ordinary ordinal utility theory by showing how one could construct an individual's indifference map by purely observing his market behaviour. Samuelson argued that "[t]he whole theory of consumer's behavior can thus be based upon operationally meaningful foundations in terms of revealed preference" (1948: 251). As has been recently shown, however, this is true only if we inter alia assume the consumer to be rational with unchanging preferences that are complete, asymmetrical, non-satiated, strictly convex, and transitive (or continuous). The theory, originally intended as a substitute for the utility theory, has, as Houthakker clearly notes, "tended to become complementary to the latter" (1950: 159).

Shortly thereafter, Samuelson argued that he was able "to complete the programme begun a dozen years ago of arriving at the full empirical implications for demand behaviour of the most general ordinal utility analysis" (1950: 369). The introduction of Houthakker's amendment assured integrability, and thus bringing the theory "to a close" (1950: 355). Starting "from a few logical axioms of demand consistency ... [one] could derive the whole of the valid utility analysis as corollaries" (1950: 370). Since Samuelson had shown the "complete logical equivalence" of revealed preference theory with the regular "ordinal preference approach," it follows that "in principle there is nothing to choose between the formulations" (1953: 1). According to Houthakker (1961: 709), the aim of the revealed preference approach is "to formulate equivalent systems of axioms on preferences and on demand functions."

But if this is all, what has revealed preference theory achieved? As it turns out, ordinal utility theory and revealed preference theory are – as Wong puts it – "not two different theories; at best, they are two different ways of expressing the same set of ideas" (2006: 118). And with regard to the theoretically solvable problem, we may still concur with Hicks that "there is in practice no direct test of the preference hypothesis" (1956: 58).

Sippel's experiments showed "a considerable number of violations of the revealed preference axioms" (1997: 1442) and thus as a theory of consumer behaviour that the revealed preference theory is of very limited value.

Today proponents of revealed preference theory have jettisoned the original attempt at building a theory on nothing but observable facts, and settled instead on the 1950s version of establishing "logical equivalences." Mas-Collel et al. note that "for the special case in which choice is defined for all subsets of X [the set of alternatives], a theory based on choice satisfying the weak axiom is completely equivalent to a theory of decision making based on rational preferences" (1995: 14). Kreps (1990: 30) holds a similar view, noting that revealed preference theory is "consistent with the standard preference-based theory of consumer behavior".

The theory of consumer behavior has been developed in order to justify a downward-sloping demand curve. While forerunners like Cournot (1838) and Cassel (1899) merely *asserted* this law of demand, the utility theorists tried to *deduce* it from axioms and postulates on individuals' economic behaviour.

Revealed preference theory tried to build a new theory and to put it in operational terms, but ended up producing a logically equivalent theory to the old one. As such it also shares its shortcomings of empirically nonfalsifiable and based on unrestricted universal statements.

As Kornai (1971: 133) remarked, "the theory is empty, tautological. The theory reduces to the statement that in period t the decision-maker chooses what he prefers ... The task is to explain *why* he chose precisely this alternative rather than another one." Further, pondering Amartya Sen's verdict of the revealed preference theory as essentially underestimating "the fact that man is a social animal and his choices are not rigidly bound to his own preferences only" (1982: 66) and Georgescu-Roegen's (1966: 192-3) apt description, a harsh assessment of what the theory accomplished should come as no surprise:

> "Lack of precise definition should not ... disturb us in moral sciences, but improper concepts constructed by attributing to man faculties which he actually does not possess, should. And utility is such an improper concept ... [P]erhaps, because of this impasse ... some economists consider the approach offered by the theory of choice as a great progress ... This is simply an illusion, because even though the postulates of the theory of choice do not use the terms 'utility' or 'satisfaction', their discussion and acceptance require that they should be translated into the other vocabulary ... A good illustration of the above point is offered by the ingenious theory of the consumer constructed by Samuelson".

Nothing lost, nothing gained!

When talking of determining people's preferences through observation, Hal Varian in his intermediate microeconomics textbook, for example, has "to *assume* that the preferences will remain unchanged" and adopts "the convention that ... the underlying preferences ... are known to be strictly convex." He further *postulates* that the "consumer is an optimizing consumer." If we are "willing to add more *assumptions* about consumer preferences, we get more precise estimates about the shape of indifference curves" (2006: 119-123, author's italics). Given these assumptions, and that the observed choices satisfy the consistency postulate as amended by Houthakker, one can always construct preferences that "could have generated the observed choices." This does not, however, prove that the constructed preferences actually generated the observed choices since "we can only show that observed behavior is not inconsistent with the statement. We can't prove that the economic model is correct."

The case of revealed preference theory is a splendid example of unsuccessful attempts by neoclassical economics to deduce a law of demand from the neoclassical postulates of rational choice – and of the rather intellectually dishonest efforts at shoving foundational problems under the rug in mainstream economics textbooks.

3   The Law of Demand and the Sonnenschein-Mantel-Debreu theorem

As is well-known, Keynes criticized neoclassical economics for making the *fallacy of composition*, which basically consists of the false belief that the whole is nothing but the sum of its parts. Keynes argued that this was not so, and that *a fortiori* an adequate analysis of society and economy couldn't proceed by just adding up the acts and decisions of individuals. The whole is more than a sum of parts. A good example is the neoclassical justification for the existence of *The Law of Demand* – when the price of a commodity falls, the demand for it will increase – on the aggregate.

In a widely used undergraduate economics textbook, we read:

> "Because the quantity demanded falls as the price rises and
> rises as the price falls, we say that the quantity demanded is
> negatively related to the price. This relationship between
> price and quantity demanded is true for most goods in the
> economy and, in fact, is so pervasive that economists call it
> the law of demand: other things equal, when the price of a
> good rises, the quantity demanded of the good falls, and
> when the price falls, the quantity demanded rises... To

analyse how markets work, we need to determine the market demand, which is the sum of all the individual demands for a particular good or service... The market demand curve shows how the total quantity demanded of a good varies as the price of the good varies, while all the other factors that affect how much consumers want to buy, such as income and taste, amongst other things, are held constant" (Mankiw and Taylor, 2011: 70-71).

But although we can succeed in establishing the law of demand for an individual, it was firmly established in 1976 with in the *Sonnenschein-Mantel-Debreu theorem* – that it isn't possible to extend The Law of Demand to the market, unless one makes ridiculously unrealistic assumptions such as individuals having *homothetic preferences* – which implies that all individuals have *identical* preferences. This is only conceivable if there is only one actor – the (in)famous *representative actor*. So, yes, it is possible to generalize The Law of Demand – as long as we assume that on the aggregate level there is only one commodity and one actor. Is this reasonable? Of course not. Once again, pure nonsense!

How has neoclassical economics reacted to this devastating finding? Judging from how Mankiw, Taylor and myriads of other neoclassical economists, basically by looking the other way, ignoring it and hoping that no one sees that the emperor is naked.

Having perused some of the most frequently used neoclassical textbooks of economics at the undergraduate level, I can only conclude that the presented models try to describe and analyze complex and heterogeneous real economies with a single rational-expectations-robot-imitation-representative-agent. That is, with something that has absolutely nothing to do with reality; and not even amenable to the general equilibrium analysis since Hugo Sonnenschein (1972), Rolf Mantel (1976) and Gérard Debreu (1974) *unequivocally* showed that there did not exist any condition by which assumptions on individuals would guarantee either stability nor uniqueness of the equilibrium solution.

So what modern economics textbooks present to students are really models built on the assumption that an entire economy can be validly modeled as a representative actor. Of course one could say that it is too difficult on undergraduate levels to prove this and defer to master and doctoral courses. It could justifiably be reasoned that way – if what you teach your students is true, if The Law of Demand is generalizable to the market level and the representative actor is a valid modeling abstraction! But in this case it's demonstrably known to be false, and therefore is nothing but scandalous intellectual dishonesty, like telling your students that 2 + 2 = 5 and hope that they will never run into Peano's axioms of arithmetics.

For almost forty years neoclassical economics itself has lived with a theorem that shows the impossibility of extending the microanalysis of consumer behaviour to the macro level (unless making patently and admittedly insane assumptions). Still after all these years pretending in their textbooks that this theorem does not exist – none of the textbooks I investigated even mention the existence of the Sonnenschein-Mantel-Debreu theorem – is really outrageous.

Almost a century and a half after Léon Walras founded neoclassical general equilibrium theory, when economists still have not been able to show that markets *move* economies *to* equilibria. What we do know is that unique Pareto-efficient equilibria do *exist.* But what good does that do? As long as we cannot show, except under exceedingly unrealistic assumptions that forces exist which lead economies to equilibria – the value of general equilibrium theory is next to nil. As long as we cannot demonstrate that forces operate under reasonable, relevant and at least mildly realistic conditions to move markets to equilibria, there is no reason to takje this 'theory' seriously.

Simply assuming the problem away or continuing to model a world full of agents behaving as economists – "often wrong, but never uncertain" – and still not being able to show that the system under reasonable assumptions converges to equilibrium, is a gross misallocation of intellectual resources and time. Getting around Sonnenschein-Mantel-Debreu using representative agents may be very expedient from a purely formalistic point of view. But from a scientific point of view it is hardly relevant or realistic.

In microeconomics we know that (ideal) aggregation really presupposes homothetic (identical preferences) something that almost never exist in real economies – if they do, it means that you and multi-billionaire Richard Branson have the same preferences. However, if these patently unreal assumptions are *not* fulfilled, there is no guarantee of a straightforward and constant relation between individuals (micro) and aggregates (macro). The results given by these assumptions are *a fortiori* not robust and do not capture the underlying mechanisms in the real economy. And as if this impossibility of ideal aggregation was not enough, there are obvious problems with the microeconomic equilibrium that one tries to reduce macroeconomics to. Decisions of consumption and production are described as choices made by a single agent. But then, who sets the prices on the market? And how do we justify the assumption of universal consistency between the choices? Models critically based on particular and odd assumptions – and are neither robust nor congruent to real world economies – are of questionable value.

4 On Keynes and wage rigidity

Among intermediate neoclassical macroeconomics textbooks, Charles Jones's textbook *Macroeconomics* (2010) is perhaps one of the better alternatives. Unfortunately it also contains utter nonsense. In a chapter on "The Labor Market, Wages, and Unemployment" Jones writes:

> "The point of this experiment is to show that *wage rigidities* can lead to large movements in employment. Indeed, they are the reason John Maynard Keynes gave, in *The General Theory of Employment, Interest, and Money* (1936), for the high unemployment of the Great Depression" (Jones, 2010: 187).

Although Keynes in *General Theory* devoted substantial attention to wage rigidities, he certainly never argued that wage rigidities were "the reason ... for the high unemployment of the Great Depression."

Since unions/workers, contrary to classical assumptions, make wage-bargains in nominal terms, they will – according to Keynes – accept lower real wages caused by higher prices, but resist lower real wages caused by lower nominal wages. However Keynes argued it is incorrect to attribute "cyclical" unemployment to this diversified agent behaviour. During the Depression, money wages fell significantly and – as Keynes noted – unemployment still increased. Thus, even when nominal wages decrease, they do not reduce unemployment.

In any specific labour market, lower wages could, of course, increase the demand for labour. But a general reduction in money wages would leave real wages more or less unchanged. The reasoning of the classical economists was, according to Keynes, a flagrant example of the *fallacy of composition*. Assuming that since unions/workers in a specific labour market could negotiate real wage reductions -via lowering nominal wages- unions/workers in general could do the same.

At the macro level wage cuts increase the risk of more unemployment. It's an *atomistic fallacy* to think that a policy of general wage cuts could strengthen the economy. On the contrary, the aggregate effects of wage cuts would, according to Keynes, be catastrophic, starting a cumulative spiral of lower prices that would make the real debts of individuals and firms increase since the nominal debts would not be affected by the general price and wage decrease. In an economy that more and more has come to rest on increased debt and borrowing this would be the entrance-gate to a debt deflation crises with decreasing investments and higher unemployment, bringing a depression.

So, lowering nominal wages would not clear the labour market. Lowering wages – and possibly prices – could, perhaps, lower interest rates and increase investment. But to Keynes it would be much easier to achieve that effect by increasing the money supply. In any case, wage reductions was not seen by Keynes as a general substitute for an expansionary monetary or fiscal policy. Even if potentially positive impacts of lowering nominal wages exist, there are also more heavily weighing negative impacts – management-union relations deteriorating, expectations of on-going lowering of nominal *wages causing delay of investments, debt deflation, etc.*

Keynes actually argued in *The General Theory*, that the classical proposition that lowering nominal wages would lower unemployment and, ultimately, take economies out of depressions, was ill-founded and basically wrong. To Keynes, flexible nominal wages would only make things worse by leading to erratic price-fluctuations. The basic explanation for unemployment is insufficient aggregate demand, which is mostly determined outside the labor market.

To neoclassical theory unemployment is voluntary, since it is only adjustments of the hours of work that these optimizing agents make to maximize their utility. Keynes on the other hand writes in *General Theory*:

> "The classical school [maintains that] while the demand for labour at the existing money-wage may be satisfied before everyone willing to work at this wage is employed, this situation is due to an open or tacit agreement amongst workers not to work for less, and that if labour as a whole would agree to a reduction of money-wages more employment would be forthcoming. If this is the case, such unemployment, though apparently involuntary, is not strictly so, and ought to be included under the above category of 'voluntary' unemployment due to the effects of collective bargaining, etc ... The classical theory ... is best regarded as a theory of distribution in conditions of full employment. So long as the classical postulates hold good, unemployment, which is in the above sense involuntary, cannot occur. Apparent unemployment must, therefore, be the result either of temporary loss of work of the 'between jobs' type or of intermittent demand for highly specialised resources or of the effect of a trade union 'closed shop' on the employment of free labour. Thus writers in the classical tradition, overlooking the special assumption underlying their theory, have been driven inevitably to the conclusion, perfectly logical on their assumption, that apparent unemployment (apart from the admitted exceptions) must be due at bottom to a refusal by the unemployed factors to accept a reward which corresponds to their marginal productivity ...

Obviously, however, if the classical theory is only applicable to the case of full employment, it is fallacious to apply it to the problems of involuntary unemployment – if there be such a thing (and who will deny it?). The classical theorists resemble Euclidean geometers in a non-Euclidean world who, discovering that in experience straight lines apparently parallel often meet, rebuke the lines for not keeping straight – as the only remedy for the unfortunate collisions which are occurring. Yet, in truth, there is no remedy except to throw over the axiom of parallels and to work out a non-Euclidean geometry. Something similar is required to-day in economics. We need to throw over the second postulate of the classical doctrine and to work out the behaviour of a system in which involuntary unemployment in the strict sense is possible" (Keynes, 1936 [1964], chapter 2).

Unfortunately, similar distortions of Keynes's views can be found in textbooks of the "New Keynesian" – a grotesque misnomer. How is this possible? Probably because these economists have but a very superficial acquaintance with Keynes's own works, and rather depend on second-hand sources like Hansen, Samuelson, Hicks and the likes. Fortunately there is a solution to the problem. Keynes's books are still in print. Read them!

5 Conclusion

Economics textbooks often have an introductory chapter where it is explained "how economists think" and why the use of models is so proliferate in economics. In Mankiw's *Macroeconomics* (2001) we read:

"Young children learn much about the world around them by playing with toy versions of real objects. For instance, they often put together models of cars, trains, or planes. These models are far from realistic, but the model-builder learns a lot from them nonetheless. The model illustrates the essence of the real object it is designed to resemble... Economists also use **models** to understand the world, but

> an economist's model is more likely to be made of symbols and equations than plastic and glue. Economists build their 'toy economies' to help explain economic variables ... They are useful because they help us to dispense with irrelevant details and to focus on important connections ... How should we react to the model's lack of realism? ... The art in economics is in judging when a simplifying assumption ... clarifies our thinking and when it mislead us. Simplification is a necessary part of building a useful model ... Yet models lead to incorrect conclusions if they assume away features of the economy that are crucial to the issue at hand ... When using a model to address a question, the economist must keep in mind the underlying assumptions and judge if they are reasonable for studying the matter at hand" (Mankiw, 2001: 6, 7, 10-11).

When pursuing today's more widely used economics textbooks, it turns out that the theories and models presented are imaginary worlds where the descriptions made are extremely tenuous and to a large degree disconnected to the specific contexts of the targeted system than one (usually) wants to (partially) represent.

This is not by chance. These closed formalistic-mathematical theories and models are constructed for the purpose of being able to deliver purportedly rigorous deductions that may somehow be exportable to the target system. By analyzing a few causal factors in their "laboratories" they hope they can perform "thought experiments" and observe how these factors operate on their own and without impediments or confounders. Unfortunately, this is not so, since economic causes never act in a socio-economic vacuum. Causes have to be set within a context to be operational, and for this a structure has to take a specific form, but instead of incorporating structures that are true to the target system, the settings made in economic models are based on formalistic mathematical tractability.

In the textbook models presented they appear as unrealistic assumptions, usually playing a decisive role in getting the deductive machinery to deliver "precise" and "rigorous" results. This, of course, makes exporting to real world target systems problematic, since these models – as part of a deductivist covering-law tradition in economics – are thought to deliver general and far-reaching conclusions that are externally valid.

But how can we be sure the lessons learned in these theories and models have external validity, when based on highly specific unrealistic assumptions? As a rule, the more specific and concrete the structures, the less generalizable the results. Admitting that we *in principle* can move from (partial) falsehoods in theories and models to truth in real world target systems does not take us very far, unless a thorough explication of the relation between theory, model, and the real world target system is made. If models *assume* identical preferences, representative actors, rational expectations, market clearing and equilibrium, and we *know* that real people and markets cannot be expected to obey these assumptions, the warrants for supposing that conclusions or hypothesis of causally relevant mechanisms or regularities can be bridged, are obviously non-justifiable. To have a deductive warrant for things happening in a closed model is no guarantee for them being preserved when applied to an open real world target system.

Economics textbook writers ought to do some ontological reflection and heed Keynes's (1936 [1964]: 297) warnings on using laboratory thought-models in economics:

> "The object of our analysis is, not to provide a machine, or method of blind manipulation, which will furnish an infallible answer, but to provide ourselves with an organized and orderly method of thinking out particular problems; and, after we have reached a provisional conclusion by isolating the complicating factors one by one, we then have to go back on ourselves and allow, as well as we can, for the probable interactions of the factors amongst themselves. This is the nature of economic thinking. Any other way of applying our formal principles of thought (without which, however, we shall be lost in the wood) will lead us into error."

If not, we will have to keep on wondering on what planet these textbook writing economists are living.

References

Cassel, G. (1899) 'Grundriss einer elementaren Preislehre', *Zeitschrift für die gesamte Staatswissenschaft,* 55.3: 395-458.

Cournot, A. (1838) *Recherches sur les principles mathématiques de la théorie des richesses.* Paris. Translated by Bacon, N. T. (1897), as *Researches into the Mathematical Principles of the Theory of Wealth.* New York: The Macmillan Company.

Debreu, G. (1974) 'Excess demand functions', *Journal of Mathematical Economics* 1: 15–21.

Georgescu-Roegen, N. (1966) 'Choice, Expectations, and Measurability', In: *Analytical Economics: Issues and Problems.* Cambridge, Massachusetts: Harvard University Press.

Hicks, J. (1956) *A Revision of Demand Theory.* Oxford: Clarendon Press.

Houthakker, H. (1950) 'Revealed Preference and the Utility Function', *Economica* 17 (May): 159-74.

Houthakker, H. (1961) 'The Present State of Consumption Theory', *Econometrica,* 29 (October): 704-40.

Jones, C. I. (2010) *Macroeconomics: economic crisis update.* [Updated ed.], International student ed., New York: W. W. Norton.

Keynes, J. M. (1964 [1936]) *The General Theory of Employment, Interest, and Money.* London: Harcourt Brace Jovanovich.

Keynes, J. M (1979) *The collected writings of John Maynard Keynes. Vol. 29,* 'The general theory and after: a supplement'. London: Macmillan.

Kornai, J. (1971) *Anti-equilibrium.* London: North-Holland.

Kreps, D. (1990) *A Course in Microeconomic Theory.* New York: Harvester Wheatsheaf.

Mankiw, G. (2001) *Macroeconomics.* Worth Publishers. 5th ed.

Mankiw, G. and Taylor, M. (2011) *Economics.* Andover: South-Western Cengage Learning. 2nd ed.

Mantel, R. (1974) 'On the characterization of aggregate excess demand', *Journal of Economic Theory*, 7: 348–353.

Mas-Collel, A. et al. (1995) *Microeconomic Theory*. New York: Oxford University Press.

Samuelson, P. (1938) 'A Note on the Pure Theory of Consumer's Behaviour', *Economica*, 5 (February): 61-71.

Samuelson, P. (1938a) 'A Note on the Pure Theory of Consumer's Behaviour: An Addendum', *Economica*, 5 (August): 353-4.

Samuelson, P. (1947) *Foundations of Economic Analysis*. Cambridge, Massachusetts: Harvard University Press.

Samuelson, P. (1948) 'Consumption Theory in Terms of Revealed Preference', *Economica*, 15 (November): 243-53.

Samuelson, P. (1950) 'The Problem of Integrability in Utility Theory', *Economica*, 17 (November): 355-85.

Samuelson, P. (1953) 'Consumption Theorems in Terms of Overcompensation rather than Indifference Comparisons', *Economica*, 20 (February): 1-9.

Sen, A. (1982) *Choice, Welfare and Measurement*. London: Basil Blackwell.

Sippel, R. (1997) 'An experiment on the pure theory of consumer's behaviour', *Economic Journal*, 107: 1431-44.

Sonnenschein, H. (1972) 'Market excess demand functions', *Econometrica*, 40 (3): 549–563.

Varian, H. (2006) *Intermediate Microeconomics: A Modern Approach*. New York: W. W. Norton & Company, 7th ed.

Wong, S. (2006) *The Foundations of Paul Samuelson's Revealed Preference Theory* (revised ed.) London: Routledge & Kegan Paul.

CHAPTER 2

Challenging the current economics curriculum: creating challengers and changes

Asad Zaman

1 Introduction

How does it happen that we have given our quiet assent to a situation where the richest 85 individuals have more money than the bottom 3.5 billion? Where vultures wait for starving children to die, while others eat luxurious meals on private resort islands? Where horrendous military and commercial crimes leading to deaths, misery, and deprivations of millions are routinely committed by highly educated men with multimillion dollar salaries in luxury corporate and government suites?

A core component of the answer to these critical questions is that we have been educated to believe that this is a normal state of affairs, which comes about through the operation of iron laws of economics. Economic theories currently being taught in universities all over the world are an essential pillar which sustains the economic system currently in operation. These theories state that we (human beings) are cold, callous, and calculating. Microeconomic theory says rational individuals are concerned only with their own consumption. They are callous; completely indifferent to the needs of others. They maximize, calculating personal benefits to the last penny. They are cold – their decisions are not swayed by emotions of any kind. All this theorizing is not without power – it creates the world we live in, and the rules we live by.

We have even been taught that laissez-faire automatically brings about the best possible outcomes. We are told that the rich are efficient wealth producers and deserve their wealth, just as the poor deserve their poverty. To create a labor market to sustain capitalist production processes, we have been trained to believe that our lives are for sale to the highest bidder.

Besides, we have been educated to believe that we are powerless to change things. We have been trained to laugh at the idea that human lives are infinitely precious. We have been made to forget that each moment of our lives is unique – each moment contains potentials which never existed before, and will never come into being again. Only by re-defining what is worth living for, and what is worth dying for, can we strike at the heart of the capitalist process of production.

When we talk about curriculum change, we are talking about creating new theoretical foundations to observe and intervene in the world we live in. This is not a project for the faint-of-heart, especially because the rich and powerful spend huge amounts of wealth and energy in preserving this status-quo, and resist efforts to change these social realities with all their might. The project of speaking truth to power is severely handicapped by our education which conditions our vision of the truth. Our theories of knowledge state that good and evil do not exist. We have been taught rules of intellectual discourse which forbid appeals to the heart and soul. We have thereby been deprived of our most powerful weapons in the eternal battle against evil. Modern education has turned us into soulless zombies, consumption and sex machines, human resources, and inputs into the production function for wealth. The vast majority of the populace has been paralyzed with poisonous ways of thinking, and the small minority which retains the capacity for thought and action has also been badly damaged by these same poisons.

Before talking about curriculum change, we must redeem our souls. How can this be done? The first step in curriculum change requires the creation of teachers who have a clear understanding of the challenge that we face. These teachers must de-program themselves to cleanse their hearts. Given that we battle against overwhelming odds, our teachers must be rocks of courage, fortitude, and stamina. Also essential is a sense of humor to enable us to laugh at the massive forces arrayed against us – without this, we would die of despair. Also required is a deep commitment to the cause, which is giving hope to and enriching the lives of billions living, entirely un-necessarily, in abject conditions. Our hearts must be full of compassion, and feel the sharp pangs of the pain felt by the parents who have to choose between buying expensive medicines for the sick child, or food for the family. We have to empower ourselves, and believe that we can make a difference.

The world we live in is constructed from structures of thought that we have internalized, far more than bricks and concrete. Unfortunately, many of these dominant structures are poisonous to our own happiness as well as general welfare of mankind. Changing our ways of thinking is not just a matter of reading and understanding. Rather, the process involves acquiring new ways of looking at the world and new tools for manipulating reality – eerily parallel to the taking of a reality pill in a popular movie. Healing ourselves requires time, effort and cooperation of like-minded friends. A first step in creating a new curriculum must be detoxification of our own minds and hearts. In terms of the Gandhian precept, we have to '*Be the change that you wish to see in the world.*' This requires analyzing the nature of the toxins we have ingested, and their removal. Some of the broad areas which require work are listed below.

2 Rethinking the human being: redeeming the heart and soul

Materialism led to the belief that thoughts were fluid secretions of the brain. Descartes thought that the soul was a gland in that brain[1]. Since the gland was not found, and we couldn't isolate, quantify, measure or weigh them, we came to believe that souls do not exist. We have been trained to believe that the heart is *only* an organ which pumps blood. This education leads us to override direct physical evidence provided by our own body of how our hearts respond to danger, thrill, anxiety, love, sorrow and happiness. Even though the essence of humanity is spirituality, this word has been removed from our lexicon, making us unable to think clearly about its meaning and significance in our daily lives.

One of the elements responsible for this loss is logical positivism, which denies existence to subjective experiences which are not "observable," and

---

[1] Descartes: "There is a little gland in the brain where the soul exercises its functions more particularly than in the other parts of the body." (In: *The Passions of the Soul*, Part 1: 31). No such organ was found, leading to the conclusion that souls do not exist.

cannot be subjected to scientific scrutiny. One of the leading proponents of positivism, A. J. Ayer, recanted later in life, saying that denying the reality of inner emotional states was akin to "feigning anesthesia" (Ayer, 1964: 101). We have been trained to feign anesthesia regarding our souls for so long that we have actually become numb, unable to feel the stirrings of our souls. The root of spirituality is compassion – the ability to directly and intuitively sense the pain that others feel. We are born as spiritual beings; babies laugh in merry company, and can sense the grief of others. The most spiritual of humans have deep hearts, which are connected on the spiritual level with all other human beings. Selfish behaviour requires us to seal our hearts to the pain we inflict on others in pursuit of our own interests. When this is encouraged in the name of assertiveness, and "looking out for number one", then hearts eventually become dead to the pain of others, and spirituality also dies. Selfish behaviour is self-defeating in that when the heart becomes dead to the pain of others, it also becomes incapable of feeling any genuine emotions. All pleasures become mechanical; on the purely physical level. For such people, the ideal state of affairs – heaven – is having an electrode implanted in the pleasure centers of the brain. It is only because of remnants of spirituality that utilitarian people have not yet proposed this logical conclusion to the quest for maximum happiness for all – a Matrix world, where simulated experiences replace reality.

The modern world has created an environment virulently hostile to the development of spirituality. The ideas of Machiavelli were repugnant to most, when soul-dead people were rare. For those whose hearts are spiritually linked with those of others, it is not possible to contemplate rule by fear, treachery, and cruelty, as hurting others is like hurting oneself. However, today, Machiavellian policies rule the roost, in a world full of zombies, where it is possible to state on public TV that it is worth killing half a million children to achieve political goals[2].

The first task of one who seeks to change the curriculum, so as to create a better world, must be to seek spiritual development. When we can sense the

---

[2] US Ambassador to UN, Madeleine Albright said this on "60 Minutes" in a CBS interview on 12th May 1996. Later expressions of regret only provide hypocritical cover to the truth expressed in a rare moment when the mask slipped. Regrets were only about expressions used, and never about the acts committed.

invisible ties that bind us all together as human beings, then it becomes easy to work for together for causes that go beyond our small and finite lives. Also these spiritual ties provide the energy required to swim against the currents. Hearts speak to other hearts directly. Thus, winning others to our cause is much easier when our hearts are aligned. But how can we achieve spiritual development? This is much harder since the past century has been overwhelmingly materialist, making both teachers and training materials rare. Furthermore, general state of arrested spiritual development makes it difficult to recognize and evaluate teachers, and to distinguish between the genuine and the fake. So we can only conclude with the highly unsatisfactory, but nonetheless true maxim: "Seek, and ye shall find." Whereas the roots of spirituality lie in compassion, the full-fledged tree with branches and leaves and fruits is a miracle beyond belief. We shall strive harder for spiritual development when we understand that it is learning how to be fully human, to achieve the potential for excellence buried within our souls, that is at stake.

Every human is like a seed which can grow into a tree if given the appropriate environment. Without nurturing spiritual growth, tremendous potential remains unrealized. How can we achieve the potential of excellence which lies within our souls? There is consensus among a wide variety of spiritual traditions that meditation, solitude and concentration are essentials – perpetual bombardment with trivial stimuli via social networks, electronic games, and other forms of entertainment are the exact antithesis, a serious obstacle to spiritual development. As Sen (2001) has cogently argued, development is really about the development of human capabilities – instead of the development of technologies or machinery as it is often taken to be. The primary human capabilities are deeply tied to spiritual development, which influences all that humans can become. Sen's (2001) capabilities approach offers a radically different to development, and deserves serious study by curriculum challengers.

3 Rethinking the nature of human knowledge

The fundamentally flawed theory of logical positivism became the dominant philosophy of knowledge in the second quarter of the twentieth century.

According to this theory, human knowledge is built on the basis of logical analysis of sense-data – incontrovertible objective empirical facts. This theory is deeply deficient on two counts. Firstly, sense data is defined as objective, whereas we experience this world entirely subjectively. Our experience of the world blends the objective out-there with the subjective mental structures we use to analyze external stimuli. People who wear glasses which invert the world soon learn how to process the image and correct it to put the world right side up again. Thus human knowledge is a blend of stimuli generated by the external world, and of internal mental structures, both physical and ideological, used to process and analyze the external world. The positivists attempted to ignore these internal mental structures and theories that we use to process the sense data. How deeply the positivist worldview has penetrated into common parlance and thought is evidenced by the sentence: "Just give me the facts – (I don't want your opinions)." The speaker and the audience are often entirely unaware that the idea that the two – facts and opinions – can be clearly separated is the dubious conclusion of a speculative philosophical position riddled with contradictions. Furthermore, the strategy of demeaning and denigrating the subjective is important in coercing us into feigning anesthesia; denying the validity of our internal experienced reality and accepting false fancy theories which conflict with our experience.

Secondly, to compound this mistake, positivists denied the existence of internal and experiential knowledge. For example, the knowledge of good and evil that is built into our hearts, and is the basis for morality, does not qualify as knowledge according to the positivists[3]. Similarly my knowledge of myself based on introspection does not derive from external sense data. Once self-knowledge was denied legitimacy, ignorance about the nature of human beings became rampant. The once dominant, and still highly influential, school of behavioural psychology reduced human beings to robots which could be programmed by stimulus and response. The founder of this school, urged us to move "beyond freedom and dignity," which are essential constituents of our humanity.

---

[3] As evidence, consider the discovery that facial expressions of emotions are universal, and not culturally conditioned. This implies that emotions, how to express them, and how to recognize them, is hard-wired in our make-up. Similarly, basic moral judgments are universal, not culturally conditioned.

We have direct experience of our freedom to choose between alternative courses of action. To accept the idea that we are subject to economic laws, that a mathematical formula can predict our behavior, is the equivalent of feigning anesthesia. Only when we understand that economic laws are what we choose to make them, we will become aware of our own responsibility for the billions living in extreme poverty. A central question that we must face is: what is the good life? Answers to this question determine the nature of the preferred economic system, and also the policies that are required to achieve it. Without explicit discussion, current economic theories assume that the good life is defined by maximum consumption. The superficiality, and essential falsity of this answer, can be established by studying humanities, which record the vast variety of lives which could serve as our models. Throughout history, wise human beings have debated and discussed merits of different alternatives; while there are many alternatives, there is near universal consensus that greed and selfishness are antithetical to well being. Unfortunately, positivist conceptions of knowledge denied any value to the study of the meaning of life. Declining enrolments in humanities attest to the currently inferior status of this type of knowledge.[4] To reverse these trends, we must re-define the concept of knowledge. Real knowledge is acquired by life experiences, and the only way to expand this is by studying the experiences of others who have thought deeply about life and its meaning. Only after achieving an understanding of the social nature of human beings can we design an economic system which supports and enables human beings to lead rich and meaningful lives.

4 Goals and perspectives for human existence

The central questions of human existence have been shunted to the side as if they were un-important or irrelevant. Even if we agree with Sartre (1996) that "existence precedes essence," we must grapple with the problem of creating meaning in our lives with the deadly seriousness that it deserves. "A life unexamined is not worth living" precisely because failure to examine

---

[4] In what might be considered the ultimate sell-out, a recent meeting at Stanford University to address the issue of declining enrolments decided to highlight the job-prospects of humanities graduates to attract more students.

leads to meaningless lives. Bertrand Russell (1903 [2002]) was one of the atheists who understood the significance of the choice he had made. He writes poetically:

> "That man is the product of causes which had no prevision of the end they were achieving; that his origin, his growth, his hopes and fears, his loves and his beliefs, are but the outcome of accidental collocations of atoms; that no fire, no heroism, no intensity of thought and feeling, can preserve an individual life beyond the grave; that all the labours of the ages, all the devotion, all the inspiration, all the noonday brightness of human genius, are destined to extinction in the vast death of the solar system, and that the whole temple of Man's achievement must inevitably be buried beneath the debris of a universe in ruins – all these things, if not quite beyond dispute, are yet so nearly certain, that no philosophy which rejects them can hope to stand. Only within the scaffolding of these truths, only on the firm foundation of unyielding despair, can the soul's habitation henceforth be safely built" (Russell, 1903 [2002]: 39).

Russell was a brave man. He realized that "unyielding despair" is a consequence of accepting an accidental universe, and sought to make it a foundation for his philosophy. He also thought that people believed in religion because they were cowards; because they could not live with the "unyielding despair" which follows from the rejection of religion. For the most part, today's atheists and religious people alike have not contemplated the consequences of their choices, accepting as basis for belief or disbelief trite platitudes offered as imitations of thought. The capitalist society needs workers to labor at meaningless jobs for meaningless money, the one-dimensional men of Marcuse (1964), and not thinkers. Human lives are full of mystery, subtlety, infinite complexity of emotions, and paradoxes. Understanding must often encompass the simultaneous truth of entirely conflicting and contradictory narratives, going beyond binary logics.

As even the Cheshire cat knew, the path to be chosen depends on the goals to be achieved. If human lives are meaningless, then all economic systems are the same. Current economic theories treat work/labor as a chore and burden, something which everyone seeks to avoid, and must be paid to do. Many studies show that work can be extremely meaningful, and provide purpose to our lives. Given that huge numbers of people spent the majority of our hours at work, providing enriching work environments could lead to vast increases in human welfare, in ways not conceivable within current curricula of economics.

Only after we clearly define the goals and purpose of human existence, can we consider the question of which kinds of economic, social and political systems would be helpful in achieving these goals. The value of our lives, and the satisfaction we feel, is directly tied to the grandeur of our vision for what we propose to do with this life. There is substantial empirical evidence that those who follow dominant paradigms of hedonism and instant gratification lead shallow and meaningless lives which do not even succeed on the narrow goal of providing happiness[5]. Deep and long term satisfaction depends on cultivating universally acknowledged praiseworthy character traits of courage, compassion, honesty, responsibility, sacrifice, etc. Our curriculum changers must have a high vision, seeking selflessly to serve humanity. The project of curriculum change can only be carried out by those with such a perspective, since others will not be able to make the efforts and sacrifices required.

5 Rescuing morality in economics

Prior to positivism, morality was considered as an essential component within the fold of human knowledge, all of which was united by a common purpose. However positivists argued that moral judgments were as meaningless as a cry of pain, and could not be any part of scientific knowledge. This came to be widely believed, and had a dramatic impact on University education. As Reuben (1996) has documented in "The Making of the Modern University: Intellectual Transformation and the Marginalization of Morality," universities abandoned their moral mission, and confined themselves to teaching technology. This has led to the development of moral

---

[5] See for example Lyubomirsky, 2008.

midgets like Oppenheimer who described the spectacular fireworks that would be generated by the Atom bomb, before explaining that all people within 2/3 miles would die[6]. McNamara and colleagues, graduates of the finest educational institutes in the USA, took pride in achieving high kill rates, amounting to more than half a million in Vietnam[7]. Obama takes pleasure in signing death-lists of people assassinated by drone strikes[8], knowing full well that collateral damage from these strikes kills thousands of innocents.

Since wars form an essential component of capitalism, stunting the growth of morality is a matter of high priority for educational systems of capitalism. This is accomplished by childhood training with video games, to teach children to shoot humans and enjoy watching gore and guts spill out. It culminates with sophisticated lectures by Michael Sandel (2011) on Justice to Harvard undergraduates. In this first lecture he explains that while they might think that they will become better persons, in fact the course will NOT accomplish this goal. Rather it will cause them to question settled belief and shake their assumptions about the nature of good and evil. Then he constructs highly artificial scenarios where inner moral certainties can be called into question – for example, should we eat a fellow human being on boat if survival depends on it? Should we kill a few to save a larger number of lives? He uses these rare and pathological examples to deceive undergraduates into thinking that morality is always relative. He ends the lecture by arguing that we have debated moral issues for centuries without making any progress on it (unlike science), and thus implies that knowledge about morality is not really possible. All of this is necessary to disarm these undergraduates of inborn moral certainties, so that they can participate in wars that destroys millions of innocent lives. Those whose consciences survive these soul-washing attempts commit suicides when the horror of what they have done sinks in.

Nearly all policy choices that we make in economics involve moral questions, but economic analysis as currently taught simply ignores the

---

[6] http://www.thenewatlantis.com/publications/the-agony-of-atomic-genius
[7] http://www.nytimes.com/1995/04/09/world/mcnamara-recalls-and-regrets-vietnam.html
[8] http://www.washingtontimes.com/news/2013/nov/4/obama-brag-new-book-im-really-good-killing-drones/

moral issues, while pretending to be an objective and positive science. Accordingly Zaman (2012), making scarcity the central problem of economics involves assuming nine different normative propositions, which receive no mention in standard textbooks. Similarly, Hausman and MacPherson (2006) have discussed how deeply morality is involved within economics. Leaders of a revolution in economics must not only know how to discuss morality, they must lead by example and strive to be moral in their life choices.

6 Overcoming market mentality

Understanding the thesis of Karl Polanyi's (1944) "The Great Transformation: The Political and Economic Origins of Our Time" is essential for those seeking radical curriculum changes. Polanyi narrates the story of how a paternalistic, regulatory economy (PRE) was transformed into a self-regulated market economy (SRME). Each type of economy has associated social norms which are in harmony with the economic system. The social norms of the PRE are based on responsibility and cooperation, while the SRME requires individualism and competition. The two types of norms are antithetical to each other, and it is impossible for one to evolve into the other. Rather, the great transformation took place when existing socio-economic structures were crushed and alternative structures were put in their place. This also led to the creation of a market society based on market norms, which are hazardous to human life on this planet. It is not possible to summarize the thesis of Polanyi here, but we discuss two important elements of market societies[9]:

1. Tying social status to wealth production.
2. Creation of artificial commodities in Land and Labour.

6.1 The pursuit of wealth

Whereas traditional societies value and celebrate courage, scholarship, athletics, beauty, spirituality, wisdom, market societies value money as the

---

[9] See Zaman (2010) for a summary.

single most important marker of social status. This is because everything is for sale in market societies. Whereas the idea was shocking when first presented, today value of human lives is routinely calculated via their capability to produce wealth. This reduction of humans to human resources has had disastrous effects on society. It has been widely recognized that the pursuit of wealth with complete disregard for social consequences was one of the root causes of the global financial crises of 2007-8.Many have remarked that financial firms sought to deceive investors into buying fraudulent instruments so as to make money for themselves at expense of others. The result of these crises was the rise of homelessness and hunger in the USA at record levels.

Among the myriad harmful consequences, perhaps the most important is the destruction of the family. The single most important function in a society is raising children, since the future of the society is shaped by it. Declining social status due to the zero wage attached to this labor of love led to the feminist movement, which demanded jobs and equal pay for women. Even now, women feel embarrassed to say "I am just a housewife" and prefer to show that they possess some skill valued by the market. This is because the market society equates worth to income. When the core societal function of rearing children receives low value, the fabric of society dissolves. Today more than 50% of children in USA and Europe are born out of wedlock, and will not receive upbringing within a stable family environment. A report on 'Fractured Families' in Britain stated that:

> "This Report paints a worrying picture of family breakdown in the UK. We now have one of the highest divorce rates in the Western world and the fabric of family life has been stripped away in the past thirty years. This study also shows more clearly than ever the destructive effects of family breakdown upon millions of children, as well as the links between family breakdown and addictions, educational failure and serious personal debt" (Centre for Social Justice, 2006).

To counteract this phenomenon, our teachers must cleanse their hearts of the love of wealth for its own sake. Among the top regrets of terminally ill people in hospices is the neglect of social relationships in pursuit of wealth; the choice of career over family. We must learn to value social relationships above wealth. We must emphasize responsibilities and commitments over short run hedonistic pleasures. By valuing friends over fortunes, and preferring simple lifestyles to luxury we can *be* the most effective proofs of failure of microeconomic theories.

6.2 *Artificial commodities of land and labor*

One of the important and deep insights of Polanyi (1944) is that the market economy requires the commodification of human lives as well as our environment. Land and labor are not natural commodities – these cannot be manufactured at any price. Labor is the stuff from which our lives are made, and making this a marketable commodity involves cheapening and degrading of human lives. Similarly, we live on the land which supports our lives in many ways; considering this as a marketable commodity does great injustice to our habitats, and this orientation is responsible for the massive amount of environmental damage we see today.

As market mentality generates ways of thinking which are directly opposed to natural human tendencies, change requires radical re-orientations in our social structures for living and working together. Whereas market societies function on the basis of greed and competition, humane societies have mutual responsibility, cooperation, brotherhood and generosity as prized values. Unfortunately, while institutions continue to pay lip service to these higher ideals, the practice has shifted away to pure profit seeking at expense of all morality. Cynics say that it is always like this, and high sounding words always serve as a cover for base motives, but there is very strong evidence that this is not true. There has been a definite and visible shift away from social mentality to a market mentality. Numerous Wall Street executives have written about the gradual shift from a service oriented culture, helping clients to manage wealth, to a purely profit oriented culture, even at expense of clients. Medicine is considered a noble profession because doctors aim to serve mankind, they do not aim to serve themselves at the expense of humanity. However, there has been a noticeable shift from the service motive to the profit motive, in all areas. Radical re-structuring of MBA programs is required to re-conceptualize the firm as an entity which earns profits in order to provide a service to the community. Teaching the opposite, that all is fair in pursuit of profits, has led to a situation about which Harvard MBA Professor Zuboff (2009) writes that "I have come to believe that much of what my colleagues and I taught has caused real suffering, suppressed wealth creation, destabilized the world economy, and accelerated the demise of the 20th century capitalism in which the U.S. played the leading role." Curriculum changers face the challenge of reversing these trends in order to bring the ideals of service to the foreground, which is no easy task.

Similarly the reduction of land to a commodity has led to a loss of appreciation for its unique features and for the fact that the land sustains our lives. Famous economists are on the record as saying that extinction of a species is an event and not a tragedy. The market vision only sees firewood and minerals, and turns a blind eye to the millions of years that have gone into creation of rainforests and coral reefs; in fact, these environmental resources are literally "priceless" in the sense that they cannot be recreated at any cost. We are on the brink of environmental catastrophes, and have even gone beyond the point of no return in some areas. The frightening prognosis of "Collapse," offered by Jared Diamond (2006) can only be averted by the recognition that the land and the biological fauna and flora it sustains is not a commodity, and cannot be produced at any cost. The task facing us as teachers is to develop an appreciation of the amazingly complex wonders which surround us, as well as the intricate and fragile ecosystems where all things work together harmoniously. We must open our hearts to the painful tragedy of the last of its kind Australian bird which issues a mating call, when there is no one left to hear it. Only the transmission of such feelings to students will enable the creation of activists required to carry out the mission selflessly seeking to provide better lives to all humans and animals inhabiting the planet.

7 The metaphor of the machine

Sustainable development theories have arisen from the desire to save the planet from the depredation caused by our treatment of the planet as a dead source of resources freely available for our exploitation. Also, our failure to intervene effectively stems partly from our acceptance of the idea that there are "economic laws" which operate inexorably – outside the boundaries of human will. Both of these deeply damaging ideas stem from our acceptance of the metaphor of the machine as a representation of the world around us. In a neglected gem, Colin Turbayne (1962) has analyzed the dramatic impact of metaphors in our lives. In particular, the post-Newtonian transition from the world as an organism to the world as a machine provides essential support to these misconceptions at heart of current economic theories.

In the field of thought, human capabilities are very limited, forcing us to rely on crude representations of complex realities. Metaphors play an important role in this process, by providing striking new representations of familiar objects, leading to new ways of thinking and inter-action. Prior to emergence of the modern world, a familiar metaphor for the world we live in was "Mother Earth" which was an affectionate homage of respect to the fact that the planet provides for all of our needs. This metaphor guided our inter-actions with our environment. The central thesis of Turbayne is that modernity replaced this with a new metaphor of the world as a machine, which has had a powerful effect on how we deal with planetary resources. Turbayne (1962: 5) writes that:

> "Descartes and Newton ... (were both originators and) ... unconscious victims of the metaphor of the great machine. These two great "sort-crossers" of our modern epoch have so imposed their arbitrary allocation of the facts upon us that it has now entered the consciousness of the entire Western World. Together they have founded a church, more powerful than that founded by Peter and Paul, whose dogmas are now so entrenched that anyone who tries to re-allocate the facts is guilty of more than heresy, he is opposing scientific truth. For the accepted allocation is now identified with science".

This is similar to Weber's (1963: 270) argument that the modern world elevated the rational and intellectual to disenchant the world, removing the mystery and wonder, as well as the sacred elements. Machines are dead and cannot feel pain. Therefore we need not hesitate in doing violent surgery, damaging fragile ecosystems and destroying and re-arranging the machine parts in any way we choose to serve us better. It should be obvious that our current treatment of planetary resources is based far more on the machine metaphor, as opposed to the Mother Earth metaphor. Conventional economic theory is guilty of this same disrespect to the finite resources of a planet, not taking into account costs of depletion or environmental damage. Schumaker (1999) and Douthwaite (1995) have argued that if we take these costs into account, we would conclude that net cost of all the apparent growth is negative[10].

The metaphor of the machine is extremely powerful, and has penetrated deeply into the modern minds. This has led to environmental disaster, as well as resignation to enormous amounts of oppression and injustice as the outcome of inexorable operations of a large machine beyond our powers to remedy. We must fight metaphor with metaphor. While a return to the mother Earth is useful, a new and more powerful metaphor is "Gaia" the living planet. We are all bound together in a complete, harmonious, and integrated eco-system, where all parts are living, conscious, and cooperate with each other to produce good results. Use and promotion of this metaphor can counteract the damage done by the machine metaphor, and is an essential aspect of efforts to achieve better living conditions for all humans on the planet.

8 Conclusions

The root of the problem, and the rot, goes far deeper than is commonly realized. The great transformation, the transition to a market economy and the dis-enchantment of the world replaced fundamental ways of thinking about the world, and the basis of social interaction. In Zaman (2009), I have shown how social science arose as an attempt to find intellectual and rational answers to questions previously answered by religion. Unfortunately, the head is incapable of discovering the reasons of the heart, as was widely realized by intellectuals in the early twentieth century. Instead expanding the framework for thought and action, intellectuals abandoned morality and

---

[10] See Zaman (2014) for extended discussion.

spirituality as un-scientific. In Zaman (2013), I have explored at length the disastrous consequence that resulted from this deification of science.

This framework for formulating the problem is necessary to lay out the immense challenges facing those who would reform the economics curriculum. Small evolutionary steps simply will not do, because the change required is revolutionary. Furthermore, change is required in both spirit and form, and just technical interventions, modifying the math and diagrams to include new elements, will not suffice, to bring about desired results. Without an appreciation of the magnitude of the task, reform efforts are bound to fail. Current reform efforts take most of the neoclassical framework as given, and identify some specific areas as target for change and reform. This would produce only superficial change, because such reforms fail to go to the root of the problem. An intense labor over centuries was required to destroy old paradigms and replace them with the modern, secular and rational conceptions of the world. Clearly there were deep flaws in the ancient worldviews which motivated and inspired these heroic efforts by the modernizers. We do not advocate a return to some mythical idealized old world. Rather, recognition of the deep flaws in modernist views requires us to replicate their efforts, in rejecting the modern paradigms and setting our sights on an unknown world which will emerge as a result of our struggles. The challenge facing us reformers is to throw off the shackles of modern thought, in order to re-integrate the heart and soul with economic teachings. The prize is tremendous: enabling billions of human beings to lead richer, fuller, more meaningful lives. The risks of getting damaged in the battle are equally large, proportional to the magnitude of the task. Teamwork is essential as the task is too large for individuals. Uptil now, heterodox efforts have been weak and ineffective because of lack of teamwork. While it is difficult to do, it is essential to build a rainbow coalition, united by our concern for the welfare of mankind, while holding extremely diverse views and lifestyles. The burning question is, are we up to the challenge?

References

Ayer, A. J. (1964) "The Concept of a Person and other essays". London: Macmillan and Sons.

Centre for Social Justice (2006) 'Fractured Families,' *The State of the Nation Report,* 14 December, London: The Centre for Social Justice.

Diamond, J. (2005) *Collapse: How Societies Choose to Fail or Succeed*: revised edition. NY: Penguin.

Douthwaite, R. J. (1995) *The Growth Illusion: How Economic Growth has Enriched the Few, Impoverished the Many, and Endangered the Planet.* Tulsa: Council Oak Books.

Hausman, D. M. and McPherson, M. S. (2006) *Economic analysis, moral philosophy and public policy.* Cambridge: Cambridge University Press.

Ludlow, L. M. (2005) "Machiavelli and US Politics", August, http://fff.org/author/lawrence-m-ludlow/

Lyubomirsky, S. (2008) *The How of Happiness.* NY: Penguin.

Marcuse, H. (1964) *One Dimensional Man*, London: Sphere Books.

Polanyi, K. (1944 [2001]) *The great transformation: The political and economic origins of our time.* Beacon Press.

Reuben, J. A. (1996) *The Making of the Modern University: Intellectual Transformation and the Marginalization of Morality*, Chicago: University of Chicago Press.

Russell, B. (1903 [2002]) 'A Free Man's Worship' reproduced in *The Basic Writings of Bertrand Russell, 1903-1959,* edited by Russell, B., Egner, R.E., Denonn, L.E. and Slater,J. (1992), http://www.positiveatheism.org/hist/russell1.htm

Sandel, M. (2011), *Harvard University's Justice* with Micheal Sandel, Episode 01: The Moral Side of Murder, http://www.justiceharvard.org/about/justice-book/

Sartre, J-P. (1996) *Being and Nothingness*, NY: Philosophical Library.

Schumaker, E. F. (1999) *Small is Beautiful. Economics as if people mattered... 25 years later with commentaries.* Hartley & Marks Publishers.

Sen, A. (2001) *Development as Freedom*, NY: Oxford University Press.

Turbayne, C.M. (1962) *The myth of metaphor.* New Haven: Yale University Press.

Weber, M. (1963) *The Sociology of Religion*, Boston: Beacon Press.

Zaman, A. (2009) 'Origins of Western Social Science', *Journal of Islamic Economics, Banking and Finance*, vol 5, number 2: 9-22, May-August.

Zaman, A. (2010) 'The Rise and Fall of the Market Economy', *Review of Islamic Economics*, Vol. 14, No. 2: 123-155.

Zaman, A. (2012) 'The Normative Foundations of Scarcity', *Real-World Economics Review*, issue 61, 26: 22-39, September.

Zaman, A. (2013) *Deification of Science and Its Disastrous Consequences*, April, http://ssrn.com/abstract=2260052

Zaman, A. (2014) 'Evaluating the Costs of Growth', *Real-World Economics Review*, issue 67, 9: 41-51, May.

Zuboff, S. (2009) 'The Old Solutions have become the New Problem,' *Businessweek*, July 2, http://www.businessweek.com/managing/content/jul2009/ca2009072_489 734.htm

Part Three

**Current gaps in
economics curriculum**

CHAPTER 3
The role of methodology in the economics curriculum

Sheila C. Dow

1 Introduction

The purpose of this chapter is to argue that methodology should be in the core of the economics curriculum. Methodology is often taken to mean simply the selection and application of methods within a given approach. But methodology is much more than that. It allows us to understand why different approaches to economics exist and how we might analyse and foster constructive communication between them. More fundamentally it helps us to understand and discuss our subject. It should therefore be a central feature of a curriculum designed to teach the subject. But at another level, understanding of methodology also provides a basis for considering curricular reform.

In what follows, we consider first in more detail what is meant by methodology. Following a reflection on the context for curriculum reform, the methodological issues underlying this reform are set out. This is followed by a discussion of the role, timing and content of methodology in the curriculum itself.

2 The meaning of methodology

Methodology includes as a subfield discussion of choice of methods, such as over which econometric method to use, how to use it and how to assess its results. But this kind of discussion rests on huge methodological assumptions: about how the subject matter is being understood, what place theory and evidence play in building up knowledge about it, and therefore how far econometric techniques are appropriate to the question at hand. In other words, by far the more important discussion concerns the methodological *approach* as prior to any discussion of specific methods.

Within mainstream texts, discussion of methodology in the full sense is discussed only, if at all, in the opening chapter. But then this discussion consists of assertions about the subject matter of economics and about the economist's 'way of thinking', i.e. about the particular mainstream methodological approach. Parkin, Powell and Matthews (2012) and Mankiw and Taylor (2006) make typical such statements, although in more detail than other introductory texts. Economics is assumed to be concerned with rational choice. Theory is equated with models, which are constructed by applying deductive logic to the rationality axioms, where the models' assumptions are regarded as simplifications of reality. Testing of these models' predictions is the subject matter of separate econometrics courses. By implication, the theory which best fits the facts is deemed to be the most scientific.

This understanding of methodology reflects the general (simplified) understanding of the type of methodology which arose from the philosophy of science literature in the 1930s and 1940s. The implication of this philosophy was that it was feasible, and indeed desirable, to distinguish between science and non-science, and to establish not only the best theory but also the best methodology. But logical positivism has since been discredited in the philosophy of science literature. In any case traditional philosophy of science has failed on its own terms in economics. The evidence from the economics literature is that neither deductive reasoning nor confirming evidence has been enough to establish which is the best theory or methodology – additional factors must explain the dominance of the mainstream approach. There have for example been cases where discovery of logical flaws (as in the Cambridge capital controversies) has not dislodged theories. Also contrary evidence has not proved decisive, as in the emergence of the financial crisis within what mainstream theory had theorised as a self-stabilising financial system. Alternative, non-mainstream, approaches and their theories are not addressed by reason and evidence, but rather are dismissed as falling outside the mainstream definition of what constitutes 'scientific' economics. Mainstream textbooks thus present their version of economics as definitive.

According to the traditional approach to methodology (exemplified by Blaug 1980), episodes of defense of the mainstream *in spite of* reason and evidence indicate, not only an over-simplified understanding of traditional philosophy of science, but also poor scientific practice. But now a range of methodological approaches to understanding and clarifying why economics is as it is, exists. The field of methodology has become much more complex and wide-ranging than its traditional form. It has grown into a field of its own, with an international organisation (the International Network for Economic Method) and an academic outlet, the *Journal of Economic Methodology*. Methodology now encompasses all the issues surrounding the co-existence of different legitimate methodological approaches, as well as the study of different theories and methods within each approach.

This new field of methodology is equipped to analyse different methodological approaches by taking account of such matters as the range of types of reasoning which can be applied, the scope for different interpretations of evidence and the sociological structure of the economics profession, including the sociology of economic education (Hands, 2001; Dow, 2002; Boumans and Davis, 2010). This type of methodology includes analysis of different understandings of the nature of economic systems and therefore how we characterise economics itself. It can cover what is and what is not regarded as a good argument, or even what counts as an argument within the economics discourse. Is discussion of moral values separable from economics or integral to it, for example? Methodology thus deals with economics in its fullest sense.

3 The methodological context of curriculum reform

The content of the economics curriculum has long been a matter for discussion. It has been driven sometimes by institutional arrangements, such as the national benchmarking exercise in the UK designed to standardise (not to reform) core economics teaching across all public universities. This type of exercise itself makes a strong methodological presumption, that the subject matter and the approach to it can reasonably be standardised. This standardisation has been promoted further by the dominance of teaching to mainstream textbooks. While these textbooks may include reference to differences of opinion within economics, the resolution of these differences is portrayed as a straightforward matter of logic and evidence. Textbooks may refer also to the history of economic thought, but only in Whiggish terms of demonstrating how theory has advanced (Roncaglia, 2014). Theory is presented in formal mathematical terms and becomes increasingly technical as teaching advances, with an increasing emphasis on acquiring the relevant technical training.

There has long been an argument that this approach to the curriculum is unduly narrow, reflecting the increasing hold of mathematical formalism in the second half of the twentieth century charted, and critiqued, by Blaug (1999). Colander and Klamer (1987) gathered evidence of disaffection among graduate students in the US with a curriculum which prioritised technical mastery over policy relevance. In 2000 French economics students led a call for teaching by means of debates, encouraging similar student calls elsewhere and setting in train the development of the Post-autistic Economics movement (Fullbrook, ed., 2003) and ultimately the emergence of the World Economics Association. The calls from students were not for replacing the mainstream as such but for a different mode of teaching which would provide students with the training as a basis for understanding economics better and also making up their own minds as to their preferred approach. This was a methodological argument for pluralism in economics education, which was part of a more general methodological argument for pluralism.

This argument for curricular reform (as well as for pluralism) has gained force with the 2007-09 financial crisis and its aftermath. The crisis has exposed the methodological presumptions of the mainstream approach and the resulting neglect in the curriculum of alternative methodological approaches. It has also exposed the lack of preparation students had generally been given for contemplating what might be required methodologically in considering any other form of analysis of the crisis. More widely the crisis has exposed the lack of understanding among economists, not only of the economy, but also of economics itself. It is the meta-methodological perspective, that there are several approaches that might be taken to economics, none of which can be demonstrated to be best, which therefore underpins the argument for curricular reform. Methodological issues are central to the argument for curricular reform.

Curricular reform should include attention to providing students with methodological training, not only to understand the pluralist framework of their education but also to understand the different methodological perspectives and learn how to analyse them. The same methodological reasoning underpins arguments for including history of economic thought in the curriculum (Dow, 2009; Roncaglia, 2014). The methodological argument for curriculum reform includes the argument for methodological content.

4 The role, timing and content of a methodology addition to the curriculum

At present most students are presented with a few pages at best at the beginning of their introductory textbooks about the nature of economics and its methodology, never to meet methodological enquiry again in the core curriculum. But in these few textbook pages a whole methodological approach is set out as a *fait accompli*, specifying a particular version of the subject matter and specifying how knowledge is to be constructed. The typical assertions as to the equation of models with theories, and the classification of the assumptions of models as simplifications involve huge methodological leaps. Yet, by covering this ground at the very beginning of economics education in this simplistic way, these textbooks lull students into thinking that no significant issues are involved.

The role of methodology in the curriculum should instead provide some grounding in the philosophy of science as it applies to economics so that there is awareness, whenever later courses proceed with one approach or another, of what is assumed about the nature of the subject matter and the best way to build knowledge about it. Once students have acquired some methodological awareness, the course is set for them to pick up methodological ideas and to better understand the contents of their other courses. But to acquire this awareness in the first place would clearly require much more substantive teaching than the kind of cursory treatment currently provided in mainstream textbooks.

It might be thought that this would be far too ambitious for students when they first encounter economics. But it is instructive to recall the UK higher education debates in the nineteenth century about the timing of philosophy education. On the one hand the predominantly Oxford-based approach required a prior foundation of other academic knowledge, so that philosophy was only taught, if at all, late in the degree. Philosophy could then be applied to their prior specialist knowledge of other subjects. On the other hand the Scottish approach started the higher education curriculum with moral philosophy, on which all other subjects then built (an approach which persisted until the 1970s). The Oxford approach taught subjects as specialisms, focusing on what was regarded as the best theory, while the Scottish approach taught subjects historically, explaining the different approaches (e.g. to mathematics, as well as to philosophy) taken at different times to address different problems. This provided the environment for the birth of modern economics, taught as topical applications of moral philosophy within which students could engage.

Introducing students to economics through methodology may sound daunting, but it can be done in simple ways, leaving the use of the more impenetrable technical terms and more sophisticated methodological analysis until later specialist courses. Methodology can be taught implicitly, e.g. by making it clear that economics is up for discussion. Thus, as with the Scottish students in the eighteenth century, the philosophical material could be made more accessible by pursuing it in terms of topical issues, especially debates in society at large on economic topics. Thus for example different theoretical explanations for the 2007-09 financial crisis could be explored in broad terms by exploring the assumptions made about the nature of the economy and which are the acceptable forms of argument (Dow, 2009). Similarly, the millennium generated a lot of reflection on the state of economics. Weintraub (1999) set out in a very accessible way a range of different accounts of economics at the millennium which would arise from different methodological/historiographical positions. This exercise was a blend of history of thought and methodology, a good example of how history of thought can form part of this introductory teaching. Again this might be thought to be daunting for students new to economics. But in fact it is not uncommon for introductory courses in other social sciences to start with great political economy figures such as Smith and Marx, putting standard introductory economics teaching to shame.

While this kind of introductory material could not go into much depth either on methodological or economic theory, it is the awareness it generates on which ever more advanced material can be built. But more advanced economics would need to be taught with this methodological awareness in mind. Once students are armed with some basic concepts their further studies are seen through different eyes. Once students understand the concept of dualism for example they will see it everywhere in mainstream theory and understand theory better as a result. Once students understand that methodological approach is contestable, they will be better able to engage in argument and understand better the arguments in the literature and in society more widely. This is an important aspect of education.

Much of the recent research in methodology is directly applicable in teaching in a range of fields, since it provides descriptive accounts of different bodies of research. Thus for example there is a growing interest in methodological issues for experimental economics[11]. The priority should be to have methodological awareness permeating all teaching. The standard approach is to teach a preferred theory, referring to other theories (if at all) in order to demonstrate the superiority of the preferred theory. A methodologically aware approach is to explain the different philosophical underpinnings of competing theories, possibly in order to make an argument for one set of theory over another, but nevertheless regarding this as a matter, not just for fuller understanding, but also for potential debate. The idea of teaching by reference to debates was central to the French students' demands in 2000.

What is being proposed is particularly challenging for teachers not accustomed to teaching in this way. Some transitional programme would be required to raise the methodological awareness and knowledge of teaching staff. A particular incentive to engage with this exercise would be provided by the reactions they can expect were they to follow the traditional pattern of teaching; students who are introduced at the very start to methodology will find it hard to accept unsupported assertions as to what economics is and

---

[11] See for example the special symposium in the *Journal of Economic Methodology*, Volume 18 (2), 2011.

how economists think. It would take time for methodological awareness to become established. But an excellent start is being made by the next generation of teachers, the students who are currently actively seeking and promoting curricular reform.

References

Blaug, M. (1980) *The Methodology of Economics, or how economists explain.* Cambridge: Cambridge University Press.

Blaug, M. (1999) 'The Formalist Revolution or What has Happened to Orthodox Economics after World War II', in R E Backhouse and J Creedy (eds.), *From Classical Economics to the Theory of the Firm: Essays in Honour of D. P. O'Brien.* Cheltenham: Elgar, pp. 257-80.

Boumans, M. and Davis, J. B. (2010) *Economic Methodology: understanding economics as a science.* London: Palgrave Macmillan.

Colander, D. C. and Klamer, A. (1987) 'The Making of an Economist', *Journal of Economic Perspectives* 1: 95-113.

Dow, S. C. (2002) *Economic Methodology: an inquiry.* Oxford: Oxford University Press.

Dow, S. C. (2009) 'History of Thought and Methodology in Pluralist Economics Education', *International Review of Economic Education*, 8(2): 41-57. https://ideas.repec.org/a/che/ireepp/v8y2009i2p41-57.html

Fullbrook, E. ed. (2003) *The Crisis in Economics. The post-autistic economics movement: the first 600 days.* London: Routledge.

Hands, D. W. (2001) *Reflection without Rules: Economic Methodology and Contemporary Science Theory.* Cambridge: Cambridge University Press.

Krueger, A. O. et al. (2001) 'Report on the Commission on Graduate Education in economics', *Journal of Economic Literature,* 29: 1035-53.

Mankiw, R. G. and Taylor, M. P. (2006) *Economics.* London: Thomson.

Parkin, M.; Powell, M. and Matthews, K. (2012) *Economics.* London: Pearson. European edition, 8th edition.

Roncaglia, A. (2014) 'Should the History of Thought be included in Undergraduate Curricula?', *Economic Thought,* 3,1: 1-9.

Weintraub, E. R. (1999) 'How Should We Write the History of Twentieth-Century Economics?', *Oxford Review of Economic Policy*, 15: 139-52.

CHAPTER 4
Should the history of economic thought be included in undergraduate curricula?

Alessandro Roncaglia[1]

1 The Mainstream View[2]

"Economic theory [...] finds no necessity for including its history as a part of professional training". In the decades since Gordon (1965: 126) stated this view, it has remained a mainstream tenet. It was already a mainstream tenet thirty years earlier, in the 1930s, when economists belonging to the then dominant Marshallian tradition such as John Hicks and Dennis Robertson argued that there was no point in wasting time reading the classical economists.[3] (Later, after the Sraffian Revolution and in opposition to it, Hicks began to refer to classical economists in his writings, but some mistakes appear to confirm his earlier attitude).[4]

The declining role of the history of economic thought in undergraduate and graduate curricula has been signaled, and discussed, in a stream of papers.[5] In all likelihood, this trend has both cultural and political reasons. Tentatively – the subject would deserve specific in-depth analysis – we might suggest two distinct but possibly interacting aspects. On the one side, we have the axiomatization of economics: a method which hypostatizes the assumptions,

---

[1] This chapter has been previously published as Roncaglia, A.. "Should the History of Economic Thought be Included in Undergraduate Curricula?", *Economic Thought*, Vol 3, No. 1, 2014.
[2] For earlier statements of my views, see Roncaglia (1996 and 2005), on which I have drawn in parts of the present paper.
[3] Letter by Robertson to Keynes, 3 February 1935, in Keynes, 1973, vol. 13, p. 504; letter by Hicks, 9 April 1937, in Keynes (1973, vol. 14, p. 81)
[4] For instance, in the first edition of *A theory of economic history*, Hicks (1969: 168) erroneously stated that Ricardo had never made use of numerical examples in his *Principles*. On the revival of the history of economic thought in the wake of the Sraffian Revolution in the 1970s, cf. Marcuzzo and Rosselli (2002).
[5] Cf. in particular the papers collected in Weintraub (ed.) (2002). More recently, Caldwell (2013: 754) optimistically pointed to "some recent hopeful signs of change" which however appear limited to HOPE stronghold, Duke University.

which are adopted for logical reasons and, once adopted, no longer require a discussion of their historical roots. On the other side, we have had the repercussions of the confrontation between Communist and Western systems – a heated confrontation, notwithstanding the label of Cold War –, with a widespread (and, as a matter of fact, largely erroneous) identification of Classical and Marxian economics, where history of economic thought (HET) was perceived as the Trojan horse for infiltrating Western culture with anti-capitalist ideas.[6]

According to Gordon, history of economic thought is not useless since it can help students in gradually scaling the heights of economic theory,[7] but it remains a detour in comparison with direct perusal of contemporary economic theory. From this point of view, we may add, HET's pedagogical usefulness is reduced whenever there is discontinuity in the development of the analytical toolbox with no change in the underlying worldview, as in fact happened after the Second World War with the publication of Samuelson's *Foundations* (1947).

Of course, this does not mean that specialists should not be allowed to devote themselves to it: as with other cultural ventures, "we study history because it is there" (Gordon, ibid). And there is a subtle justification for

---

[6] The identification of HET with heterodox economics has been lamented by, for instance, Weintraub (2002: 6): "if most economists understand the history of economics as an attack on mainstream economics, they will be hostile to the subdiscipline and its claims on common resources of faculty positions and students' time." I agree in principle that such an identification is wrong: each point of view, within economics as well as within any other social science, has a right, and indeed has the need, to reflect on its own roots and on the differences with other viewpoints; moreover, such research helps open confrontation between opposing viewpoints. Whatever their viewpoint, historians of thought should share the common philological requirements of fidelity to the text to be interpreted and attention to the context, and this should help in the inter-viewpont debate (as an example, I always enjoyed – and learned from – my debates with Samuel Hollander). However, Weintraub makes a different point, concerning the (fundamentalist, Taliban-like) attitude of the majority of mainstream economists towards the heterodox minority, and in this respect very little can be said, apart from the fact that such an attitude should be rejected by any liberal mind, whatever the point of view adopted in economic research.

[7] A similar position is held by Blaug (2001: 156): "I never understood the calculus I learned at school until I read accounts of the Newton-Leibnitz disputes about 'the fundamental theorem of the calculus'". This experience however is by no means a common one among students of mathematics.

inserting it in graduate economic curricula (a justification now apparently overlooked, since HET rarely gets a look, even there), which we may derive from one of the leading mainstream scholars in the field, Jacob Viner.

According to him, although theoretical research comes uppermost, HET may contribute to the formation of researchers. As Viner (1991: 385 and 390) says, "the pursuit of broad and exact knowledge of the history of the working of the human mind as revealed in written records", namely "scholarship", implies "a commitment to the pursuit of knowledge and understanding": "once the taste for it has been aroused, it gives a sense of largeness even to one's small quests, and a sense of fullness even to the small answers […] a sense which can never in any other way be attained". In this sense, HET is important for the education of researchers, even if it is not necessary for their training. To the many people who are not willing to recognize this, Viner, with his aristocratic bent, might have answered by paraphrasing John Stuart Mill (1863: 281): "It is better to be a human being dissatisfied than a pig satisfied, better to be Socrates dissatisfied than a fool satisfied. And if the fool, or the pig, are of a different opinion, it is because they only know their own side of the question".

Along much the same lines as Viner, namely considering HET as an activity inferior to theorizing, useful but not strictly required for the training of economists, we find the other leading historian of economic thought of the 20th century, Joseph Schumpeter. According to him, studying economists of the past is pedagogically helpful, may prompt new ideas and affords useful material on the methods of scientific research in economics. "We stand to profit from visits to the lumber room provided we do not stay there too long" (Schumpeter 1954: 4), where the qualification sounds self-ironical, considering the amount of time Schumpeter himself spent in "the lumber room"). In other terms, studying previous economists' accomplishments should not take too much of the contemporary economist's time out of theoretical and applied research. HET may nevertheless be useful, for among other things a reason similar to the one given by Viner: it "will prevent a sense of *lacking direction and meaning* from spreading among the students" (Schumpeter, 1954: 4; italics in the original).

In other terms, even in the context of a single paradigm, HET can help in understanding economic theories, by pointing to the social, political and cultural context of their origins and their diffusion, such as what problems they aim at solving, or which ideas they support or oppose.

2 The hidden assumption of the mainstream view

Schumpeter implicitly pointed to other reasons, which we shall consider below, for attributing to HET an important role in economists' basic training; however, as we shall see, such reasons acquire vital significance only when a common attitude prevailing among mainstream economists is rejected. Within the mainstream approach, explicitly or – more often – implicitly (and – quite important – not necessarily), a sort of positivist attitude dominates: economic knowledge grows over time, through accumulation of new theories and new empirical knowledge; the personalities of the economists, their ethical values or their basic vision of the world (their *Weltanshauung*) are external to the field of economic science and should rather be considered as belonging to the field of cultural history, together with the history of mathematics or physics.

As a matter of fact, viewing HET as belonging to the general field of the history of culture (or the history of sciences) rather than the broad field of economics is an attitude taken by some contemporary historians of economic thought.[8] This viewpoint was taken to its extreme consequences in the – luckily unsuccessful – attempts to remove HET from economic research classifications, first in Australia (by the Australian Bureau of Statistics in 2007) and then in the European Union (by the European Research Council in 2011).[9] My view is that HET belongs to both fields: a good practitioner of HET should be both knowledgeable in economic theory and in the history of culture.[10] Since the present paper is concerned with the role of HET in economic curricula, it is quite natural for the relationship between HET and economic theory to dominate the argument. As for the partition of academic careers, an opening to HET should be left in both

---

[8] Cf. for instance Schabas (1992).
[9] The story is told by Kates (2013).
[10] On this point cf. also Marcuzzo (2008).

fields, depending on the individual researcher's specialized contributions, as is the case in many other bridge disciplines.

Underlying the mainstream view on the limited usefulness of HET is a clear – though never explicitly stated – assumption, namely that there is but one correct approach to economics. We may label this a "cumulative view": economics does change over time, but with steady progress in the understanding of economic reality, piling up new theories and new facts. As mentioned above, the toolbox of the economic theorist may change (for instance, from Marshallian U-shaped cost curves to axiomatic Arrow-Debreu general equilibrium theory), but the underlying pillar – in short, the notion of market equilibrium between supply and demand – remains the same. From this viewpoint, the provisional point of arrival of contemporary economics incorporates all previous contributions in an improved way.

The "cumulative view" has, as its methodological (but often implicit and occasionally unconscious) background, a positivist view of science: economic theories based on deduction from first principles (scarcity of resources, agents' preferences, demand and supply equilibrium) are either logically consistent and hence true given the premises, or logically contradictory and hence false; factual statements are once again either empirically confirmed or contradicted; science progresses as theories and knowledge of facts cumulate.

This viewpoint has been supported by mainstream historians of economic thought from Jacob Hollander (1904; 1910) to Samuel Hollander (1973; 1979), through an interpretation of classical economists aligning them with the supply-and-demand-equilibrium view, so that they can be considered as perceptive but defective precursors of later views. This explains the importance of Piero Sraffa's (1951) reinterpretation of Ricardo (and with him of the whole classical economists' approach) as embedded in a different paradigm, which can be succinctly expressed as the "picture of the system of production and consumption as a circular process" (Sraffa, 1960: 93). In fact, in the 1960s and 1970s the debate between the contending paradigms proceeded along two parallel paths: the "Cambridge controversies" in the theory of capital and distribution (as illustrated for instance in Harcourt, 1972) and debates in the history of economic thought concerning, for instance, the role of supply and demand in the Classical (Smith's or Ricardo's in particular) theory of value and distribution.

3 The role of HET when the existence of different approaches to economics is recognized

As soon as we recognize the existence of different (and contending) paradigms,[11] the history of economic thought acquires a new, much more relevant, role. This is where Schumpeter's distinction between different stages in economic theorizing is relevant.

As is well known, in the first pages of his *History of Economic Analysis* Schumpeter (1954: 41-42) identifies distinct stages in economic research: i) the 'pre-analytic cognitive act' or 'vision', meaning by this a vague vision of the issue to be considered and some tentative hypotheses as to the direction of research; ii) conceptualisation, namely 'to verbalise the vision or to conceptualise it in such a way that its elements take their places, with names attached to them that facilitate recognition and manipulation, in a more or less orderly schema or picture'; iii) model building and, finally, iv) the application of such models to the interpretation of economic reality. What matters to us here is the second stage, quite often overlooked, although Schumpeter himself attributes great importance to it.

Conceptualization, in fact, becomes an essential aspect of the economist's work when the vision that the researcher is trying to develop differs from the visions adopted/developed by other theoreticians. It is in this stage that the theoretician can clarify the distinct character of her/his own representation of the world: not only the relative importance attributed to different aspects of the real world, but also and especially the perspective from which each aspect is viewed. Conceptualization is a complex activity, where for instance the requirement of consistency (which of course still holds) has a different, broader meaning as compared with the formal coherence required of

---

[11] It is beyond the scope of this paper to discuss the critiques of positivism and the alternative methodological views of Kuhn, Popper, Lakatos, McCloskey, etc.. For a concise survey of some of these views from the point of view of the history of economic thought cf. Roncaglia (2005, chapter 1).

mathematically-framed theories; in any case, conceptualization represents the (explicit or implicit) foundation for clarifying the connection between such mathematically-framed theories and the real world. For example, a formal model of functional income distribution relies on a class representation of society; analysis of financial managers' incentives relies on the conceptualization of a managerial (large corporations) economy rather than an economy based on small competitive firms.

It is not usual for mainstream theoreticians to overlook the role of this stage in economic research. This is because the underlying vision of the economy is common to all of them (though with different nuances) and is considered the only possible one. Supply and demand reasoning reigns supreme; differences between streams of mainstream economics are a matter of the framework to which supply and demand analysis is applied, as for instance when introducing market forms different from perfect competition, imperfect and asymmetric information, and the like. Thus, it is only these latter aspects that are considered when illustrating the conceptual foundations for the activity of model-building.

On the other hand, there are profound differences in the visions of the economy underlying Classical, Keynesian and neoclassical-marginalist economics. In order to understand them, recourse to the history of economic thought is necessary: it is only when seeking through HET a direct understanding of the visions of the world of a Smith, a Ricardo, a Keynes, a Jevons or a Walras that we can perceive these differences, and the true content of the different concepts referred to in formal analyses of the economy.

Let me make myself clear: this does not mean that HET is only useful from a non-mainstream point of view; a better understanding of the meaning of the concepts utilized in economic theorizing is essential whatever the researcher's own preferred approach. It is also essential – but this is a different, additional element – for a serious debate between contending approaches.[12] HET does not belong to heterodox economics: it belongs to

---

[12] Confrontation between contending approaches is useful for the scientific community at all levels, from the international community at large down to the individual university department level. This can be maintained on three accounts: as

every approach; it is useful, nay necessary, for economists of all persuasions. Confrontation with alternative viewpoints is in fact essential to mainstream economists for a better understanding of their own conceptual foundations.

The reason why HET appears to be more strongly connected to heterodox economics is precisely that these are minority approaches, so that confrontation is vital for them, as a means for climbing in the general opinion of the economic profession, while HET is vital for this confrontation, given its role, discussed above, for clarifying the different world-view adopted by mainstream economics as well as by each group of heterodox economists. Debate between contending approaches should be the salt of serious research activity: the majority rule should not be adopted as a criterion for damnation of dissenting views (as John Stuart Mill thought for the political field at large). From a slightly different context, let me recall Kula's (1958: 234) beautiful eulogy of history: "To understand the others: this is the historian's aim. It is not easy to have a more difficult task. It is difficult to have a more interesting one."

4 An illustration: Classical and Marginalist conceptualizations of the economy[13]

Let us briefly consider, by way of illustration, the main differences between the classical and the marginalist/neoclassical conceptualizations of the economy.

---

a stimulus to demonstrate by research that the adopted viewpoint is a progressive scientific research program; as a push to greater clarity in presenting research results; as a source of criticism essential to a conjecture-confutation scientific process. Departments in which different approaches coexist are more lively than departments where one single faith reigns supreme; this liveliness attracts bright students and constitutes a basic element in their formation as researchers. Of course this requires a strong morality and scientific openness.

[13] This outline presentation of the differences between contending approaches (for which I have drawn on Roncaglia, 2010) ignores important differences internal to each approach. We also leave aside a basic notion brought to the fore by the Keynesian approach, namely the notion of uncertainty (on the differences between the Keynesian and the Knightian notion of uncertainty, cf. Roncaglia (2009); it is this latter notion which has been embodied in the mainstream conceptual framework). For fuller illustration of the different views, cf. Roncaglia (2005).

The economics curriculum: towards a radical reformulation

The classical economists saw the economy as first and foremost characterized by the division of labour. There is not only separation of tasks within each production process, but also specialization of the different productive units turning out different (bundles of) commodities. Thus, at the end of each productive process, each productive unit - and each sector, or in other words each set of productive units utilizing similar production processes and producing similar commodities - needs to recover its means of production in exchange for at least part of its products. This gives rise to a web of exchanges which are necessary for the economy to subsist. Indeed, analysis of the conditions necessary for the vitality and sound functioning of a market economy based on the division of labour is the main object of the classical approach. Thus, according to the classical economists, in a market economy the exchange ratio between commodities must be such as to allow each sector to recover physical production costs and obtain profits constituting sufficient incentive to continue activity. Taking into account the dominant technology and a uniform profit rate – corresponding to the assumption of free competition, or in other words the absence of obstacles to capital movements from one sector to another – the classical economists set out to determine production prices: those prices, that is, which are compatible with regular continuation of economic activity. Within their approach, income distribution between profits and wages is not univocally determined by technical givens, and is commonly treated as an open (economic, but also socio-political) issue.

According to the marginalist/neoclassical approach, economic agents have at their disposal given amounts of scarce resources (or original endowments), which are then utilized to satisfy their needs and desires (directly, through exchange and consumption, and indirectly, through production processes in which productive resources are transformed into consumption goods and services). Indeed, analysis of the conditions under which resources are optimally allocated to the satisfaction of human needs and desires is the main object of the marginalist approach. The market here is a point in time and space where demand and supply meet: its archetype is the market fair, and in more recent times the stock exchange or, more precisely, the old-fashioned continental exchanges, based on call markets, even more than the continuous dealing Anglo-Saxon exchanges which constitute the rule in contemporary economies. (In the classical approach, as pointed out above, the market is a web of commodity flows, recurring period after period, which link up all sectors of the economy.) As an implication of this viewpoint, within the marginalist approach the notion of prices refers to indicators of the relative scarcity of goods and services available at each given moment in time to satisfy the needs and desires of economic agents. This implies assuming the relative intensity of needs and desires as given data in addressing the problem. In the classical approach, on the other hand, prices are indicators of relative difficulty of production;[14] the problem here is how to express in terms of value – in terms of a single magnitude, that is – all the different physical costs while at the same time respecting the distributive rules of a capitalist economy; consumption choices are analyzed, rather, by reference to (social) habits evolving over time. Similar differences can be illustrated for the notions of social classes and the analysis of income distribution, the notion of competition and the analysis of market forms, and so on.

5 The role of HET in undergraduate and in graduate curricula

Let us conclude by summarizing the implications of the arguments illustrated above for the role of HET in undergraduate and graduate curricula.

In the first case, a systematic illustration of the history of our discipline is a way to present undergraduate students with the different approaches which have existed over time, often simultaneously, and their rise and fall (which, by the way, should appeal to mainstream economists, who should find a reason of pride in being not the only ones around but – pro tempore at least – those emerging as winners from a centuries-long debate).

An execrable practice in drawing up undergraduate curricula is to include only the study of the mainstream approach in its various components. The customary excuse is that presenting a single truth and avoiding controversy simplifies life for the students – with, once again, the covert assumption that

---

[14] "Relative" here refers to comparison between the different production processes; in marginalist analysis, instead, "relative" refers to demand-supply comparison which, in a general equilibrium approach, concerns simultaneously all the goods and services in the economy.

there is only one single 'true' approach in economics. This authoritarian attitude implies that eighteen-year-olds may have the right to vote in political elections but they still remain so simple-minded as to get confused when confronted with a simple fact of life, namely that there are different and often conflicting viewpoints for all aspects of life, including how a market economy works. On the contrary, and even if students were unable to make up their own minds about contending economic approaches – provisionally, of course, and keeping an open mind, as we all should do – it is of the utmost importance that they be educated to take pluralism in their stride, in economics as in any other subject matter. Thus, in undergraduate education, HET has a crucial democratic role, confronting students with the idea that there are different approaches to economics, and providing them with some notion of the conceptual foundations of such approaches: the background they emerged from and their evolution in response both to theoretical debate and to historical events. This helps towards a better understanding and evaluation of formalised theories/models, thus constituting a prerequisite for serious study of economic theory.

In the case of graduate curricula, assuming that they are directed to prepare economists for a research career, and assuming that the existence of different approaches is an already acquired component of undergraduate education, HET has a twin formative role. First, HET educates to evaluating the content of concepts and, in connection with the study of economic history (another under-represented but necessary component of economic curricula), the shift such a content undergoes over time, partly in response to theoretical developments and partly in response to changes in economic reality, namely to history; hence, acquisition of the rhetorical method of confrontation. Second, HET educates to a method – the philological method of faithfulness to text and context – which is different from those exercised in theorizing or in applied research and which is most useful in understanding the world confronting us, where culture and ideas are such an important component of the economic environment.[15] The philological method is also important for its formative character in the ethics of research: attention to details and openness to confrontation with different points of view, absence

---

[15] This is, from a somewhat different viewpoint, the aspect stressed by Viner and discussed above.

of definitive truths but consciousness of degrees of superior or inferior quality in the analysis.

The declining role if not the absence of HET from undergraduate and graduate curricula is not so much a problem for the confraternity of HET practitioners. What we mainly lose is room for the employment of our students, while an already established practitioner of this discipline can move to the fields of history of culture, or history of science. It is above all a problem for the economics discipline at large. In fact economics, a-historically interpreted as model building and applied analysis based on econometric exercises, is losing ground to business schools and to faculties of political and social sciences, and especially to sociology – which, a century ago, was a sub-discipline internal to economics itself. Economics without HET is a body without soul.

References

Blaug, M. (2001) 'No history of ideas, please, we're economists', *Journal of Economic Perspectives*, 15: 145-64.

Caldwell, B. (2013) 'Of positivism and the history of economic thought', *Southern Economic Journal*, 79: 753-67.

Gordon, D. (1965) 'The role of the history of economic thought in the understanding of modern economic theory', *American Economic Review*, 55: 119-27.

Harcourt, G. C. (1972) *Some Cambridge controversies in the theory of capital*. Cambridge: Cambridge University Press.

Hicks, J. (1969) *A theory of economic history*. Oxford: Oxford University Press.

Hollander, J. (1904) 'The development of Ricardo's theory of value', *Quarterly Journal of Economics*, 18: 455-91.

Hollander, J. (1910) *David Ricardo - A centenary estimate*. Baltimore; repr. New York: McKelley, 1968.

Hollander, S. (1973) *The economics of Adam Smith*. Toronto: University of Toronto Press.

Hollander, S. (1979) *The economics of David Ricardo*. Toronto: University of Toronto Press.

Keynes, J. M. (1973) *The General Theory and after*, in *Collected writings*, vols. 13 (*Part I: preparation*) and 14 (*Part II: defense and development*), ed. by D. Moggridge. London: Macmillan.

Kates, S. (2013) *Defending the history of economic thought*. Cheltenham: Edward Elgar.

Kula, W. (1958 [1990]) *Riflessioni sulla storia*. Venezia: Marsilio (English translation, *The problems and methods of economic history*, Aldershot: Ashgate, 2001).

Marcuzzo, M. C. (2008) 'Is history of economic thought a "serious" subject?', *Erasmus Journal for Philosophy and Economics*, 1: 107-23.

Marcuzzo, M. C. and Rosselli, A. (2002) 'Economics as history of economics: the Italian case in retrospect', in Weintraub (ed.): 98-109.

Mill, J. S. (1863 [1987]) *Utilitarianism*, reprinted in Mill J.S. and Bentham, J., *Utilitarianism and other essays*, ed. by A. Ryan. London: Penguin Books.

Roncaglia, A. (1996) 'Why should economists study the history of economic thought?', *European Journal of the History of Economic Thought*, 3: 296-309.

Roncaglia, A. (2005) *The wealth of ideas*, Cambridge: Cambridge University Press.

Roncaglia, A. (2009) 'Keynes and probability: an assessment', *European Journal of the History of Economic Thought*, 16: 489-510.

Roncaglia, A. (2010) 'The origins of social inequality: beavers for women, deer for men', in A. Birolo, D. Foley, H. Kurz, B. Schefold, I. Steedman (eds.), *Production, distribution and trade: alternative perspectives. Essays in honour of Sergio Parrinello*. London: Routledge, pp. 289-303.

Samuelson, P. A. (1947) *Foundations of economic analysis*. Cambridge (Mass.): Harvard University Press.

Schabas, M. (1992) 'Breaking away: history of economics as history of science', *History of Political Economy*, 24: 187-203.

Schumpeter, J. (1954) *History of economic analysis*, ed. by E. Boody Schumpeter. New York: Oxford University Press.

Sraffa, P. (1951) 'Introduction', in Ricardo D.,. *Works and correspondence*, 10 vols., ed. by P. Sraffa, Cambridge: Cambridge University Press, 1951-55, vol. I, pp. xiii-lxii.

Sraffa, P. (1960) *Production of commodities by means of commodities*. Cambridge: Cambridge University Press.

Viner, J. (1991) *Essays on the intellectual history of economics*, ed. by D.A. Irwin. Princeton: Princeton University Press.

Weintraub, R. (ed.) (2002) *The future of the history of economics*. Annual Supplement, *History of Political Economy,* 34.

Weintraub, R. (2002) 'Will economics ever have a past again?', in Weintraub (ed.): 1-14.

Acknowledgments

Thanks are due to Donald Gillies, Grazia Ietto, Cristina Marcuzzo and Annalisa Rosselli for reading and commenting on a previous draft. Thanks are also due to Andres Bedoya and especially to Constantinos Repapis and Nicholas Theocarakis for their contributions in the *Economic Thought* Open Peer Discussion forum on this paper, which has accordingly been substantially revised.

CHAPTER 5

The multinationals' age is everywhere but in the economics curriculum

Grazia Ietto-Gillies

1 Introduction

The title of this paper paraphrases a famous statement by Robert Solow (1987)[1] and it deliberately exaggerates the application to the multinational companies (MNCs) or transnational companies (TNCs) as I prefer to call them to emphasise their ability to operate across nation-states and not just in several of them.

My own limited experience as a scholar in the subject and a teacher for many years in a business school is the following. Most economics departments have, for a very long time, shied away from research and pedagogy into the TNCs. However, research and teaching into this subject has flourished in the last thirty years. The subject is taught in a variety of institutions ranging from Business Schools to Development Studies, Geography, Human Resources, Marketing and Strategy Departments. Business Schools have tended to be interested in both the TNC as an institution and in its defining modality: foreign direct investment (FDI). The interest of other type of departments tends to focus mainly on FDI.

Moreover there is a very active and wide community of researchers in the subject. They are united under the banner of 'International Business' which includes a very large number of scholars from a variety of disciplines. They have both research and pedagogic interests and they talk to each other and collaborate across disciplines.

The research and teaching has been mainly unorthodox in approach though not necessarily radical. However, the neoclassical paradigm has established roots into this growing successful field from the mid 1980s. Scholars of New

---

[1] 'You can see the computer age everywhere but in the productivity statistics' (p. 36).

Trade Theories – such as Markusen, Krugman and Venables – have moved into the field and developed New Trade Theories applied to multinational corporations. This has made the subject more acceptable in neo-classical circles and may be responsible for an increasing inclusion of the field into pedagogy in economics departments. The appearance of a textbook – highlighting only this approach – to the explanation of why MNCs exist and operate across countries may have helped the process (Barba, Navaretti and Venables, 2004).[2]

2 A brief excursion into the theoretical background

The theory of TNCs starts with the seminal work of Stephen Hymer, a Canadian student working at the MIT under the supervision of Charles Kindleberger. His thesis (1960, published 1976), has novel insights such as: (1) the distinction between portfolio and direct foreign investment and their different motivations and determinants; (2) the role of control in investment decisions; and (3) the role of structural market imperfections and market power in the decisions of international firms. Hymer's later work – before his early death in a car crash – was more radical in its analysis of the effects of international firms on developing countries, on labour and on the constraints they posed on the policies of national governments (Hymer, 1966; 1971; 1972; 1975)

Other theoretical developments followed and some became very successful. They deal with a variety of aspects of international business though the unifying theme is strategies and behaviour of TNCs. The International Product Life Cycle theory of Raymond Vernon (1966) was also developed at Cambridge (Massachusetts) at the Harvard Business School. The environment in which it was developed may have given it the specific

---

[2] There are many textbooks on the MNCs or on international business in general. Most of them take the strategy/marketing route. Dicken (2003) has a geographical perspective. Ietto-Gillies (2012) analyses TNCs and their activities largely from an economics point of view. It deals with Concepts (Part I); Pre-WWII theories (Marxists and Neoclassical) in Part II. Part III deals with most of the theories developed since Hymer's including all those mentioned in Section two of this chapter. In Part IV the book considers effects of TNCs' activities. Large parts of the material in this chapter derive from this book.

multidisciplinary and dynamic characteristics. On the other side of the Atlantic – at the University of Reading - some scholars were developing a Coasian theory of the MNCs based on transaction costs: the internalization theory (Buckley and Casson, 1976) originating with McManus (1972). John Dunning' interest in MNCs dates back to the late 1950s; his 1977 and 1980 papers put forward a theory which aims to explain all modes of international business activities from trade to licensing to direct investment. His eclectic approach developed the notion of a three-prong set of advantages: pertaining to firms – the ownership advantages; pertaining to countries – the locational advantages; and those related to internalization advantages, i.e. to the choice between developing business activities in-house or externalizing them. Dunning's theory took off in a big way and became the staple of research and pedagogy particularly in business schools. The underlying schematic framework made it easy to apply to most cases, but there lies the problem: The theory became almost tautological in its all-embracing scope, a fault that Dunning recognized and tried to redress (Dunning, 2000a and b).

A more strategy and marketing approach is present in the very dynamic theory developed by the Scandinavian School. Johanson and Wiedesheim-Paul (1975) and Johanson and Vahlne (1977) explained the stages and modalities of penetration of foreign markets that international companies go through. Their approach is rooted in a multidisciplinary approach that considers issues of strategy, marketing and management as an essential part of the decision-making process.

Multidisciplinarity is present also in the Evolutionary Theories approach to the TNCs (Cantwell, 1989; Kogut and Zander, 1993) all of which have roots in Nelson and Winter (1982). They stress the learning function within TNCs and the advantages it generates. The international environment in which they operate allows TNCs to learn from the different countries in which they operate. This puts them in a stronger position on the innovation front and thus gives them competitive advantages. However, there are constraints to learning and to the diffusion of knowledge internally and externally to companies. The organizational structure of companies may facilitate or hinder the transmission and spread of knowledge, whether the diffusion is to other parts of the company or to the localities in which TNCs operate or from the local environment to their subsidiaries. Many of the works dealing with these latter aspects originated in the organizational and managerial literature on TNCs (Bartlett and Ghoshal, 1989; Gupta and Govinbdarajan 1991, 2000; Hedlund, 1986).

The 1980s saw the publication of a new approach to theories of the TNCs by well-known economics scholars, specifically: Helpman (1984); Markusen (1984 and 1995); Krugman (1985, 1987; 1991 a and b; 1998); Krugman and Venables (1996); Venables (1998). The approach was developed on the back of their successful and established New Trade Theories of trade and – on the international business side – on the back of the internalization and of the eclectic theories. The overall approach is one of partial equilibrium analysis in which MNCs are profit maximizers under specific cost conditions derived from ad hoc assumptions. It is a theory of location of production in which assumptions about fixed costs at the firm level – over and above any fixed costs at the plant level – lead to a multi-plant organization of production. This approach is specific to spatial location and is one that geographers have been considering for a long time though, usually, without the mathematical techniques used by the New Trade theorists. Krugman (1991a) acknowledges the relevance of geography for economics and economic theories. At the theoretical level their approach is largely spatial and therefore as applicable to inter-regional location of production as to inter-national location. In other words there is not much which is nation-states specific. Not much that might highlight the differences in a US company based in Michigan deciding to invest in Texas or California as against the same company decisions to invest in the UK or Bulgaria or Tunisia. In practice – and not surprisingly – the models are not corroborated by the empirics. Krugman (1998: 15) writes on this point: "preliminary efforts ... have found that such models are not at all easy to calibrate to actual data; in general, the tendency toward agglomeration is stronger in the models than in the real economy!"

3 TNCs and economics: an uneasy relationship

It may be seen as too facile to state that the TNCs' activities do not figure – or not enough – in the economics curriculum. And this is not just because I do not have hard evidence; it is also because it could be pointed out that many other areas of economics do not figure prominently or enough to satisfy scholars in the fields.

Indeed, regarding the TNCs it could be claimed that the theory of the firm does figure prominently in the curriculum and if the TNCs are taught in a couple of lectures within a module on the firm, that should suffice. Moreover, it could reasonably be queried whether there is a need for specific theories of the TNCs over and above theories of the firm. In this section I want to deal with this query before (in the next section) developing the case for the relevance of TNCs for research and pedagogy from both a micro and macro perspective.

To the lay person it would seem obvious that we need to study the activities of the most important economic agents operating today: transnational companies. Moreover, it would seem obvious that we must try and explain their most relevant activity: international production/foreign direct investment.

However, there are strong reasons – linked to both methodology and subject matter – why economic researchers have been unable or unwilling to fit the TNC and its activities into the main body of their theories. There are also very good reasons why the topic should now be given a stronger role in the economics curriculum and research. To both of these I now turn.

Let us begin with trying to see the reasons why the transnational as such has no specific place in economic theory particularly in macroeconomic theory. Let us assume for a moment a wholly theoretical world in which all national barriers and frontiers have come down; one single currency circulates; a single tax regime is in operation; the labour market and social security system are unified. In other words, the world becomes one single country/nation-state and is governed as such. In such a world we would have no theory of international production: there would be no need for it. We would work within the confines of spatial location theory to explain where production is located and with theories of the firm, business governance and market structure to explain the growth of firms, their organization and their behaviour *vis-à-vis* other firms. Thus we would not need a theory of transnational companies to understand *who* invests, *where* and *why*.

In fact we do not attach much relevance to the identity of the investors when they originate from other regions within the same nation-state, for example, when a Texan firm invests in Massachusetts or a Piemontese firm invests in Calabria. Why should we consider the origin of the firm as relevant when it is from a foreign country?

In general, when analysing economic activities, economists tend to ignore the actual nationality of the investor. Instead, the main focus has been on such issues as: the firm in general or in relation to its size; the market structure of an industry; the production, investment or trade of the macro economy independently of the nationality of the firm producing, investing or trading. This is exactly what we do when we study, for example, international trade theory: we analyse the comparative conditions and advantages of the trading countries and/or the impact of trade on them independently of the national identity of the exporter firm. Why should we bother with such identity when the operator is someone investing in many countries?

Economists traditionally have looked into the identity of the investor, when analysing the investment by public versus private firms. The reason for this is clear: the public investor is supposed to have different *objectives* compared with the private one and therefore the characteristic 'private versus public' does matter. However, this is not the case when the investor is a TNC. Whether the firm is foreign or domestic, multinational or a uninational firm, the objectives are not different; they are profit or profit-related objectives.

In fact, the reason why in our case the uninational or multinational character of the investor matters has nothing to do with objectives but with *strategies*. The argument for specific studies of the TNCs and for their incorporation into the main body of the economics curriculum is the existence of nation-states. In other words theories of transnational companies and of foreign direct investment are needed because we have nation-states and frontiers and these have a bearing on firms' strategies. Such strategies affect the levels and patterns of world investment and production. They also affect the economic and social context in which other agents – such as labour, uninational firms or governments – operate. They do, in particular, affect the context of government policy. This is the main reason why a study of TNCs and their activities is important, and indeed essential, for an understanding of the activities of firms, industries and national economies in the global context.

4 Why the activities of TNCs should be an essential part of the curriculum

The relationship between micro and macro economics has never been easy. These have mostly been and still are two separate and not consistent parts of economics and they are taught as such. Yet the emergence and growth of large TNCs – and many TNCs are large though a growing number of smaller firms are becoming transnationals – has made the separation and inconsistency more glaring. Moreover, the nature and activities of TNCs also raise questions for the traditional categories of economics and its curriculum. Macroeconomics tends to be largely nation-based; the theory of the firm tends to be geographically and country neutral; the theory of international trade tends to be country or region based. But the main actor in all these elements – the TNC – operates in many geographies. Moreover, though their country of origin and residence is still very relevant, they operate *across* nation-states; they also operate in a variety of modalities – from direct production abroad to licensing and franchising to subcontraction – of which exports and imports are only one.[3]

Looking at TNCs as firms, the case for a separate theoretical approach to their existence, growth and activities rests on the fact that the existence of nation-states – across which they operate – gives them opportunities for strategies to enhance their power and improve their position and profitability.

Zetlin (1974: 1090) argues that power (and control) "is essentially relative and relational: how much power, with respect to whom?" Companies' power has usually been analysed in relation to market power and, therefore, with

---

[3] However, trade is a very important modality from the perspective of countries and the global economy. TNCs are responsible for some 80 percent of world trade. Moreover, one third of world trade takes place on an intra-firm basis, i.e. between units of the same TNC which are located in different countries (UNCTAD, 2013: fig. IV.14 and Box IV.3: 135-6).

respect to rival firms. In fact, many theories of the TNC deal – to a greater or lesser degree – with strategic behaviour towards rival firms (Vernon, 1966; Knickerbocker, 1973; Graham, 1978; 2000; Cowling and Sudgen, 1987; Cantwell, 1989; 1995; Dunning, 1993; Buckley and Casson, 1998). However, power may also relate to other players in the economic system and specifically labour, governments, suppliers/distributors, subcontractors.

Power is used in the resolution of conflicts, particularly those over distributional issues arising from production or market conditions. In the case of conflicts with rivals, the distribution relates to market shares; in the case of labour, the conflict is over distribution between profits and wages; in the case of conflicts with governments' the issue is distribution over the overall surplus and how much should go to the private sphere – companies – or public sphere – governments and taxpayers.

Ietto-Gillies (2012: ch 14) argues that operating across countries gives companies a stronger bargaining power towards labour and towards governments. In turn this results also in a stronger position towards rival companies. The stronger bargaining power of TNCs is linked to specific features of nation-states, i.e., that each nation-state has a different regulatory regime governing the country's economic, social and political life. Specifically each nation-state has its own:

- Rules and regulations regarding the social security system and in particular different regimes regarding labour.
- Fiscal regimes.
- Currency regimes.
- Regime of industrial policy with regard to incentives to businesses.
- Rules and regulations regarding environmental and safety standards.

The existence of different regulatory regimes across nation-states allows companies that can truly plan, organize and control across frontiers to develop strategies for taking advantage of differences in such regulatory regimes. This is particularly true when the strategies aim to enhance power *vis-à-vis* actors who cannot – or not yet – plan and organize across national frontiers, or not to the same extent as TNCs. The advantage of transnationality can manifest in relation to labour, in negotiations with governments, towards suppliers, risk spreading, and the acquisition of knowledge and innovation.

Some of the advantages involve distributional issues and conflicts particularly in relation to labour and governments. However, any advantage towards labour, governments or suppliers will eventually lead to competitive advantages towards rival firms. The advantages deriving from risk spreading and acquisition of knowledge and innovation directly put the TNC in a better position towards rivals. Advantages towards rivals, whatever their origin, involve distribution over market shares.

The enhanced bargaining power towards labour given by transnationality derives from the fact that: (a) social security and labour markets regulations differ across countries; moreover, labour organization and solidarity is low across countries but relatively higher within a single country. This leads to a fragmented labour force across the national frontiers and thus to lower bargaining power for the labour force employed by the same TNC in many countries. It therefore leads to the opportunity for TNCs to exploit such fragmentation to gain better conditions in bargaining for wages and conditions.[4] Other labour fragmentation strategies are also implemented, usually contemporaneously, and relate to the organization of production. Externalization of some activities by large companies and public sector institutions leads to a more fragmented labour force and thus reduces its bargaining power within a country. Internationally, some companies may pursue strategies of both geographical – by nation-state – and organizational fragmentation. In fact, many sub-contracting activities take place at the international level.

The ability to operate across countries also gives TNCs bargaining power in negotiating incentives for inward investment with governments in different countries. Some playing off of governments against each other may also occur at the intra-country, or regional level whenever regions of the same country are free to set their own conditions for attracting foreign investment.

---

[4] This is evident in the strategies of the car manufacturer FIAT during the last few years. The management has achieved a new, favourable bargaining context for the company by pitting Italian, American and Polish work forces against each other.

The current moves towards possible devolution of regions within the UK, Italy or Spain will be in the interest of TNCs who can extract better conditions from different regulatory regimes within the same country.[5]

Operating across countries may also give a better bargaining position towards suppliers who tend to be smaller companies operating in one or two countries only. Over and above these advantages deriving from the bargaining position, transnationality offers advantages in terms of risk spreading. It also gives advantages in terms of knowledge acquisition from different geographical, economic and social contexts and in its diffusion among the different units of the company, as mentioned earlier in section two.[6]

These considerations make the case for a full and independent treatment of TNCs as part of the theories of the firm. Their ability to plan, organize and control activities across national frontiers gives them opportunities for strategic behaviour over and above that of any uninational company and independent of size. Thus transnationality can be turned into a considerable advantage. A full understanding of this issue requires an analysis in terms of strategic behaviour, which is best done in the context of a multidisciplinary approach. Thus any proper analysis of TNCs must move away from cost efficiency and equilibrium models in favour of real life strategic analysis. If the latter leads to less precise results, so be it. It is better to be imprecisely correct than precisely wrong.

5 The relevance of TNCs in the macro context

The above discussion of power of the TNCs in bargaining with governments takes the perspective of the companies, i.e. the micro perspective. However, the size, scope and power of TNCs towards governments, labour and other stakeholders and their relevance in general to the economies of single countries – especially when not very large – raise issues about the

---

[5] In 2014 the British media reported that the White Paper on Scottish devolution includes the plan to lower the corporation tax to attract foreign direct investment into an independent Scotland.
[6] See also Frenz and Ietto-Gillies, 2007; Filippetti et al., 2011 and 2012.

relevance of TNCs for the macro environment.[7] They therefore raise issues at the policy level and at the level of our categories in economics.

The relevance on the macro environment derives from the TNC's sheer power to affect employment, production, productivity and most of the variables key to growth and prosperity. At the government level their bargaining power affects the fiscal position of countries via the incentives given to them including those related to taxation. Moreover, on the taxation side corporations that operate in many countries have wide scope for the manipulation of transfer prices.

Transfer prices are charged by one part of the company (headquarters or one of the subsidiaries) to another part for the internal transfer of goods and services. When the internal transfer of goods and services takes place across borders as part of transnational activities, the corporations have the opportunity to develop pricing strategies that maximize the overall returns for the company as a whole. Such strategies may lead to the so-called 'manipulation of transfer prices,' where manipulation refers to the setting of prices for internal transfers at different levels compared with the prices which might be charged for arm's-length transactions, i.e. different levels compared with the actual or potential market prices. Why would a company want to manipulate transfer prices? In what conditions and for what reasons would such a manipulation lead to higher company-wide profits?

The most common – and best known – reason[8] for the manipulation of transfer prices is the minimization of the overall tax liability of the company. A company faced with tax liabilities in many countries is also likely to be faced with different tax rates in different countries as part of their different regulatory regimes. If the company can disclose most of its profits in the

---

[7] Rahoul Deodhar (http://curriculumconference2013.worldeconomicsassociation.org/the-multinationals-age-is-everywhere-but-in-the-economics-curriculum/#comments) - in his comment to the conference paper from which the current chapter derives – points out that 'TNCs straddle macro-economic advantages and micro-economic advantages'.

[8] On transfer prices see also Eden (2001). For a more extensive discussion on reasons and effects of the manipulation of transfer prices see Ietto-Gillies (2012: ch. 20).

country with the lowest tax rate, it will avoid the charge of higher tax rates on some of its profits.

Companies that engage in international vertically integrated strategies of production have wide scope for transfer of components across countries and therefore have wide scope for manipulating transfer prices. However, such a manipulation can occur also in the pricing of services transferred between different parts of the company. These can be factor services – like the services of a highly skilled technical expert or manager – or product services. Many of these services or components are specific to the company and may not have a market price. Detection of possible manipulation of transfer prices may, therefore, be difficult. However, it is not impossible if reference is made to costs rather than market prices.

The issue of the effects of manipulation of transfer prices has come to the media fore in late 2012 during a probe by a House of Commons Public Accounts Committee into the low tax returns of major TNCs – such as Amazon, Starbucks and Google - for their UK operations. The large media coverage pointed out that it was a matter of where the companies chose to declare profits. They have also been keen to stress that whatever practices the companies were using, they were legal and so the issue was mainly one of ethics and morality rather than one of legality. I would like to point out the following. First, I do not know the details of how each of the companies ended up paying little or no corporation tax in a country where they seem to be doing quite well. However, if – and I stress if – the process was helped by invoicing at prices different from the potential arm's-length ones, or at prices with little or no relationship to the actual costs of goods and services being transferred, then there may be legal questions to be asked by clever and willing Inland Revenue officials.[9] Moreover, if the law allows companies to pay no tax in countries where they have a considerable amount of profitable business, then questions must be raised for the law and the government of the country. In my view it is not so much a moral/ethical issue as one of law,

---

[9] The Organization for Economic Cooperation and Development (2010) gives detailed guidelines for companies and tax administrators on how to – respectively – set and monitor transfer prices. These guidelines are of use to other stakeholders and to general policy makers.

of law enforcement, of accounting skills and resources by tax revenue offices and of government policies. This makes the activities of TNCs all the more intertwined with macroeconomic analysis and policy.

The manipulation of transfer prices has considerable effects on: (1) the tax revenue of individual countries and of the world as a whole; (2) their Balance of Payments position; (3) the size of the distribution of surplus between public and private spheres. For all these reasons I consider that inclusion of the study of TNCs in the economics curriculum is essential for a proper understanding of both the micro and macro context of real economies in the XXI century.

6 Summary and conclusions

The paper starts with the provocative assertion that TNCs have very little impact on today's economics curriculum. It aims to show that an understanding of modern economies cannot be obtained without an understanding of how TNCs operate. It then touches on the development of theories of the TNCs in the last 50 years. It considers the relationship between economics and the study of TNCs arguing for the relevance of inclusion of such a study for both the micro and macro curricula. At the micro level the issue of strategic behaviour by TNCs is considered in relation to the opportunity for strategies offered by transnationality. Such opportunities are related to the enhanced bargaining power open to TNCs. Some macro issues of TNCs' activities and behaviour are considered particularly in relation to the manipulation of transfer prices.

The TNCs are here to stay. The organization of production across different nation-states and geographies has been a reality for the best part of the XX century and beyond. It has been greatly enhanced by the use of digital technologies in the planning of production and in the development of markets. In many respects the TNCs are a force for progress in their organizational and technological innovation. However, as private companies their interest does not always coincide with the interests of society as a whole. It is the role of governments to properly channel the potential and activities of TNCs in the interest of other stakeholders. It is for us economists to try and understand how they operate; the effects of their activities; and what policies may be needed to maximize the benefits – or minimize the costs - of their activities for economies and societies. It is our duty as researchers and educationalists (a) to delve into this important aspect of our real economies in a way that leads to a better understanding of them. If this requires collaboration with other disciplines, we should welcome it; and (b) to include very widely this important part of the real economy into our economics curricula. Anything else may be a betrayal of our mission as researchers and educationalists.

References

Barba Navaretti, G. and Venables, A. J. (2004) *Multinational Firms in the World Economy*. Princeton and Oxford: Princeton University Press,

Bartlett, C. A. and Ghoshal, S. (1989) *Managing Across Borders: The Transnational Solution*. Boston, MA: Harvard Business School Press.

Buckley, P. J. and Casson, M. C. (1976) 'A long-run theory of the multinational Enterprise' In: Buckley, P. J. and Casson, M. C. (eds.), *The Future of the Multinational Enterprise*. London: Macmillan, 32-65.

Buckley, P. J. and Casson, M. C. (1998) 'Analyzing foreign market entry strategies: extending the internalization approach', *Journal of International Business Studies*, 29, 3: 539-62.

Cantwell, J. (1989) *Technological Innovation and Multinational Corporations*. Oxford: Blackwell.

Cantwell, J. (1995) 'The globalisation of technology: What remains of the product cycle model?', *Cambridge Journal of Economics*, 19, 1: 155-74.

Cowling, K. and Sugden, R. (1987) *Transnational Monopoly Capitalism*. Brighton: Wheatsheaf.

Dicken, P. (2003) *Global Shift: Reshaping the Global Economic Map in the XXI Century*, London: Sage Publications, 4th edition.

Dunning, J. H. (1977) 'Trade, location of economic activity and the NINE: a search for an eclectic approach'. In: Ohlin, B., Hesselborn, P. O. and Wijkman, P. M. (eds.), *The International Allocation of Economic Activity*. London: Macmillan, 395-431.

Dunning, J. H. (1980) 'Explaining changing patterns of international production: in defense of the eclectic theory'. *Oxford Bulletin of Economics and Statistics*, 41 (4), 269-95.

Dunning, J. H. (1993) *The Globalization of Business*. London: Routledge.

Dunning, J. H. (2000a) 'The eclectic paradigm as an envelope for economic and business theories of MNE activity', *International Business Review*, 9: 163-90.

Dunning, J. H. (2000b) 'The eclectic paradigm of international production: a personal perspective, In: Pitelis, C. and Sugden R. (eds.) *The Nature of the Transnational Firm*, London: Routledge, ch. 5: 119- 39.

Eden, L. (2001) 'Taxes, Transfer Pricing, and the Multinational Enterprise', In: Rugman. A.M. and Brewer, T. L. (eds.), *The Oxford Handbook of International Business*, Oxford: Oxford University Press, ch. 21: 591-619.

Frenz, M. and Ietto-Gillies, G. (2007) ' Does multinationality affect the propensity to innovate? An analysis of the third UK Community Innovation Survey', *International Review of Applied Economics*, 21, 1: 99–117.

Filippetti, A., Frenz, M. and Ietto-Gillies, G. (2011) 'Are innovation and internationalization related? An analysis of European countries'. *Industry and Innovation,* 18, 5, July.

Filippetti, A., Frenz, M. and Ietto-Gillies, G. (2012) 'The role of internationalization as a determinant of innovation performance. An analysis of 42 countries', *Centre for Innovation Management Research, CIMR, Research Working Paper Series*, No. 10, presented at the 32nd EIBA conference 2012 at the University of Sussex, Brighton, UK, Dec 7-9.

Graham, E. M. (1978) 'Transatlantic investment by multinational firms: a rivalristic phenomenon? *Journal of post-Keynesian Economics*, 1, 1, Fall.

Graham, E. M. (2000) 'Strategic mangement and transnational firm behaviour: a formal approach', in C.M. Pitelis and R. Sugden (eds.), *The Nature of the Transnational Firm*, London: Routledge, 2nd edition, ch. 7: 162–73.

Gupta, A. K. and Govindarajan, V. (1991) 'Knowledge flows and the structure of control within multinational corporations', *Academy of Management Review*, 16, 4: 768–792.

Gupta, A. K. and Govindarajan, V. (2000) 'Knowledge flows within multinational corporations', *Strategic Management Journal*, 21, 4: 473–496.

Hedlund, G. (1986) 'The hypermodern MNC – a heterarchy?', *Human Resource Management,* 25, 1: 9–35.

Helpman, E. (1984) 'A simple Theory of International Trade with Multinational Corporations', *Journal of Political Economy*, 92, 3: 451-471.

Hymer, S. H. (1960 [1976]) *The International Operations of National Firms: a Study of Direct Foreign Investment*. Cambridge, MA: MIT Press.

Hymer. S. H. (1966) 'Direct foreign investment and the national economic interest', In: Russell, P. (ed.) *Nationalism in Canada*, Toronto: McGraw-Hill, 191-202.

Hymer, S. H. (1971) 'The multinational corporation and the law of uneven Development', In: Bhagwati, J. W. (ed.), *Economics and World Order*. London: Macmillan, 113-40. Reproduced in Radice, H. (ed.) (1975), *International Firms and Modern Imperialism*. Harmondsworth: Penguin, 113-35.

Hymer, S. H. (1972) 'The internationalisation of capital', *The Journal of Economic Issues*, 6, 1: 91-111.

Hymer, S. H. (1975), 'The Multinational Corporation and the law of Uneven Development', In: Radice, H. (ed.) *International Firms and Modern Imperialism*, Hammondsworth: Penguin Books, 113-135.

Ietto-Gillies, G. (2012) *Transnational Corporations and International production. Concepts, Theories and Effects*. Chelthenham, UK and Northampton, MA, USA: Edward Elgar. Second Edition.

Johanson, J. and Vahlne, J-E. (1977) 'The Internationalization Process of the Firm- A model of Knowledge development and increasing Foreign Market Commitment' *Journal of International Business Studies*, 8, 1: 23-32.

Johanson. J. and Wiedersheim-Paul, F. (1975) 'The Internationalization of the Firm: Four Swedish Cases', *Journal of Management Studies*, October, 305-22.

Knickerbocker, F. T. (1973) *Oligopolistic Reaction and Multinational Enterprise*. Cambridge, MA: Division of Research, Graduate School of Business Administration, Harvard University.

Kogut, B. and Zander, U. (1993) 'Knowledge of the Firm and the Evolutionary Theory of the multinational Corporation', *Journal of International Business Studies*, 4th quarter: 625-45.

Krugman, P. (1985) 'Increasing Returns and the Theory of International Trade', *National Bureau of Economic Research Working Papers*, No. 1752, November.

Krugman, P. (1987) 'The narrow moving band, the Dutch Disease and the competitive consequences of Mrs Thatcher: Notes on trade in the presence of dynamic scale economies', *Journal of Development Economics*, 27: 41-55.

Krugman, P. (1991a) *Geography and Trade*, Cambridge, MA: The MIT Press.

Krugman, P. (1991b) 'Increasing Returns and Economic Geography', *Journal of Political Economy*, 99: 483-99.

Krugman, P. (1998) 'What's new about the new economic geography?', *Oxford Review of Economic Policy*, 14, 2: 7-17.

Krugman, P. and Venables, A. (1996) 'Integration, specialisation and adjustment', *European Economic Review*, 40: 959-967.

McManus, J. (1972) 'The theory of the international firm', in Paquet, Gilles (ed.), *The Multinational Firm and the Nation State*, Don Mills, Ontario: Collier-Macmillan, 66–93.

Nelson, R. R. and Winter, S. G. (1982) *An Evolutionary Theory of Economic Change*, Cambridge, MA: Harvard University Press.

Organization for Economic Cooperation and Development (OECD) (2010) *Transfer Pricing Guidelines for Multinational Enterprises and Tax Administrators*, Paris: OECD

Solow, R.M. (1987) 'We'd Better Watch Out', *New York Times Book Review*, 12 July.

United Nations Conference on Trade and Development (UNCTAD) (2013) *World Investment Report. Glabal Value Chains: Investment and Trade for Development*, Geneva: United Nations.

Venables, A. J. (1998) 'The Assessment: Trade and Location', *Oxford Review of Economic Policy*, 14, 2: 1-6.

Vernon, R. (1966) 'International investment and international trade in the product Cycle', *Quarterly Journal of Economics*, 80: 190-207.

Zetlin, M. (1974) 'Corporate ownership and control: the large corporation and the capitalist class', *American Journal of Sociology*, 79, 5: 1073-119.

CHAPTER 6

Teaching finance: a real world approach

Maria Alejandra Madi

1 Introduction

In the last few decades, the long-run process of financial expansion turned out to be characterized as the "financialization" of the capitalist economy where monopoly-finance capital became increasingly dependent on credit and financial bubbles (Foster, 2009). In this scenario, there has been broad recognition that the current operation of the financial markets has not generated sustainable economic and social development. Indeed, current financial dynamics promoteds economic and social vulnerability .

As a matter of fact, the global economy suffered 244 financial crises in the period between 1975 and 1998: 158 currency, 54 banking and 32 twin (currency and banking) crises (Kaul et al., 2003). These crises were more frequent in emerging countries: 116 currency crises, 54 banking crises and 32 twin crises. After 2008, United States and many European countries, among others, also suffered financial instability.

The most recent global crisis has shown sources of financial fragility: the financial innovations regarding asset, liability and capital management in the banking sector, the movement toward securitized finance, the growing importance of institutional investors in the management of "financial savings" within the shadow banking system, besides the random investors' behaviour in a context of capital account openness (The Economist, 2011). More to the point, economic systemic contradictions and tensions in the political and social spheres have been created by financial globalization (Guttmann, 1998). Output and employment losses partially illustrate the economic and social costs.

Indeed, the recent Great Financial crisis has restated the menace of deep depressions among the current economic challenges while livelihoods were subordinated to speculation, financial instability and the bailout of domestic financial systems. Looking backward, in the context of the 1930 Great Depression, John Maynard Keynes pointed out that the evolution of capital markets increases the risk of speculation and instability since these markets are mostly based upon conventions whose precariousness affects the rhythm of investment and increased pressures on the political sphere.

Considering this background, teaching finance in the 21st century presupposes a great heterogeneity between national economic structures, institutions and social outcomes of the capital accumulation process. In this setting, real-world institutions are overwhelmed by tensions, contradictions and forces of resistance that reinforce market failures. In truth, our understanding of the financial phenomena supports an emphasis on the historical dimensions of economic dynamics. In this context, the economist is able to deal with *"mankind and the ordinary events business of life"* – recalling Marshall – so as to analyze the social and economic challenges. The target of economics education is the comprehension of reality in its economic dimensions, that is to say, the understanding of the practices and ideas that support the evolution of the production and reproduction conditions of material life for further policy intervention.

This chapter points out *what we should teach in undergraduate courses in order to understand finance from a real-world perspective – both in microeconomics and macroeconomics curriculum.* The understanding of the financial challenges requires new perspectives in a significant learning process where the target should be a solid reflection-base to think and a critical attitude towards the political, economic and social reality. Our approach emphasizes the "institutions-history-social structure" nexus instead of the "rationality-individualism-equilibrium" nexus of mainstream economics.[1]

Section 1 presents a conceptualization of finance. The following sections present four main topics that should be addressed in a real-world economics curriculum: finance and instability, finance and labor, banking dynamics, financial regulation. Finally, the conclusions call for reforms of economics

---

[1] On the characterization of these paradigms see Davis (2006).

education since we need real world economists to re-conceptualize financial problems.

2 Conceptualizing finance

The economics curriculum should consider that the concept of finance is not just related to management techniques, procedures or product phenomena but involves institutions, behaviours and policies. In a monetary economy, accordingly Keynes (1936), money, as the institution that founds the exchange system, links the present and future. The existence of a monetary economy of production is founded on credit relations, organized markets of financial assets, speculation and uncertainty. Indeed, in a framework of uncertainty and speculation, a set of interrelated portfolios and cash flows between banks, income-producing firms and households may influence the evolution of credit, the pace of investment, and the valuation of capital assets.

As Keynes argued, the tensions between money as a public good, issued by central banks, and money as a private good, created by banks, is inherent in the capitalist institutional set up. On behalf of these tensions, trust is crucial in finance. Indeed, the foundations of trust are conventional, that is to say, socially and historically built (Madi, 2014). However, risk is inherent to finance, as Bagehot warned in his classical book *Lombard Street*:

> "The peculiar essence of our banking system is an unprecedented trust between man and man: and when that trust is much weakened by hidden causes, a small accident may greatly hurt it, and a great accident for a moment may almost destroy it" (1873 [1999]: 158).

Keynes highlighted that the capitalist system has endogenous mechanisms capable of destabilizing the levels of spending, income and employment. At the heart of his theory, Keynes suggested a reconsideration of the understanding of the relations among individuals, society and governments within the markets where institutions and conventions could shape human behavior. Aware of the need to overcome the concept of rationality that overwhelms the *homo oeconomicus*, his contribution enhances a more extended understanding of financial decisions. Thus, his approach enhanced a more fruitful apprehension of the real-world where the outcomes of business decisions are not submitted to stochastic behavior, that is to say, they are not predictable.

Takng into account the current global scenario, the shift in economic activity from production to finance is one of the main contemporary issues (Foster, 2009). As Aglietta (1979) argued in the late 1970s, the monetary and financial system not only expands access to finance but also leans on the appropriation of social wealth. Indeed, financial capital exercises control over the cycles of productive capital, thanks to centralized money at their disposal. The conditions of investment, production and consumption express the social nature of money or, in other words, reveal that money is a social institution. Nevertheless, profit-seeking financial activities create new tensions in the possibilities of economic and social reproduction (Madi and Gonçalves, 2007).

Finance fosters the capital accumulation process that develops through time and involves credit contracts. From the Keynesian tradition, Hyman Minsky (1991) argued that finance could be apprehended in a changing historical framework where tensions arise between regulation and the strategies of innovative profit-seeking banks. Financial innovations impact banks' assets, liabilities, and capital. As a result, they could provoke sudden changes in market dynamics and financial stability. Considering the non-neutral role of finance through the business cycle, post-Keynesian economics emphasizes that financial instability relies on endogenous-driven fluctuations of credit and the money supply.[2] According to Minsky, in a monetary economy, credit relations, speculation and uncertainty decisively affect the investment path, leading to endogenous credit crunches. In other words, growing investment puts pressure on the demand for funding – a function of bankers'

---

[2] Among post-Keynesians: while the post-Keynesian horizontalist approach points out that central banks accommodate any increase in banks' demand for reserves as a result of increasing loans (Lavoie, 1984 and 1992; Rochon, 1999a and 1999b); the-post Keynesian structuralist approach highlights that the money supply also depends on the asset and liability management practices of banks (Wray, 1990 and 2012a; Pollin, 1991; Palley, 1996 and 1997).

expectation of future incomes. Increased investment and consumption leads to higher profit rates and present value of capital assets.

Credit booms intensify while liquidity preference declines and, as a result, the resulting portfolios turn out to be extremely vulnerable to changes in interest rates, asset prices, credit strategies and monetary policies. When profits decline, as they inevitably do, credit and external sources of funding generally become restricted. In the liquidity crisis, the nation state must restate the public nature of money. Indeed, in a context of uncertainty and speculation, the tensions between money as a public and as a private good overwhelms central banks' actions, as we are seeing in the current bail-outs.

3 Finance and Instability

If students could look at the current global economic downturn in terms of the lessons from Minsky, they could certainly state that the outstanding features of this crisis should be focused within the financial sector. The recent American financial crisis is an example of how the financial industry encouraged speculation dependent on future housing prices, the future price of securitized assets and the renewal of lending operations. Banks encouraged speculative and Ponzi operations that depended on the future prices of houses, the future prices of the securitized assets and the renewals of lending operations.

With a real world approach to finance in the economics curriculum, it is especially important to understand the current challenges to the financial markets, given Minsky's emphasis that the financial institutions play a crucial role in determining investment through the business cycle. The process of financial deregulation has been overwhelmed by transformations in the investment pattern since corporate decisions have been increasingly subordinated to speculative financial commitments (Minsky, 1975). The financial conception of investment has increased in the context where financial innovations aimed to achieve fast growth with lower capital requirements could be used by managers to favor short-term financial performance (Fligstein, 2001).

Financial instability is viewed as a result of speculation and uncertainty. Higher levels of investment put pressure on the demand for funding – a function of bankers' expectation of future incomes. Increased investment leads to higher profit rates and present value of capital assets. The credit boom intensifies while liquidity preference declines and the resulting portfolios are extremely vulnerable to changes in interest rates and asset prices. When profits decline, as they inevitably do, credit and external funding turn out to become restricted.

Influenced by the business cycle approach to economic dynamics of Michael Kalecki (1990), Minsky considered the role of finance in the business cycle and developed the financial instability hypothesis which states that financial crises are inherent in the capitalist economy after financial deregulation in the 1970s. In his own words: *"it is finance that acts as the sometimes dampening, sometimes amplifying governor of investment. As a result, finance sets the pace of investment"* (Minsky, 1975: 130).

While considering the factors that determine investment, the autonomous component of aggregate demand, Minsky stated how credit markets affect investment transactions which are financed initially through debt and ultimately through profits resulting from the previous levels of investment and asset prices. His approach relies on the endogenous nature of financial instability and criticized the competitive market paradigm of neo-classical economics. Under Minsky´s perspective, investment dynamics is based on the existence of a monetary economy where credit relations, speculation and uncertainty are decisive to affect the investment path, leading to endogenous credit crunches. When profits and asset prices begin to decline, the credit crunch also restricts external financing for those transactions. In this scenario, the liquidity crunch might be dampened by the Central Banks' interventions as a lender of last resort while the Big Government supports private profits in order to enhance the recovery of aggregate demand (Madi and Gonçalves, 2008).

During the last thirty years, most governments around the world have supported the long-run process of financial expansion that turned out to be characterized as the "financialization" of the capitalist economy (Foster, 2009). Here monopoly-finance capital became increasingly dependent on bubbles that, both in credit and capital markets, proved to be global sources of endogenous financial fragility. Financial and currency crises have also revealed that monetary and supervisory authorities do not cope with the complexity of the global, profit-seeking, innovative and speculative portfolios of investors and banks. Central banks, in a context of financial liberalization, do not face financial disturbances easily. Indeed, credit squeeze, volatility in the valuation of assets, the menace of recession, the shift of investors toward liquid and safe assets, among other factors, put pressure on central banks and treasuries.

What Brunhoff, Chesnais and Flassbeck could add to our students' understanding of real world finance is that domestic monetary systems, in a context of financial liberalization and inconvertible currencies, do not face financial disturbances easily. The financial crises and the erratic movements of key-currencies have shown that central banks do not control the complexity of global, innovative and speculative markets. Otherwise, central banks´ actions are not independent from private and public pressures. There are social and political tensions inherent to the current crisis: the impacts on livelihoods, the loss of social cohesion and the subordination of society to the bailout of the financial systems. In fact, the tensions that emerged within the markets have been shifted to the political sphere.

Another important issue to include in the macroeconomics curriculum is that financial crises highlight exchange rate and balance of payments vulnerability in the context of current international financial architecture where the evolution of exchange rates depends on the hierarchy among monetary policies and the arbitrage/speculation within financial markets. In this regard, Brunhoff (1998) points out that financial instability means price instability in financial asset markets. The instability of exchange rates is a co-related question since domestic currencies assume the role of financial assets. Chesnais (1998: 51) also emphasized the interactions between monetary and exchange rate markets while explaining that:

"A pattern of high financial return was universally imposed by financial markets, with local variations, depending on the influence of financial arbitrages on domestic monetary policies. The evaluation of domestic currencies in exchange markets was submitted to this new financial regime, as well as the practices of Central Banks".

In this setup, the level of domestic interest rates is subordinated to the main features of the new international financial pattern – high returns and low inflation. This idea is also discussed by Flassbeck (2002) who analyzes the viability of unilateral options of exchange rate regimes in a multilateral world where the advance of market globalization continues despite the lack of global institutions or yet the absence of a global approach to economic policy. Under his perspective, the canonic discussion between fixed or flexible exchange rate regimes sets aside the essence of the current financial global problem, that is, the destabilizing effects of the increasing capital mobility and the loss of autonomy of economic policy.

In the current international financial architecture, exchange rate crises may also happen on behalf of abrupt reversals of capital flows. According to Keynes, this should be explained in a context of uncertainty where portfolio decisions are not submitted to stochastic behaviour, that is to say, they are not predictable:[3] the process of decision making is in actuality based on conventions. Considering this background, the vulnerability of domestic currencies, as a result of changes in market opinions, is not independent of the global financial cycle that threatens the sustainability of the exchange rate regimes.

In fact the macroeconomic curriculum should address that autonomous monetary management collapsed under the 2008 global financial crisis. Since the 1980s the so- called New Consensus Macroeconomic (Arestis, 2009), founded on the "belief" in the potential of the self-regulated markets to promote economic growth, turned out to favor financial accumulation and social exclusion.[4] In this scenario, the ability of central banks and treasuries

---

[3] The role of expectations and private strategies is crucial in Keynes´ analysis. The principle of uncertainty is based on the idea that the past is irrevocable and the future is unknown. In the capitalist economy, money means the representation of wealth, the link between present and future. Money has a non-neutral nature, or yet, it affects spending and portfolio decisions.
[4] The American philosopher Charles Peirce warned that any method of fixing "belief" may be called the method of tenacity. In his opinion, beliefs will be unable to hold

to promote financial stability and inclusive growth has been reduced by the power of markets. In the real world, central banks' actions are not independent from private and public pressures. The increasing growth of sovereign-debts imposes the adoption of government austerity programs that mainly rely on taxpayers. As a result, the social tensions that have emerged within the markets have been shifted to the political sphere and proved to challenge money as a public good.

If we encourage students to look at the microeconomic foundations of the current global economic downturn in terms of the lesson learned from Minsky, they could observe that outstanding features of this crisis emerged from banks' speculative and Ponzi portfolios that are dependent not only on the future price of housing and securitized assets but also on the renewal of households' lending operations. As Bagehot (1873) clearly said: banks trade money. In the current financial scenario, the interconnections between credit and capital markets foster the growth of banks' and institutional investors' assets. The other side of the "coin" shows higher corporate leverage and household debt. As a result, all society has been subordinated to trading private money.

At the center, however, is the concept of capital that has been a controversial issue at the heart of economics education since the conceptualization of capital enhances deep implications on the apprehension of the economic, social and political dimensions of reality. Among recent contributions to this debate, Thomas Piketty new book has discussed on behalf of his data sets and explanation for increasing disparities in wealth and income in the context of neoliberalism. Among critical readers of his approach to explaining growing inequality, David Harvey's concern emphasized that his argument relies on a mistaken definition of capital. In short, although there is much that is valuable in his data sets, Piketty's explanation seems to be founded on a neoclassical theoretical background where capital is mainly a factor of production. Indeed, it is defined as the *stock of all assets* held by private individuals,

---

their ground in practice as the social impulse is against it. On the fixation of belief in science see Peirce (1877).

corporations and governments that can be traded in the market (no matter whether these assets are being used or not).

Under Harvey's Marxist approach, the definition of capital as a stock of assets excludes the idea of *capital as a social process* where money is used to make more money often, but not exclusively, through the exploitation of labor power. Following Harvey's concern, we need to highlight that the nexus between the current global scenario and inequality encloses inner tensions between the hypertrophy of finance and the expectations of society about citizenship, labor and income. In the current historical context, labor markets have become a key variable in macroeconomic and business adjustments. In truth, capital mobility has favored the regulation of social relations based on growing flexibility. In contemporary capitalism, the global institutional architecture has favored capital mobility and short term investment decisions - increasingly subordinated to rules of portfolio risk management. While recent changes in productive organization have been based on competitiveness and corporate governance criteria, job instability and fragile conditions of social protection have forced the reorganization of survival strategies. Thus, workers must redefine their skills or become informal entrepreneurs. Given the decreasing power of workers in recent decades, it is not surprising that both the globalization process and its outcomes have favored the concentration of wealth and changes in social behavior.

While money is an end in itself, social behavior has been overwhelmed by the "profit motive", as Karl Polanyi warned in his masterpiece *The Great Transformation*. Consequently, in the last decade, special interest groups have increased spread and social cohesion has diminished. Indeed, the conflicts between solidarity and particular interests have revealed the current inner tensions reshaping ethical societies. Growing social violence and civil wars, as Eric Hobsbawm clearly said, are some of the outcomes of the current relations between national states, the free markets and societies in the global order.

4 Finance and labor

Since the 1980s, under the aegis of finance capital, finance regulates the pace of investment, which in turn determines income and employment (Minsky, 1986). Workers have increasingly changed consumption patterns and expanded their spending due to credit access policies implemented under the auspices of the World Bank (2004). Indeed, the innovative and speculative global financial markets have not only systematically influenced consumer preferences, but have also increased pressure on the political sphere. The target of credibility has globally overwhelmed the policy making process in order to address global investors' expectations (Grabel, 2001). In this setting, social and infrastructure spending has become restricted by policy rules based on government surplus targets.

Any macroeconomics curriculum for the 21st century should address that, in the last decades, the dynamics of investment and employment has been discussed primarily in financial terms. Managers and owners of firms considered their organizations in terms of short-term financial performance. Debts, stock market evaluation, mergers and acquisitions are part of investment decisions where firms turned are understood as a set of assets: its operational divisions and product lines might be bought or sold in order to achieve higher short-term profits. While corporate decisions have been increasingly subordinated to speculative financial commitments, the adjustment on the labor force has been subordinated to short-term profit targets.[5] The financial conception of investment has increased in the context where financial innovations aimed to achieve fast growth with lower capital requirements could be used by managers to favor short-term financial performance (Fligstein, 2001). Managers and owners of firms have privileged short-term financial performance and shareholder value. Changes in corporate ownership, through waves of mergers and acquisitions, have created new business models where companies turn out to be bundles of assets and liabilities to be traded.

Hence, current corporate governance has privileged mobility, liquidity and short-term profits based on high levels of debt. Along with these new global

---

[5] This financial commitment is currently being observed in private equity funds' business and labor strategies. See for example, Gonçalves and Madi (2014).

business strategies, new perspectives on social reproduction have been driven by short-term profits and competition. Mergers and acquisitions have subordinated ownership changes, financial restructuring and company efficiency. In truth, working conditions have been constantly reorganized and reconfigured by finance. Finance has fostered systemic contradictions and tensions in both social and political spheres (Chesnais, 1998). The evolution of aggregate demand, employment and income, as Keynes warned, has highly revealed the endogenous fragility of capitalist economies, the random behavior of investors and the narrow interconnections between capital and credit markets.

Economics education should emphasize that the evolution of real-world finance results from economic forces historically shaped by the social dimension of the markets and the political nature of society. Considering this methodological background, both the microeconomics and macroeconomics curriculum should favor the understanding of the evolution of the capitalist relations of production. In the last decades, this evolution has revealed changing labor organizing principles to cope with the dictates of the financial accumulation pattern: flexible production; redefinition of tasks and kinds of control, job rotation and suppression of skilled workers. Current market flexibility and informality have been connected with the increasing growth of insecurely-employed and low-skilled workers. Indeed, changes in power forces, technology, income distribution and wealth do affect the levels of employment and working conditions (Robinson, 1959).

5 Banking dynamics

The understanding of banking dynamics requires deep changes in microeconomic courses to emphasize the dynamics of non-financial markets. Besides, there is the need to open up more integrated theoretical and analytical perspectives in order not to obfuscate the micro and macro interrelationship of our current financial problems.

Commercial banks manage a set of assets and liabilities with a variety of maturities, risks, and regulatory requirements. These banks have to meet domestic and foreign markets in order to fundraising deposits, non-deposit borrowings, and wholesale funds, while the central bank is the ultimate fallback refinancing institution. Liability management involves strategies aimed to refinance the banks' liabilities (Saunders, 1994). The process of innovation in the search of alternatives to bank financing result not only because of competitive market forces, but also due to banking regulation and to monetary policy. Innovation, as Schumpeter (1912 [1934]) argued, is the key to capitalist development.

According to Minsky (1991), financial innovations are not just techniques or product phenomena, but involve institutional changes because banks and their practices are also subject to innovation. As financial innovations impact banks' assets, liabilities, and capital, they could provoke sudden changes in financial stability. For example, such financial innovations could increase the amount of credit through the endogenous money creation since the new loans are considered profitable by banks. Classic reading on this subject should consider the contribution of Tobin (1963) who explained why commercial bank loans are not restricted by the previous amount of deposits because banks could be active in fundraising as a result of expected risks and returns.

In practice, banks analyze the multiple risks to which they are exposed. Since the 1980s, acknowledging that many different types of risk are related and overwhelm assets and liabilities (Dermine and Bissada, 2007), banks have increasingly adopted an integrated approach called asset-and-liability management (ALM). This management approach aims to look at how bank assets and liabilities can match up in the most effective way to mitigate risks, accomplish legally capital adequacy requirements, and achieve expected earnings. On the assets side of their balance sheet, banks deal with the composition of discretionary portfolios, including loans, currencies, bonds, securities, and other trading assets. Banks assess the magnitude of the risks, owing to imbalances in the balance sheet composition, and figure out how to mitigate them. For example, banks could be interested in asset securitization, so as to enhance credit and liquidity risk management. Besides, banks could change the maturity of their deposits when rapid shifts in the level of interest rates are expected. In this case, accounting methods, such as gap analysis or duration analysis, could also maintain a controlled gap between the maturities of assets and liabilities. ALM could also be used to analyze currency and other trading-related risks. As a result, financial innovations could include off-balance-sheet banking and hedging techniques, such as currency futures and swaps to control balance sheet exposures. As a result, banks set aside additional capital for potential losses. These management practices are becoming increasingly similar whether an institution is chartered as a commercial bank, a savings bank, an investment bank, or an insurance company (Saunders and Cornett, 2002).

Indeed, economics education should emphasize the changing environments where decisions are taken. Banking management could be apprehended in a changing historical framework where tensions between the regulation of capitalist finance and the strategies of innovative profit-seeking banks arise. The global crisis that erupted in 2008 showed that innovations regarding banks' management have reinforced the risks associated with individual banks or non-bank financial institutions as well as systemic risk. In other words, these practices have potentially materialized the risk of collapse of the financial system with deep negative consequences for society.

The microeconomics of banking management practices should focus on the non-neutrality of banks' strategies and decisions. Hence, financial innovations need a permanent policy attention since banks could make ineffective the central banks' policies and could also build a speculative debt structure in spite of the financial regulation, as Kaldor (1982) and Minsky (1986) previously warned.

6 Rethinking financial regulation

The recent global financial crisis exposed the inner economic, social and political tensions that overwhelm the outcomes of the reality of the self-regulated markets. These questions have long been ignored in the competitive market paradigm of neoclassic economics that constitutes the New Macroeconomic Consensus agenda and most of the economics curriculum. The New Macroeconomic Consensus' monetary rules as a guideline for central banks' actions rescued Friedman´s contribution to monetary policy (Friedman 1963a and 1968; Friedman and Schwartz, 1963b).

In a pluralist economic curriculum, Friedman's classical reading is relevant since his critique against the state interventionism modified, on behalf of individual freedom, the rules of economic policy in the global order after the 1970s. Since then, a low and stable inflation has been widely recognized as the main target of macroeconomic policies in a changing context toward the financial accumulation pattern. Indeed, an "inflationary targeting" monetary system emerged in the international economy.[6] In the framework of the New Macroeconomic Consensus conception of monetary policy, the short-term interest rate instrument of central banks would be adjusted in response to recent changes in inflation and real gross domestic product. As a matter of fact, this agenda shares the fundamental presumption of post war macroeconomics: the nation state is able to control all the macroeconomic outcomes by means of the available economic policy tools.

Beyond the emphasis of the New Macroeconomic Consensus on price stability, there was the "belief" that markets, without state intervention, were inherently stable. From this perspective, financial crises are the result of wrong economic policy options. Financial crises are a monetary phenomenon: expansionary monetary policies do not favor domestic and external equilibrium. The ex-ante saving-investment disequilibrium is stimulated by the money supply and credit expansion and causes financial imbalances. In other words, the attempt to keep the domestic income level too high *vis-à-vis* its non-inflationary level is related to the causes of the crises (Madi, 2004).

The monetarist theoretical foundations rely on the exogenous nature of the money supply and the duality "real versus monetary", while it does not consider the active role of money or even banks' speculative behavior. Under the monetarist approach, the autonomous monetary policy, aimed to stabilize prices, subordinates the evolution of fiscal policy. Besides,

---

[6] During the inflation of the 1970s, the rational expectations' approach to monetary policy emphasized the role of monetary policy in price stabilization. Nevertheless, the early 1980s was a transition period in terms of monetary policy (Taylor, 1999). After the recognition that the demand for money appeared to be less stable there was a shift from the money stock side to the short-term interest rate side of monetary policy. Increasingly, the Taylor rule became the framework of monetary policy not only in the United States but also globally, due to the consensus built around the empirical successful results of the Taylor rule to fit aggregate data.

achieving general macroeconomic equilibrium under the case of a constant money growth policy rule requires flexible exchange rates in the context of capital account openness. Following this policy recommendation, the operation of floating exchange rates would permit the adjustment of domestic prices to costs in the international order and the free markets would express rational choices

Under the free market paradigm, financial markets efficaciously transfer funds; and furthermore, financial deregulation is necessary to increase efficiency in financial markets and, consequently, the supply of loanable funds.[7] Under this theoretical and political approach, financial market imperfections might be avoided and, eventually, corrected, since adequate monetary and financial policies would be implemented. This approach has supported current financial regulation. Among financial policies, the Basel Agreements have shaped an institutional set up in order to improve the efficiency of financial markets in the allocation of resources by means of the commitment to better risk and capital management practices in the domestic banking sectors.

The Basel "codes and patterns" – based on the conception of capital adjustment to risk in the banking sector – focused the reduction of asymmetric information on credit and capital markets, maximize investors' returns and dampen the arising agency problem. As a matter of fact, the Basel Agreements have been voluntarily adopted to spread out mechanisms of protection to avoid the financial systemic risk and favor informational transparency (disclosure). Thus, the prudential measures might be

---

[7] However, the defenders of the financial liberalization process, such as International Monetary Fund, consider that its long-term benefits can be noticed in better allocation of global saving (Fischer, 1997). Among other benefits of financial integration with foreign markets are: a) lowered cost of domestic credit, as domestic saving is complemented with foreign savings; b) the possibility of diversifying risk by acquiring positions in assets not available in domestic markets; c) the possibility of supplementing residents' investments with foreign investments, having access to new technologies and to new markets; d) the chance of delivering more efficient and complete financial services for residents in a new environment characterized by competition between domestic and foreign players. Under this perspective, financial liberalization is understood as a precondition to overcome the inefficiency of domestic financial intermediation (Madi, 2004).

supported by the dissemination of information, transparency, contingent strategies and better supervision practices. These practices, aimed to overcome the "asymmetric information" that overwhelms the contracts within the financial markets, would enhance more efficient financial leverage systems and greater transparency to financial regulators and investors (Madi, 2013).

However, from a Keynesian perspective, the understanding of financial crises and regulation highlights that the scope of domestic policies to prevent and manage a crisis is limited. As Keynes pointed out in the 1930s, the predominance of speculation and instability increases the pressures on the political sphere. Expressing concerns about the fragile institutions during the Great Depression, and its effects on income and employment, his proposals aimed to promote economic and social transformations (Keynes, 1987).

The reading of Keynes is a must in transforming the Economic curriculum. Global financial integration has augmented the exposure of countries to global macroeconomic and financial vulnerabilities. In this setup, domestic prudential financial regulation presents challenges to success. First, banking assets and liabilities are vulnerable to changes in global macroeconomic conditions. Second, the universal scope of banks' operations reveals the conflicts behind the segmentation of domestic supervision. Third, there is a delay between new regulation patterns and banking practices. At last, the consolidation of larger financial institutions, stimulated by capital adequacy requirements, information technology, the elimination of geographic restrictions and changes in the composition of financial savings have favored the action of the Central Bank as an agency that arbitrates the competitive settlement. As a result, domestic financial regulation can induce to better practices, but cannot eliminate the possibility of crisis. Global action is also necessary with coordination and coherence among multilateral institutions.

Indeed, in spite of the "belief" in free markets, the 2007-2009 crisis has restated the menace of deep depressions among the current challenges (Foster, 2009) while livelihoods were subordinated to the bailout of the domestic financial systems. At the center, however, is the discipline of economics itself and economics education, which obfuscates the political nature of economic policy decisions. Indeed, current financial global agreements have supported the "status quo", that is to say, the expansion of universal banks, private money and liquid capital markets under the World Trade Organization´s defense of financial services liberalization (Guttmann, 1998). As a matter of fact, the efficient financial model presents limits and failures when confronted with evidence. In this scenario, the "belief" in an autonomous monetary management has collapsed under the 2008 global financial crisis. Domestic monetary systems, in a context of financial liberalization and inconvertible currencies, do not face financial disturbances easily. The financial crises and the erratic movements of key-currencies have shown that central banks do not control the complexity of global, innovative and speculative markets; and central banks' actions are not independent from private and public pressures.

Taking into account these challenges, it is decisive to underline the importance of a thorough agenda of institutional reform so as restructure the international financial architecture and control the working of a capitalist economy toward sustainable growth. Recalling Minsky, *"finance cannot be left to the free markets"*. However, one of the main challenges of global institutional reform is the absence of a common project with the compliance of all countries, so as to achieve the adequate provision of liquidity, the recognition of the need of stable financial flows and new forms of debt negotiation (Griffith-Jones, 2002).[8]

Keynes' attempt to re-shape the world order in the 1940s highlighted the need of an international currency system that might only work by means of a "wide measure of agreement", that is, by means of the creation of a new international convention. In Keynes' time, this convention would rely on multiple needs: an international currency, a stable exchange rate system, redistribution of international reserves, stabilizing mechanisms, sources of liquidity, besides a central institution to aid and support other international institutions related to the planning and regulation of the world economic life. In our times, new convention-conducing institutions could foster financial re-

---

[8] The low level of representation of developing countries in multilateral institutions (International Monetary Fund, World Bank and Bank of International Settlement, for example) renders renewing the global economic policy agenda even more difficult (Griffith-Jones, 2002).

regulation and re-shape domestic policies to enhance sustainable inclusive growth. Central banks' actions should be thus subordinated.

Considering the current global scenario, we need real world economists to re-conceptualize financial problems. The understanding of these financial challenges requires new perspectives regarding knowledge, abilities and attitudes in order to rethink alternatives. Taking into account the current social and economic challenges, it is necessary to re-focus the economic policy agenda. Investment, employment and finance cannot be left to the free markets.

As the organization of economic and social institutions helps to define policy goals and outcomes, students should reflect on how to promote a new relationship between the financial and industrial spheres, which is required to promote growth and income distribution. Here, the economic agenda involves aggregate demand (fiscal and monetary) and income policies besides the articulation of financial flows in both credit and capital markets. Under this perspective, the role of monetary policy could be highlighted through the participation of central banks in redirecting flows of credit. It is necessary to influence the flows of credit and articulate them within the framework of the industrial policy that would search for alternatives to the market power of giant corporations (Minsky, 1986). It is also time to think about capital controls that might reduce the effects of sharp reversal short-term capital flows. Globalization has not been a miracle way to achieve growth.

As global finance has subordinated the outcomes of social reproduction, the main question is, as Minsky (1986) warned, *Who will benefit?* The recent global crisis has indicated that the structure and dynamics of current global finance, as a historical set of institutions, products, procedures, behaviors and policies have potentially materialized the risk of collapse of the financial system with deep negative consequences for the real economy and society. In order to support sustainable development, it's time to stimulate students to rethink global finance, as well as its policy agenda about global and corporate governance, prudential regulation and supervision of systemic risk.

In fact, any transformation in economic curriculum needs to look forward to search for more coherence in the approach to the relationship between finance and sustainable development both in micro and macro courses. This approach must emphasize a historic understanding of the business decision making process, since economic decisions are based on conventions that in turn are based on trust. Indeed, trust is a conventional concept related to the level of confidence built in a society around the future business environment, that is to say, around the legal, regulatory, macroeconomic and political setting, that is, trust has a historical and social nature. Trust deeply impacts economic and social development. It's time for explicitly introducing this discussion in the economics curriculum (Madi, 2014).

7 Final considerations

Due to changing reality, the effort in economics education should reinforce the attempt to teach real world finance founded on the conception of society as a developing entity, the contemporary problems of social development and the correlation between humanistic sciences. As Hamilton (1917) warned, economics education needs to face the challenge to reshape hierarchies within the effort of searching for the nexus between economics, history, logic, political science and sociology.

Economics education in the 21st century presupposes the recognition of the subject: the economic systems in transformation. As John Kenneth Galbraith pointed out economics is overwhelmed by an 'uncorrected obsolescence' (Siler, 2003). The concern with the idea of process in the conceptual construction of finance is handled by considering that institutions "refuse to retain a definite content" – in Hamilton's words (1919). Indeed, the study of the evolution and dynamics of the markets within a historical framework is conditioned by social and political forces.

Regarding the transformation of the economics curriculum, the consideration of a pluralist set of visions is a must. The inclusion of the reading of Marx, Schumpeter, Keynes, Hayek, Kalecki, Friedman and Minsky, for example, could be fruitful toward the challenge to comprehend the structure and dynamics of contemporary capitalism. The ability of a "real world" economist to deal with "mankind and the ordinary events business of life" should be preceded by the recognition of the boundaries of economics and of its political dimensions as a particular knowledge oriented to social and economic development issues.

References

Aglietta, M. (1979) *A Theory of Capital Regulation: The US Experience*, London: NLB,

Akyüz, Y. (2004) *Managing financial instability and shocks*, Turkish Economic Association, Discussion Paper 2004/11, http://www.tek.org.tr

Arestis, P. (2009) *Fiscal Policy within the New Consensus Macroeconomics Framework*, CCEPP WP06-09, Cambridge Centre for Economic and Public Policy, University of Cambridge.

Bagehot, W. (1873 [1999]) *Lombard Street: A Description of the Money Market*, USA: John Willey & Sons.

Chesnais, F. (ed.) (1998) *A mundialização financeira- gênese, custos e riscos*. São Paulo: Ed. Xamã.

Davis, J. (2006) 'The Nature of Heterodox Economics', *Post-autistic economics review*, issue no. 40, article 3, pp.23-30, December, www.paecon.net/PAEReview/issue40/Davis40.pdf

Dermine, J. and Bissada,Y. (2007) *Asset and Liability Management: The Banker's Guide to Value Creation and Risk Control*, London and New York: Financial Times and Prentice Hall.

Fischer, S. (1997) *Capital Account Liberalization and the Role of the IMF*. Washington, DC: IMF.

Flassbeck, H. (2002) 'The Exchange Rate: Economic Policy Tool Or Market Price?', *UNCTAD Discussion Papers* 157, Genève: United Nations Conference on Trade and Development, 2002.

Fligstein, N. (2001) *The architecture of markets,* New Jersey: Princeton University Press.

Foster, J. B. (2009) A Failed System, *Monthly Review*, March.

Galbraith, J. K. (1958) *The Affluent Society*. Boston: Houghton Mifflin Co..

Grabel, I. (2000) 'The Political Economy of "Policy Credibility"', *Cambridge Journal of Economics*, 24, 1: 1-19

Friedman, M. (1968) 'The role of monetary policy', *American Economic Review*, 58, 1: 1–17.

Friedman, M., and Schwartz, A. (1963a) 'Money and Business Cycles', *Review of Economics and Statistics*, supplement February, pp. 32-64.

Friedman, M., and Schwartz, A. (1963b) *A Monetary History of the United States, 1867 - 1960*, Princeton, NJ: Princeton University Press.

Kaldor, N. (1982) *The scourge of monetarism*, Oxford: Oxford University Press.

Gonçalves, J. R. B. and Madi, M. A. C. (2014) 'Global business and private equity strategies: current challenges to labor', *Global Advanced Research Journal of Management and Business Studies*, 3, 2, Feb.

Griffith-Jones, S. (2002) 'Una nova arquitetura financeira internacional como bem público global', In: Fendt, R. and Tedesco Lins, M. A. (eds.) *Arquitetura Assimétrica*. RJ: Fundação Konrad Adenauer. Série Debates.

Guttmann, R. (1998) 'As mutações do capital financeiro'. In: Chesnais, F. (ed.) (1998) *A mundialização financeira- gênese, custos e riscos*. São Paulo. Ed. Xamã.

Hamilton, W. (1917) 'Problems of Economic Instruction'. *The Journal of Political Economy*. 25, 1: 1-13, January.

Hamilton, W. (1919) 'The Institutional Approach to Economic Theory". *The American Economic Review*, 9, 1. Supplement, Papers and Proceedings of the Annual Meeting of the American Economic Association, March, 309-318

Harvey, D. (2014) *Afterthoughts on Piketty's Capital*, http://davidharvey.org/2014/05/afterthoughts-pikettys-capital/

Hobsbawm, E. (2007) *Globalisation, Democracy and Terrorism*. London: Abacus,

Kaul, I., Conceição, P.; Le Goulven, K. and Mendoza, R. (eds.) (2003) *Providing public global goods: managing globalization*. UNDP, New York, Oxford University Press, 2003.

Kalecki, M. (1990) *Collected Works*, Vol. I and Vol. II, Oxford: Clarendon Press 1990.

Keynes, J. M. (1936) *The General Theory of Employment, Interest and Money*, London: Macmillan.

Keynes, J. M. (1940-1844 [1987]) 'Shaping the Post-World: The Clearing Union'. In: *Collected Writings of John Maynard Keynes*, Activities 1940-1944, edited by Moggridge, D., vol. XXV. Cambridge: Cambridge University Press.

Lavoie, M. (1984) 'The Endogenous Flow of Credit and the Post Keynesian Theory of Money', *Journal of Economic Issues,* 18, 3: 771–797.

Lavoie, M. (1992) *Foundations of Post-Keynesian Economic Analysis*. Edward Elgar Publishing, Aldershot, UK.

Madi, M. A. C. (2004) *Financial Liberalization and Economic Policy Options: Brazil, 1994-2003,* Instituto de Economia, UNICAMP, Discussion Paper.

Madi, M. A. C. (2013) 'Global finance: banking dynamics, regulation and future challenges', In: *The Greening of Global Finance*, edited by Chichilnisky, G., Fah, Y.

Madi, M. A. C., Gale De Oliveira, M. and Kennet, M., UK: The Green Economics Institute, 2013.

Madi, M. A. C. (2014) *Economics and trust*, Wea Pedagogy Blog, http://weapedagogy.wordpress.com/, March.

Madi, M. A. C and Gonçalves, J. R. B. (2007) 'Corporate Social Responsibility: Credit and Banking Inclusion in Brazil', In: Bugra, A. and Agartan, K. (eds.) *Market Economy as a Political Project: Reading Karl Polanyi for the 21st Century,* Palgrave.

Madi, M. A. C. and Gonçalves, J. R. B. (2008) 'Stabilizing an Unstable Economy by Hyman Minsky', *International Journal of Green Economics*, 2, 3.

Marshall, A. (1920) *Principles of Economics*. Published: London: Macmillan and Co. Ltd.

Marx, K. (1859 [1904]) *A Contribution to The Critique Of The Political Economy*, Chicago: International Library Publishing Co.

Minsky, H. P. (1975) *Can "It" Happen Again?* Armonk: M.E. Sharpe.

Minsky, H. P. (1986) *Stabilizing an Unstable Economy*, New Haven: Yale University Press.

Minsky, H. P. (1991) 'Financial crises: systemic or idiosyncratic', *Levy Economics Institute of Bard College,* Working Paper no. 5.

Moore, B. J. (1988) *Horizontalists and Verticalists: The Macroeconomics of Credit Money*, Cambridge: Cambridge University Press.

Piketty, T. (2014) *Capital in the Twenty-First Century,* Harvard University Press, MA: Belknap Press.

Palley, T. (1996) *Post Keynesian Economics: Debt, Distribution, and the Macro Economy*. St. Martin's Press, New York.

Palley, T. (1997) 'Endogenous Money and the Business Cycle'. *Journal of Economics*, 65, 2: 133–149.

Peirce, C. S. (1877) 'The fixation of Belief'. *Popular Science,* Monthly 12: 1-15, November, http://www.peirce.org/writings/p107.html

Polanyi, K. (1944 [1971]) *The Great Transformation*. Beacon Press: Boston, 11th ed.

Pollin, R. (1991) 'Two Theories of Money Supply Endogeneity: Some Empirical Evidence', *Journal of Post Keynesian Economics,* 13, 3: 366–396.

Robinson, J. (1959) *Ensayos de economía poskeynesiana*. México: Fundo de Cultura.

Rochon, L-P. (1999a) 'The Creation and Circulation of Endogenous Money: A Circuit Dynamique Approach', *Journal of Economic Issues*, 33, 1: 1–21.

Rochon, L-P. (1999b) *Credit, Money, and Production: An Alternative Post-Keynesian Approach*, UK: Edward Elgar.

Saunders, A. (1994) *Financial Institutions Management: A Modern Perspective*, Burr Ridge, IL: Richard D. Irwin.

Saunders, A. and Cornett, M. M. (2002) *Financial Institutions Management: A Risk Management Approach,* Columbus: McGraw-Hill College.

Siler, K. (2003) 'The Social and Intellectual Organization and Construction of Economics', *Post-autistic economics review*, issue no. 22, article 3, November, http://www.paecon.net/PAEReview/issue22/Siler22.htm

Schumpeter, J. A. (1912 [1934]) *The Theory of Economic Development*, Cambridge, MA: Harvard University Press.

Taylor, J. (1999) A Historical analysis of the Monetary Policy Rules. In: Taylor, J (ed.) *Monetary Policy Rules*. London: University of Chicago Press.

Tobin, J. (1963) 'Commercial banks as creators of 'money'', In: Carson, D. (ed.), *Banking and Monetary Studies*, Homewood: Richard D. Irwin, 408-19.

The Economist. (2011) *The great unknown. Can policymakers fill the gaps in their knowledge about the financial system?,* Jan 13th, print edition.

Wray, R. (1990) *Money and Credit in Capitalist Economies: The Endogenous Money Approach*, UK: Edward Elgar.

Wray, R. (ed.) (2012) *Theories of Money and Banking*. Edward Elgar, Cheltenham.

World Bank (2004) *Making Services Work for Poor People*, World Development Report, Co-publication of the World Bank and Oxford University Press.

CHAPTER 7
Teaching economic policy in Italy
Nicola Acocella

1 Introduction

Before and just after WWII until the 1950s teaching economic policy – that part of the discipline of economic policy dealing with conditions for consistent and successful policy action – in Italy and some other European countries was confined to a set of practical rules intended to explain technical procedures of government intervention, particularly in the realm of microeconomic policies, in particular, customs policy, price controls. In Italy the contributions of Pareto and Barone (Pareto, 1906; Barone, 1908) had stimulated mathematical economics, not that of welfare economics and the theory of economic policy. Public finance had a higher status, as this discipline had developed a theory of public goods (Mazzola, 1890) well before (Wicksell, 1926) and others and a conception of the role of the state (De Viti De Marco, 1888). Theoretical contributions on the theory of international trade and balance of payment adjustments were taught under separate disciplines. A subject such as macroeconomic analysis and policy barely existed, only starting long after Keynes' (1936) contribution, which found a hard way through in Italy and some other European countries. Monetary theory was a highly developed field, but only practical policy prescriptions were taught as a part of economic policy.

This was a striking difference with that part of continental Europe, in particular in Scandinavian countries, the Netherlands and Austria, where a discipline to some extent autonomous from that of economic analysis was developing.

This development was the product of a number of circumstances: not only the prevailing political inclinations favouring an active role of the state, but also the slow but steady development of some essential seeds of the discipline up to the 1930s and some decisive innovations of that decade: the advent of Keynesian analysis; critical discussions of principles of public policy intervention by other leading economists of the time on subjects such as the compensation principle and the derivation of a social welfare function; the birth and development of econometrics.

The next section discusses the passage from the first, non-systematic, attempts of economists in Anglo-Saxon countries, Scandinavia and the Netherlands to indicate cases for government intervention to the theoretical advances in the 1930s that made it possible to devise economic policy as an autonomous discipline. Section 3 discusses the foundations and articulation of economic policy in some countries of Continental Europe and its practical absence in other European and non-European countries. Section 4 discusses developments of the discipline in Italy since the 1960s. Section 5 analyzes why developments of economic policy in Italy and other countries had a limited impact on teaching in Europe (and elsewhere). Section 6 briefly discusses the connection between teaching economic policy and research on this subject.

2 From Walras's examples of empirical policy to the seeds of the 1930s for economic policy as an autonomous discipline

Most classical writers, along with the marginalists had suggested cases where public intervention was in order, e.g., Smith (1776), Ricardo (1817), Mill (1848), Marshall (1890), and Walras (1896; 1936). But these cases were mainly what Walras called 'examples of empirical policy', rather than rational policy, stemming from no systematic and consistent assessment of the foundations and the articulation of public policy.

The first attempts to develop a systematic discipline of government intervention came from Sidgwick (1883), whose third part had economic policy as an object; Pareto (1906) and Pigou (1912; 1920), who delineated essential principles for state intervention connecting it to the preferences of citizen. These had been produced not only as an almost occasional and case-by-case by-product of analytical investigations (as it was for the 'classics'), but as a systematic corpus of principles. However, apart from their debatable foundations (utilitarianism for Sidgwick and Pigou; efficiency for Pareto), the issue of the range of action for public intervention was largely incomplete and that of its consistency was still unresolved. The former involved other cases of market failures. Some developments, as for macroeconomic market failures, had to wait for Keynes' contribution or, as for asymmetric information, much later (see Akerlof, 1970).

This situation rapidly changed after WWII as a result of four developments in the theory, some of which had taken place in the Thirties:

- advent of Keynesian thought (Keynes, 1936);
- since the end of the 1930s, development of the new welfare economics, underlining the relevance of market failures at a micro level and the suggestion to construct a social welfare function, thus contributing to the theory of justice (a summary of these advances was expressed after the war by Bator, 1958);
- in the early 1930s, the birth of the new discipline of econometrics, as a development of mathematical economics; construction of formal models to be tested against reality introduced the idea of the need for consistency of different public policies and the possibility to check their effectiveness against reality; this idea was formally stated by two of the founding fathers of the Econometric society and the Journal 'Econometrica', i.e. Ragnar Frisch and Jan Tinbergen;
- the high growth rates experienced in the Thirties and the following decade by planned economies, suggesting that governments could successfully direct economic systems.

3 Foundations and articulation of economic policy in continental Europe

These developments led to the foundation of the discipline of economic policy in particular in Scandinavia and The Netherlands. To the best of my knowledge, Zeuthen (1958) was the first successful attempt to offer a systematic and consistent summary of developments in welfare economics and the theory of economic policy, which became the cornerstone of economic policy as a separate discipline drawing mainly from economic analysis and, in addition, econometrics, political philosophy, political and social sciences.[1]

The discipline had rather solid foundations suggesting an almost complete range of microeconomic failures, anchored to the following: the non-utilitarian, Paretian principle; the Keynesian case for macroeconomic intervention to sustain employment and income; the literature on growth and development, flourishing during the Fifties out of the issue of Harrodian instability and of Myrdalian analyses, which offered reasons for government intervention. The logical difficulties raised by Arrow (1951) in deriving a social welfare function out of individual preferences were pragmatically solved by Frisch (1957), who suggested refer to politicians, who should respond to citizens through the operation of democratic institutions.

Effectiveness and consistence of public action was analysed along two lines. One was initiated by Ragnar Frisch (1949; 1950; 1957), who stated a theory of economic policy in terms of 'flexible targets': the policymaker, in the same vein as a household, tends to maximize his preferences, or to minimize a loss function in terms of quadratic deviations from a set of target values for the variables of interest, the direction later followed by Theil (1956; 1964). Instead, Tinbergen (1952; 1956) and then others developed a theory in terms of 'fixed targets', suggesting that a number of instruments at least equal to that of targets should be available to the policymaker. These foundations were enough solid to sustain reasons, rules and procedures to follow for dealing with specific practical issues, in specific historical and institutional circumstance.

Why did such a discipline – in particular the theory of economic policy – develop only in Continental Europe? This is a very difficult question to answer. I will try to indicate some of the relevant factors.

One might argue that development of economic policy was natural for countries that had adopted (indicative) planning for their economies, even if Zeuthen had warned that the theory of economic policy was not only necessary for planned economies, but also useful for less interventionist

---

[1] The importance of this book for the development of economic policy as a separate discipline in Italy must be stressed, as it was translated into Italian in 1961.

societies, whose economic policies must be coordinated. In fact, 'economic policy action changing according to moods can be extremely harmful' (Zeuthen, 1958: 133 It. tr.). Undoubtedly, complexity of economic policy and the need for coordinating the various fields of action are more acute where the goals of policy action to correct markets are more ambitious and widespread. This could rather easily explain why such a theory never developed in the United States where the dominant credo was one of scarce public interventions, with the exception of unemployment and anti-inflationary policies. In a similar vein one could say that this was the case also of Germany, where macroeconomic action was relatively less relevant and mainly directed to an anti-inflationary target. However, this explanation would not fit the case of the United Kingdom where there was a vast array of public actions, including – in addition to macroeconomic policy – extensive recourse to public enterprises and the welfare state but neither the theory of economic policy nor the discipline of economic policy developed as such.[2] A partial exception is Meade (1951; 1955). Nor would it explain the absence of a theory of economic policy in France, where the government played an important role in a number of fields and indicative plans were prepared for a number of decades after WW II.

4 Economic policy in Italy since the 1960s

A discipline of economic policy barely existed, at least until mid-1930s, in the syllabus of Italian (and, to my knowledge, French and German) tertiary courses. Trade, colonial policy and law were its main substitutes (Tiberi, Frinolli, 2006; Tiberi, Fubelli, 2006). Most Italian economists – even some leading figures such as Maffeo Pantaleoni – had espoused the Fascist and corporatist credo and could only teach how to directly control an autarchic system, practically directing credit, monetary policy, etc. to the targets stated

---

[2] An explanation could be that public intervention in Britain was so obvious that there was no need to theorize it, omitting one of the main goals of the theory of economic policy, i.e. need for consistency of various policy actions. Another partial explanation of this apparent exception of Britain to host a 'school' of economic policy could be that in the 1950s and the 1960s the attention of at least part of the academic left in Britain was directed to some alternative target to challenge this credo (a more radical critique of the prevailing economic credo, that of Neo-Ricardians). In due course, policy attitudes changed towards laissez-faire and dismantling positive policy action.

by the Fascist regime. In some cases these specific policy subjects were taught by people engaged in the administration of practical policies. The remaining free-market minority was rather resistant to the innovations introduced by Keynes and other economists abroad. Add to this that in Italy, economic policy was compressed between economics and public finance scholars, that had acquired a high status also at an international level. Moreover, the ability of Italian economists and public finance theorists to take due account of institutional and historical factors when prescribing implementation of optimal or fair policy rules left little room for an autonomous discipline such as economic policy to develop beyond very specific realms such as those of trade policy and the like, having a very high historical, institutional and social content. This was the case, e.g., of Pantaleoni[3] and, even to a larger extent, of Luigi Einaudi.[4] All in all, being almost isolated from theoretical developments abroad for the two decades before WWII, Italian economists did not possess the instruments necessary for a systematic approach to economic policy.

Towards the end of the 1930s a specific term for the discipline had been forged: Politica Economica, i.e. economic policy (e.g., see Fontana Russo, 1935),[5] although its content remained practically the same as before. The first real systematic attempt to gain breadth to the discipline by relating it (loosely) to market imperfections, devising different main directions of state intervention and distinguishing home and foreign economic policy directed to different targets, was Bresciani Turroni (1942). However, the second edition of this book (Bresciani Turroni, 1960), while deeper analytically, had a quite different content, focusing on money, international trade, balance of payments and monetary systems, losing part of the breadth of the previous edition. A textbook used at La Sapienza University of Rome until the early 1960s was Fantini (1962) whose previous editions had a different title

---

[3] Pantaleoni's static economic analysis is encapsulated in a given institutional context; his dynamic analysis proceeds along a number of institutional and social changes (see Pantaleoni, 1889; 1913). His work deserved appreciation by Schumpeter (1954) and Buchanan (1960), and among the others (Bini, 1997; De Cecco, 1995; Bellanca, Giocoli 1998).
[4] Luigi Einaudi was the prototype of Italian public finance theorists accounting for history and institutions for their policy recommendations (see, in particular, Einaudi, 1958, 1965); and Faucci (2010) and Da Empoli (2010).
[5] A previous text by this same author referred to trade treaties and policy (Fontana Russo, 1902).

(Fantini, 1943; 1948). To some extent this followed Bresciani Turroni's (1942) path, but, while containing chapters on banking, monetary, financial, transport, labor, trade and international policy, this book lacked a systematic part of the foundations and methodology of economic policy as well as macroeconomic policy. Similarly, was Franchini Stappo (1963; 1964). Thus, the task to give a new content to the discipline was left mainly to younger economists, who had the opportunity to catch theoretical innovations abroad and to import them to Italy.

In the early 1950s practically only a few Italian scholars had introduced – or were about to introduce – Keynesian thought in Italy: Giuseppe Ugo Papi, Alessandro Franchini Stappo, Vittorio Marrama, Ferdinando Di Fenizio and Federico Caffè.[6] Some had introduced progresses abroad in welfare economics (Caffè and Lombardini in 1953-1954),[7] which is apparently strange, as these were based on Paretian foundations following Pareto's method, such as Luigi Amoroso and Ernesto D'Albergo.[8] Some had done the same thing for the theory of economic policy (Caffè, Marrama and Di Fenizio).[9] In a few cases theoretical advances abroad were introduced into Italian textbooks;[10] in other cases some Italian journals hosted either important original articles by foreign authors or their translations.[11] Translations of books or collected essays as books also played an important role.[12] The intellectual openness of these economists was crucial also in their propensity to encourage their pupils to complete their preparation

---

[6] Papi (1953), Franchini Stappo (1955), Marrama (1961); Di Fenizio (1948).

[7] Caffè (1953; 1956a); Lombardini, (1954); Caffè's translation of some essays in welfare economics by Bergson, Hicks, Hotelling, Kaldor, Little, Scitovsky (Caffè, 1956b); see also Caffè's translation of Zeuthen (1958).

[8] By contrast, Pareto had a very extensive, if lagged, impact on the academic profession abroad, in particular, for what we are interested in this paper, not only for his principle of welfare but also for laying down the tools of mathematical economics that contributed to the foundation of econometrics (Tinbergen, 1949).

[9] Caffè's translation of Zeuthen (1958), Marrama (1962), Di Fenizio (1956; various years).

[10] E.g., Di Fenizio (various years), Marrama (1948).

[11] This was the case of a number of contributions by Frisch, Tinbergen, Theil, and, outside the proper realm of economic theory, Shackle and even Kurt Godel, which were published in 'L'industria', a journal edited by F. Di Fenizio, and 'Metroeconomica', founded and edited by Eraldo Fossati.

[12] F. Caffè, who didn't edit any journal, made an extensive use of translations to let Italian students and also the general public learn from foreign economic thought.

abroad, mainly in the United Kingdom and the US, but this added little to the birth and development of economic policy and in due time contributed to its demise (see next section).

By the beginning of the 1960s all the premises for devising a consistent and rather autonomous set of propositions to be called economic policy were present in Italy. The only problem was about the weights to assign to the different possible ingredients. There were two main lines along which the discipline was systematically introduced, one by Ferdinando Di Fenizio and the other by Federico Caffè.

Di Fenizio was the most popular representative of the first line. He had studied in particular Keynesian analysis and policy together with various aspects of programming and wrote a monumental course of economic disciplines in five volumes, devoted to the method in economics and economic policy; macroeconomic agents and economic flows; the consumption function; short-term diagnosis, analysis and policy; macroeconomic planning (Di Fenizio, various years). We can include in this line Eraldo Fossati (1955), dealing mainly with macroeconomic analysis and policy and to some extent with rational programming as essential ingredients of economic policy, and Adalberto Predetti, who had explored methodological issues related to economic policy with specific reference to programming (Predetti, 1973). This line of conceiving economic policy left welfare economics out of its realm. By contrast, it stressed, in addition to macroeconomic policy, the need for the consistency of government action, which was also a reflection of the first attempts to institute some kind of indicative planning emerging in Italy in the mid-1950s (with the formulation of the so-called 'Schema Vanoni', i.e. an outline of targets and instruments for Italy's development presented by the Budget Minister Ezio Vanoni).

Caffè expressed the second line of economic policy, including, in addition to the ingredients of the first line, explicit and more or less detailed references to welfare economics. Caffè had searched for all the possible key ingredients for conceiving economic policy as an autonomous discipline. Indeed he did so first by publishing two short books (Caffè, 1964), then developed into two larger volumes (Caffè, 1966; 1970). A few years later Caffè, who had been impressed by the 1968 student movements' demands, tried to cope with them by rendering the two volumes easier to read and summarizing them in a single volume, at the cost of omitting some technical and analytical passages (Caffè, 1973; 1978). Economic policy was conceived as consisting of a part discussing the ultimate targets of economic policy, derived from welfare economics; problems of social choice; planning; and specific (in particular short-term) micro-economic and macro-economic policies. Such a discipline should draw mainly from economics, but also from other social sciences, mathematics and statistics. Caffe's path was largely followed by a group of economists in Naples, led by Augusto Graziani, who wrote a book presenting foundations for public economic action, the theory of economic policy, detailed policies aiming at specific short-run or long-run targets (D'Antonio, Graziani, Vinci, 1972; 1979), as well as by Lombardini (Lombardini, 1977).

More encyclopedic, but less ample in welfare economics was Francesco Forte (1964; 1970). He had contributed to welfare economics and social choice (or was about to do so), but included only a few pages dedicated to this topic in the cited books, possibly since he considered it to be more in the realm of public finance, his main subject.[13] An original route was followed by Franchini Stappo (1976; 1982), which explored connections between the concepts of power and economic policy.

For many years these were practically the only economic policy textbooks circulating in Italy, widely adopted in many universities. Only around 1990 another generation of economists added new textbooks. Some of them following Caffè's, either deepening its analytic content or complementing and updating it (Acocella, 1989; Palmerio, 1989). Along lines similar to Caffè and D'Antonio, Graziani, Vinci, but with greater attention to social choice and positive economic policy, were Balducci Candela, 1991 (later Balducci, Candela, Scorcu, 2001), Acocella (1994; 1999) and Cagliozzi (1994). Government failures, which had been asserted first by Italian public finance theorists of the 19th century, were being placed at the forefront of many international contributions beginning in the 1960s, by some public finance

---

[13] The traditional relevance of public finance in Italy led many academics to include welfare economics and social choice in this subject, rather than in economic policy.

theorists following the schools of public choice and political economics.[14] These contributions could not be left out of the realm of economic policy, especially when conceived as including market failures.

Valli (1986; 1993) exemplifies a different approach, with almost no reference to welfare economics and the theory of economic policy, but more open to long-term issues and thus also to discussing the institutional and comparative setting, which to some extent was inspired by Di Fenizio's interest in such topics.

A few textbooks dealt with economic policy only in strict reference to analytical short-term models (Marelli, 1992; then Marelli, Signorelli, 2010) or to specific Italian problems (Bianchi, 1994). The following years saw new textbooks giving different weights to the ingredients already present in their predecessors: Ciccarone (1997) and Campiglio (1999) discussed mainly problems of welfare economics and social choice; Chiarini (2004) dealt with decision models.

5 Why a limited impact on teaching in Europe (and elsewhere)?

Some of the Italian textbooks (e.g., Acocella, 1994; 1999) have been translated into English, Polish, Chinese, Croatian. Nonetheless, the idea of

---

[14] Adherents to the school of Public choice have been numerous in Italy, as they have linked this school to some findings of the traditional Italian school of public finance, such as those of De Viti De Marco and other authors mentioned in section 1, which can be considered to be anticipatory of the content of the school of Public choice. Reference to public choice was rather ample in the main Italian textbooks of public finance and economic policy. In addition, a translation of the main sources of Buchanan, Tullock and other public choice authors was collected in the early 1980s (Da Empoli, Carrubba, 1984). The presence among textbooks of the political economics strain of research was well represented by one of the main proponents, together with Alberto Alesina, of this approach, i.e. Guido Tabellini (see Persson, Tabellini, 1990). All these theorists are high critical of government intervention. For the school of public choice, government failures are even more pronounced than those of market and constitutional rules should be devised in order to limit policy action. For the authors of the political economics approach, in addition to constitutional rules aiming at a proper functioning of the government, rules should be introduced to limit current discretionary action of the state as an effect of the role played by the private sector's expectations, which we will shortly deal with in the next section.

economic policy as a discipline starting from welfare economics and social choice, including normative and positive theories of economic policy and then dealing with specific policies and targets (taking due account of the institutional and historical mediations to make before applying economic analysis) has not been passed over to other countries. Today even in Scandinavian countries and the Netherlands it is not popular and both scholars and students have lost memory of the discipline's founding fathers. This is apparently strange. I offer three explanations: the rise of the Anglo-Saxon school (with scarce reference to history and institutions); the negative attitude of this school towards active policy intervention (including the -until recently unchecked- power of the Lucas critique), which matured from the late 1960s; absence of theoretical advances in crucial areas of the discipline. I have dealt to some extent with the first two factors elsewhere (Acocella, 2013); in the next section I briefly discuss the third one.

6 Teaching and researching in economic policy

The content of any discipline is subject to be challenged by advances from the current literature. In order to survive, it must resist critical objections, either of a logical or an empirical type. Substantive research, refinements and innovations on the issues that are the object of the discipline are necessary in order to respond to those critiques that can be incorporated in the old framework.

This is especially so if its main propositions that justify the foundations of the discipline - have been attacked either in logical terms or due to empirical correspondence and relevance. In the case of economic policy, welfare economics and social choice have not only resisted attacks, but have been able to respond to the Arrowian impossibility theorem. Decisive objections, instead, have been directed to the theory of economic policy, by the Lucas critique, which negates effectiveness of discretionary policy action. State intervention is thus questioned and should be restricted to its minimum. Rules must constrain it, in the case where it is absolutely necessary in order to ensure a reliable environment for the market to operate. This implies that one of the two main bases of economic policy as a discipline – the other being existence of market failures – falls apart and economic policy becomes a lame duck, which returns us to pre-Keynesian times. The critique based on logical considerations adds to the limitations of the realm of application of the government's discretionary action that hinges on the damages caused by politicians (as highlighted by the public choice and the political economics strands of the economic discipline). However, it has a more devastating impact, being based on logical arguments.

Economic policy in Italy was mainly built as a discipline by collecting innovations produced abroad in various areas, but with scarce additional personal research. When critiques defied the core of the discipline, there seemed to be no possibility of maintaining the construction of the discipline as it had been designed in the Scandinavian countries and the Netherlands. It is understandable, then, that this conception of economic policy found it difficult to be accepted in many other countries.

However, more recently the core of the discipline, which seemed to be defeated by the Lucas critique, has not only been shown to be exempt from this critique, when used in a strategic context, but also to be able to produce new interesting results in this context, in so far as existence, uniqueness or multiplicity of the game equilibrium is concerned.[15] One could thus hope that now this way of conceiving economic policy as a consistent and autonomous discipline will spill over from the countries from where it has some roots, although several factors may counter this including: the habits of teachers and researchers; their bias in favour of the theoretical tools they are familiar with, not to say, in some cases, of conformism; vested interests in free-market institutions; the limited extent of government action. These are all factors that would certainly run counter to some reaffirmation, at least in theoretical terms, of the power of the public institutions, when endowed with a sufficient number of instruments and well managed, not limited by preclusions and prejudices, to tame market forces and address them to desirable outcomes.

---

[15] Acocella, Di Bartolomeo, Hughes Hallett (2013), this book has been preceded and followed by a number of more specific papers, dating back, in some cases to 2005. Among the most recent ones, see Acocella, Di Bartolomeo, Hughes Hallett and Piacquadio (2014).

References

Acocella, N. (1989) *Elementi di politica economica*, Kappa: Roma.

Acocella, N. (1994) *Fondamenti di politica economica. Valori e tecniche,* Roma: Nuova Italia Scientifica (English transl., *Foundations of Economic policy. Values and techniques,* Cambridge: Cambridge University Press, 1998)

Acocella, N. (1999) *Politica economica e strategie aziendali,* Roma: Carocci (English transl, *Economic policy in the age of globalisation,* Cambridge: Cambridge University Press, 2005)

Acocella, N. (2013) 'Teoria e pratica della politica economica: l'eredità del recente passato', *Rivista di Storia Economica,* 2-3: 471-93.

Acocella, N., Di Bartolomeo, G. and Hughes Hallett, A. (2013) *The theory of economic policy in a strategic context,* Cambridge: Cambridge University Press.

Acocella, N., Di Bartolomeo, G. and Hughes Hallett, A. and Piacquadio, P. (2014), , 'Announcement wars as an equilibrium selection device', *Oxford Economic Papers,* 66, 1: 325-347.

Akerlof, G. (1970) 'The market for lemons. Uncertainty and the market mechanism', *Quarterly Journal of Economics,* 84, 3: 488-500.

Balducci, R. and Candela, G. (1991) *Teoria della politica economica,* Roma: La Nuova Italia Scientifica, 2 vols.

Balducci, R., Candela, G. and Scorcu, A.E. (2001) *Introduzione alla politica economica,* Bologna: Zanichelli.

Balducci, R., Candela, G. and Scorcu, A. E. (2002) *Teoria della politica economica. Modelli dinamici e stocastici,* Bologna: Zanichelli.

Barone, E. (1908) 'Il Ministro della produzione nello stato collettivista', *Giornale degli Economisti,* Sept./Oct., 2: 267–293, 392-414. (English trans.: 'The Ministry of production in the collectivist state', In: Hayek, F. (ed.) (1935) *Collectivist economic planning,* London: Routledge and Kegan Paul, reprinted in Marchionatti, R. (ed.) (2004), *Early mathematical economics, 1871-1915: The establishment of the mathematical method in economics,* v. IV, London: Taylor & Francis, pp. 227-63.

Bator, F. (1958) 'The anatomy of market failure', *Quarterly Journal of Economics,* 72, 3: 351-379.

Bellanca, N. and Giocoli, N. (1998) *Maffeo Pantaleoni, il Principe degli economisti italiani,* Firenze: Polistampa.

Bianchi, C. (1998 [1994]) *L'economia italiana e i problemi della politica economica,* II Ed., Milano: Guerini Studio.

Bini, P. (1997) *When economics talked to society. The life, thought and works*, In: Baldassarri, M. (ed.), *Maffeo Pantaleoni. At the origin of the Italian school of economics and finance*, London: Macmillan.

Bresciani Turroni, C. (1942) *Introduzione alla politica economica*, Torino: Einaudi.

Bresciani Turroni, C. (1960) *Corso di economia politica*, vol.2, 'Politica economica', Milano: Giuffré.

Buchanan, J. M. (1960) *'La scienza delle finanze'. The Italian tradition in fiscal theory*, In *Fiscal theory and political economy. Selected essays*, Chapel Hill: University of North Carolina Press.

Caffè, F. (1953) *Vecchi e nuovi indirizzi nelle indagini sull'economia del benessere*, Roma: Tecnica Grafica.

Caffè, F. (1956a) 'Economia del benessere', In: Napoleoni, C. (ed.) *Dizionario di economia politica*, Milano: Ed. di Comunità.

Caffè, F. (ed.) (1956b) *Saggi sulla moderna economia del benessere*, Torino: Boringhieri.

Caffè, F. (1964) *Appunti introduttivi alla politica economica*, Roma: Edizioni 'Ricerche'

Caffè, F. (1966) *Politica economica. Sistematica e tecniche di analisi*, vol. I, Torino: Boringhieri

Caffè, F. (1970) *Politica economica. Problemi economici interni*, vol. II, Torino: Boringhieri.

Caffè, F. (1973) *Elementi di politica economica*, Roma: Kappa.

Caffè, F. (1978) *Lezioni di politica economica*, Torino: Boringhieri.

Cagliozzi, R. (1994) *Profili delle lezioni di politica economica*, Napoli: Liguori.

Campiglio, L. (1999) *Mercato, prezzi e politica economica*, Bologna: Il Mulino.

Chiarini, B. (2004) *Lezioni di politica economica. Debito pubblico, aspettative razionali, fluttuazioni cicliche*, Roma: Carocci.

Ciccarone, G. (1997) *Fondamenti teorici della politica economica. Equilibrio, informazione e non linearità*, Roma-Bari: Laterza.

D'Antonio, M., Graziani, A. and Vinci, S. (1972) *Problemi e metodi di politica economica*, Napoli: Liguori; Cooperativa Editrice Economia e Commercio, Napoli, 2nd. Ed. 1974.

Nicola Acocella

D'Antonio, M., Graziani, A. and Vinci, S. (1979) *Problemi e metodi di politica economica*, vol.1: 'Aspetti di metodo. Gli interventi di breve periodo', Napoli: Liguori, 3rd. Ed.

Da Empoli, D. (2010) *Einaudi: La scienza delle finanze come scienza della libertà*, In: Acocella, N. (ed.) (2010) *Einaudi: Studioso, Statista, Governatore*, (Einaudi: Scholar, Statesman, Governor), Roma: Carocci.

Da Empoli, D. and Carrubba, S. (eds.), (1984) *Scelte pubbliche*, Firenze: Le Monnier.

De Cecco, M. (1995) Il ruolo delle istituzioni nel pensiero di Pantaleoni, *Rivista di politica economica*, 75, 3: 189-96.

De Viti De Marco, A. (1888) *Il carattere teorico dell'economia finanziaria*, Roma: Pasqualucci.

Di Fenizio, F. (1948) *Studi keynesiani*, Milano: L'Industria.

Di Fenizio, F. (1956) *La programmazione economica*, Torino: UTET.

Di Fenizio, F. (1957) *Le leggi dell'economia*, vol.1: 'Il metodo dell'economia politica e della politica economica', Milano: L'Industria.

Di Fenizio, F. (1958) *Le leggi dell'economia*, vol.2: 'Il sistema economico, i grandi attori e i flussi di reddito' and vol.3: 'La funzione del consumo', Milano: L'Industria; vol.4: 'Diagnosi, previsioni, politiche congiunturali in Italia', and vol.5: 'La programmazione globale in Italia' Roma: Isco.

Einaudi, L. (1958) *Lezioni di politica sociale*, Torino: Edizioni scientifiche Einaudi.

Einaudi, L. (1965) *Saggi sul risparmio e l'imposta*, Torino: Einaudi.

Fantini, O. (1943) *Politica economica e finanziaria*, vol. 1, 'Parte introduttiva', Padova: Cedam.

Fantini, O. (1948) *Politica economica e finanziaria*, vol. 2, 'Politica monetaria, politica del risparmio, politica del credito e politica bancaria, politica finanziaria, politica economica di congiuntura', Padova: Cedam.

Fantini, O. (1962) *Teoria e problemi della politica economica*, Padova; Cedam,7th ed.

Faucci, R. (2010) *Luigi Einaudi e la Storia*, in Acocella, N. (ed.) (2010) Einaudi: Studioso, statista, governatore (Einaudi: Scholar, statesman, governor), Roma: Carocci.

Fontana Russo, L. (1902) *I trattati di commercio e l'economia nazionale*, Roma: Soc. ed. Dante Alighieri.

Fontana Russo, L. (1935) *Corso di politica economica generale e corporativa*, Roma: Cremonese.

Forte, F. (1964) *Introduzione alla politica economica*, Torino: Einaudi.

Forte, F. (1970) *Manuale di politica economica*, 2 vols., Torino: Einaudi.

Fossati, E. (1953) *Elementi di politica economica razionale*, Padova: Cedam.

Franchini Stappo, A. (1955) *Studi sulla teoria macroeconomica della congiuntura*, Firenze: Società editrice universitaria.

Franchini Stappo, A. (1963) *Corso di politica economica*, vol. 1, Padova: Cedam.

Franchini Stappo, A. (1964) *Corso di politica economica*, vol. 2, Padova: Cedam.

Franchini Stappo, A. (1971) *Fondamenti di politica economica generalizzata*, Padova: Cedam.

Franchini Stappo, A. (1976) *Teoria del potere e politica economica*, Padova: Cedam.

Franchini Stappo, A. (1982) *L'organizzazione come struttura di potere*, Padova: Cedam.

Frisch, R. (1949) *A memorandum on price-wage-tax subsidy policies as instruments in maintaining optimal employment*, UN Document E (CN1/Dub 2), New York, reprinted as Memorandum from Universitets Socialokonomiske Institutt, Oslo, 1953.

Frisch, R. (1950) 'L'emploi des modèles pour l'élaboration d'une politique économique rationnelle', *Revue d'Économie Politique*, 60: 474-498; 601-634.

Frisch, R. (1957) *Numerical determination of a quadratic preference function for use in macroeconomic programming*, Memorandum from the Institute of Economics at the University of Oslo, No. 14, reprinted in Studies in honour of Gustavo del Vecchio, Giornale degli Economisti and Annali di Economia, 1961, 1: 43-83.

Keynes, J. M. (1936 [1973]) *The general theory of employment, interest and money*, Macmillan, London, repr. In: *The Collected writings*, vol. vii, London: Macmillan.

Lombardini, S. (1954) *Fondamenti e problemi dell'economia del benessere*, Milano: Giuffrè.

Lombardini, S. (1977) *I problemi della politica economica*, Torino: Utet.

Marelli, E. (1992) *Scuole macroeconomiche ed il dibattito di politica economica*, Torino: Giappichelli.

Marelli, E. and Signorelli, M. (2010) *Politica economica. Teorie, scuole ed evidenze empiriche*, Torino: Giappichelli.

Marrama, V. (1948) *Teoria e politica della piena occupazione*, Roma: Edizioni italiane.

Marrama, V. (1961) *Ciclo economico e politica anticiclica*, Napoli: Giannini.

Marrama, V. (1962) *Problemi e tecniche di programmazione economica*, Cappelli: Rocca S. Casciano.

Marshall, A. (1890) *Principles of economics*, London: Macmillan.

Mazzola, U. (1890) *I dati scientifici della finanza pubblica*, Roma: Loescher e C.

Meade, J. E. (1951) *The theory on international economic policy*, vol.1, 'The balance of payments', Oxford: Oxford University Press.

Meade, J. E. (1955) *The theory on international economic policy*, vol.2, 'Trade and welfare', Oxford: Oxford University Press.

Mill, J. S. (1848) *Principles of political economy with some of their applications to social philosophy*, London: John Parker.

Palmerio, G. (1993) *Politica economica*, Torino: Giappichelli.

Pantaleoni, M. (1889 [1942]) *Principi di economia pura*, Firenze: Barbera.

Pantaleoni, M. (1913) *Lezioni di economia politica,* ed. by N. Trevisonno, Roma: Castellani.

Papi, G. U. (ed.) (1953) *Studi keynesiani*, Milano: Giuffrè.

Pareto, V. (1906) *Manuale di economia politica*, Milano: Società Editrice Libraria, (reprinted by Nuova grafica, Roma, 1965).

Persson, T. and Tabellini, G. (1996), *Politica macroeconomica. Le nuove teorie*, Roma: Nuova Italia Scientifica (English ed., *Macroeconomic Policy, Credibility and Politics,* London: Harwood Academic Publishers, 1990).

Pigou, A. C. (1912) *Wealth and welfare*, London: Macmillan.

Pigou, A. C. (1920) *The economics of welfare*, London: Macmillan.

Predetti, A. (1973) *Appunti di metodologia della politica economica,* Milano: Cisalpino-Goliardica.

Predetti, A. (1989) *Temi di metodologia della politica economica*, Milano: Cisalpino-Goliardica.

Predetti, A. (1995) *Problemi metodologici della politica economica*, Milano: Cisalpino-Goliardica.

Ricardo, D. (1817 [1951]) *On the principles of political economy and taxation*, ed. by Sraffa, P. Cambridge: Cambridge University Press.

Schumpeter, J. A. (1954) *History of economic analysis*, New York: Oxford University Press.

Sidgwick. H. (1883) *Principles of political economy*, London: Macmillan.

Smith, A. (1776) *An inquiry into the nature and causes of the wealth of nations*, London: W. Strahan.

Theil, H. (1956) 'On the theory of economic policy', *American Economic Review*, 46: 360-366.

Theil, H. (1964) *Optimal decision rules for government and industry*, Amsterdam: North Holland.

Tiberi M. and Frinolli, A. (2006) 'Gli insegnamenti economici', In: Cagiano de Azevedo, R. (ed.) *La Facoltà di Economia. Cento anni di storia, 1906-2006*, Rubbettino, Soveria Mannelli.

Tiberi., M. and Fubelli C. (eds.) (2006) *Cento anni di economisti*, Facoltà di Economia, Sapienza University.

Tinbergen, J. (1952) *On the theory of economic policy*, Amsterdam: North Holland, (It. transl. ed. by Di Fenizio, F. (1955) *Sulla teoria della politica economica*, Milano: Ed. L'Industria)

Tinbergen, J. (1956) *Economic policies. Principles and design,* Amsterdam: North Holland (It. transl. ed. (1969) *Principi e metodi della politica economica,* Milano: F.Angeli)

Valli, V. (1986) *Politica economica: i modelli, gli strumenti, l'economia italiana*, Roma: La Nuova Italia Scientifica, 1st ed.

Valli, V. (1993) *Politica economica*, vol. 1. 'Teoria e politica dello sviluppo. Il caso italiano; vol. 2: 'Macroeconomia e politiche di breve periodo. Il caso italiano', Roma: La Nuova Italia Scientifica.

Walras, L. (1896 [1936]) *Etudes d'économie politique appliquée*, Paris: Pichon et Durand.

Wicksell, K. (1926 [1946]) *Lectures on political economy*, English tr., London: Routledge and Kegan Paul.

Zeuthen, F. (1958) *Videnskab og Veltfaerd I okonomisk Politik*, Copenhagen: Gads Forlag. (It. transl. edited by Caffè, F. *Scienza e benessere nella politica economica*, Torino: Boringhieri, 1961).

Part Four:

Laying the foundations for a future economics curriculum

CHAPTER 8

Five ideas that should be included in microeconomics textbooks

David Hemenway

1 Introduction

Unlike most other social sciences, economics has a single basic model that is taught to all budding economists. Like all models, the microeconomic model abstracts from reality. The model has proven to be very powerful and useful, providing important insights and policy guidance, and raising economics to the "queen of the social sciences" – the only social science with a Nobel Prize. The assumptions of the model are its strengths – and also its limitations

Textbook microeconomics assumes that (a) people are rational, and (b) tastes or preferences are exogenous – tastes are well-defined and stable, essentially God-given at birth. The advent of behavioral economics has been a breath of fresh air for microeconomics, with much of its focus on the rationality assumption, particularly the rationality of individuals (rather than of institutions). However, aside from a growing literature on the desire for social position, that people are social animals has received less emphasis along with the effect of society and culture on how tastes are formed change.

In the economic model, people are largely solitary creatures, with fixed tastes, assumed to be basically Robinson Crusoe's, each living on our own little island. Our major interaction with other humans is when we trade (including trading labor for goods). In other words, we are connected to each other primarily through markets. Economic theory in effect has, with mere punctuation changes, converted John Donne's famous saying into "No! Man Is an Island."

However, in the real world, humans are not like bears. Bears are solitary animals. An adult male spends almost all of his life away from other bears, living and dying by himself. By contrast, wolves, dolphins, and primates are social animals like ourselves. We live in societies, and we depend on others of our species for health and happiness. Humans "are social not just in the trivial sense that we like company, and not just in the obvious sense that we each depend on others. We are social in a more elemental way: simply to exist as a normal human being requires interaction with other people" (Gawande, 2009).

It is now commonly accepted that human children require nurturing from others, not just for food and protection but also for the normal functioning of their brains. Caregivers teach children how to be human. Child neglect typically has worse long term consequences than child abuse. Even for adults, one of the most severe forms of punishment is solitary confinement, where one is denied contact with other humans; indeed, it is considered psychological torture.

As biologists, sociologists and psychologists know, people do extremely little individually or independently; human nature is about grouping, flocking and herding. We are natural imitators of each other, literally "monkey see monkey do." Indeed that is how children learn.

Raising children involves not only helping them learn the natural laws of our planet (e.g., how long a day is; that clouds can bring rain), but also the customs or rules of their specific society. Children must largely adapt to these customs if they are to survive and thrive – what to wear, what to eat, what to say, how to play. Each child is different, but they almost all go through similar stages at various ages, and quickly learn and mimic most of their society's conventions.

Thus tastes are very predictable. For a boy growing up in Chicago in the 1950s, one could fairly accurately predict pretty that his favorite sport might be baseball, football or basketball, and that his favorite sports team would be a Chicago team. By contrast, soccer would probably be the favorite sport of a boy growing up in Caracas, Venezuela.

Parents are key influences on the tastes children will have as adults. For example, we know that a major risk factor for adult smoking is whether one's parents smoke, and that the best single predictor of adult gun ownership is if one was raised in home with a gun. We also know that the brain of children and adolescents are still in the process of developing and that they are more likely than adults not only to make poor long run decisions but to have malleable tastes.

Tastes are affected not only by parents, but also by peers. Adolescence is probably the most peer-driven of ages; teens tend to move, play, and even commit crimes in packs. The importance of peer approval on the behavior of adolescents cannot be overstated. How else to explain that so many US teens are currently getting tattoos?

The desire for many products depends on the purchases of others. Teens "need" cell phones because their friends have cell phones, and they will be an outsider without one. Kids want baseball gloves if their friends have gloves and are playing baseball. A generation of children wanted to read Harry Potter and go to the Harry Potter movies in large part so that they could be part of the group and talk about the stories.

Adults often want what other adults have for many similar reasons. If everyone else is watching the Superbowl, it is fun to watch it with others; you are an outsider if you missed it and everyone else is talking about it. Adults are tied together in networks of individuals. We now know that even obesity can spread through social networks, just as fads and fashions spread. What you give as gifts and when you desire to retire is largely dependent on what others are giving and when others are retiring.

Thus five of the concepts that should to be treated more fully in microeconomic textbooks are that (a) people are social animals; (b) tastes are malleable, particularly so for children; (c) children are an important part of the economy; (d) retail buyers typically have limited information, and (e) large corporations have substantial social and political power.

Perhaps the most controversial concept is that most consumers have little real knowledge about what they are buying, instead relying (sometimes correctly) on the good faith of the seller, government protection, or perhaps the invisible hand of a perfect market. My belief in the lack of knowledge of retail purchasers was formed by my experiences working for consumer advocate Ralph Nader in the 1960s, writing my doctoral dissertation on standards and product specifications (Hemenway, 1975), and my work in public health. With Nader, we documented that buyers were misled and/or incapable of knowing what they were buying – e.g., how a sizable amount of distilled water sold in supermarkets was actually tap water; that college educated consumers could not determine the low cost item among identical products; and that buyers had no idea how many rodent hairs were being sold in hot dogs.

Specifications, and standard specifications, I discovered were used almost exclusively by large buyers (e.g., corporations) who were buying in bulk and had the ability and financial incentive to know exactly what they were buying. By contrast, since learning about the quality of a product is largely a fixed cost that can be spread over the amount of the product that is being purchased, retail consumers are largely rationally ignorant. If you or I need paint, we simply go to the store; if General Motors wants paint, it writes or uses detailed purchase specifications.

Working in the health arena also made me skeptical of the knowledge of consumers. For example, the public spends tens of billions of dollars each year on quack remedies. Even though I am in the field, I personally know little about the health and safety aspects of what I buy, and what little I know often comes from government reporting requirements. Test yourself. How carcinogenic are the items in your bathroom? When you buy beef or poultry, do you know what the steers and chickens were fed.

Overall, most consumers typically lack basic knowledge needed to make informed decisions in a complex world. For example, for food consumption, studies show that consumers are wildly misinformed about dietary fat and fatty acids (Diekman and Malcolm, 2009), and for financial decisions, most lack even a rudimentary financial literacy needed to make wise choices (Lusardi, 2008).

The fifth idea, that corporations have social and political power, is well known, though rarely studied by neoclassical economists. It is, after all, more in the domain of sociologists and political scientists. It is nonetheless important for economists to remember that policies affecting corporations typically affect not only their economic but also social and political activities. Politically, for example, corporations have the power to influence who gets elected, what laws are passed, what regulations are set, and how they are implemented and enforced. Indeed, U.S. corporations have been given the human right of protected speech.

2 The cigarette story

A few years ago I read a fascinating history of the cigarette industry in the 20th century (Brandt, 2007), written from a public health perspective. Because litigation against the industry forced it to reveal internal documents, there is probably more and better information about the behavior of cigarette companies than any other industry in the United States. The cigarette story can be used to illustrate the five ideas.

From a public health standpoint, tobacco-related diseases are the largest preventable burden of mortality in the United States, and will soon hold that unenviable position for the entire world. Were they a new product, it is doubtful that cigarettes would be allowed on the U.S. market. They not only cause a multitude of diseases to the smoker (over 400,000 deaths per year in the United States), but secondhand smoke significantly increases the risk of disease to others.

2.1 People are social animals with malleable tastes

At the turn of the 20th century, cigarette smoking was widely considered a dirty habit, practiced by disreputable men and boys. Smoking was seen as a profound moral failing, and Henry Ford among others, vowed never to hire a cigarette smoker. A number of states even prohibited the sale of this noxious weed. All that would change in the next fifty years: by the mid-1950s half of American adults smoked cigarettes, and smoking was an integral part of the American lifestyle.

The social aspects of smoking were crucial to its popularity in 20th century America. The first cigarette was rarely a pleasant experience, but smokers soon grow accustomed. Still, when asked, smokers overwhelmingly cited sociability as the essential attraction of a cigarette. Only a tiny percentage cited taste as one of a cigarette's pleasures.

While almost everyone smoked their own particular brand, in repeated experiments, smokers failed to identify their brand, despite their belief that they could do so. Still, brand loyalty was fierce for this largely undifferentiated product, whose identity was fashioned not through intrinsic qualities but by cultural meaning.

Cigarettes were promoted, not only through enormous amounts of advertising, but through many other means including parades, planted magazine articles and product placement. Cigarette advertisers, armed with evidence from psychology, were sure that the public didn't really know what it wanted. It had to be given ideas about what it should like. Individuals, they believed were in a constant struggle to conform and yet be different. The industry could thrive, they believed, if it did not focus on selling the product, but on selling a way of life, with cigarettes a mechanism of self-identity.

In the 20th century, the large majority of smokers began as adolescents, and cigarettes played an important role in the rituals of adolescent identity. To smoke had meaning – for example to refrain from smoking could be considered the same as joining the sissy group of boys. Many girls in the early 20th century began smoking to break with Victorian conventions about females, to show that they were modern and up-to-date.

For women, smoking became associated with physical beauty, sexual attractiveness, and social and political equality. For men, it provided connotations of virility and strength. Movies were filled with the cigarette smoke of the leading stars.

The importance of promotion was highlighted when the Marlboro brand was successfully transformed from a luxury cigarette for women into a macho smoke for men, solely through mass marketing. Marlboro ads had little copy and instead conveyed the message almost exclusively through image.

Unfortunately for the cigarette companies, by the end of the 20th century in America, the image of smoking had changed dramatically. Anti-cigarette ads, shown on TV because of the fairness doctrine, smartly focused not only on the health aspects but the social aspects of smoking (e.g., "nobody wants to kiss an ashtray") and significantly reduced the level of smoking. In the late 20th century an RJR memo correctly reported that "the general public and its leaders are of the opinion that smoking is messy, indulgent, down-scale, non-family oriented, non-fashionable habit – one that is increasingly a smaller part of contemporary lifestyles." The companies saw that they were losing the cultural battle.

Smokers reported a declining pleasure from smoking. What was fragrant had become foul, what was attractive had become repulsive. Social conventions moved to stigmatize smokers as irrational, dirty and self-destructive. Yet while the cigarette was losing its connotation of glamour, sophistication and sexual allure in the United States, in developing nations the industry was able to construe meanings of social status, cosmopolitanism and affluence, turning Western cigarettes into status symbols among teenagers. Worldwide, each day, some 80,000-100,000 individuals (mostly children and youth) become new smokers.

2.2 Youth and children

Adolescents play a crucial role in this industry. In the United States, over 80 percent of smokers begin regular use before the age of 18. The first brand one smokes is likely to be kept for life, and the younger one starts smoking, the less likely one is able to quit. By the 1970s, with smokers dying off or quitting, companies clearly understood the need for "replacement smokers" – their future rested on the illegal buying decision of teenagers. Not surprisingly, cigarette companies promoted their cigarettes to youth and children. A 1991 study found that for children aged three to six, the recognition rate of a tobacco company cartoon character "Joe Camel" approached that of Mickey Mouse. Internal company documents made it clear to whom the appeal of Joe Camel was focused.

2.3 Consumer misinformation

Cigarettes have been called a delivery system for nicotine. Nicotine is addictive, in the same way that heroin or cocaine is, leading to dependence, tolerance, and withdrawal when ingestion is halted. In a typical year, more than two-thirds of American smokers express a desire to quit, but fewer than 10 percent who try are able to quit. To keep people smoking, companies sometimes added nicotine. For example, they knew that "light" cigarettes required increased nicotine to help sustain the addiction.

As is true for many goods, retail consumers had little detailed information about the product they were consuming. For example, cigarette companies not only secretly varied the levels of nicotine in their cigarettes, but often included additives – at least 13 of which were substances banned in food products. At mid-century, most consumers and even some researchers believed that smoking could not be very harmful, relying largely on the fact that so many people smoked. Surely everyone would know if it were deadly.

After research linked smoking to cancer and other diseases, the companies introduced filter cigarettes, with the clear implication that these would reduce the risk of disease (e.g., Kent's micronite filter, "just what the doctor ordered"), which they did not. Most filter cigarette smokers believed the claims. Similarly, the introduction of low tar and light cigarettes did not reduce the risk of smoking, but as the companies understood, many smokers were convinced and switched to low tar and light cigarette brands.

When the science began overwhelmingly to show that cigarettes caused many diseases, the industry undertook a PR strategy to produce and sustain scientific skepticism and controversy. Although there was virtual consensus even among industry researchers – who were not permitted to publish their findings – for decades the companies were able to create the impression of strong controversy and scientific debate about the relationship between cigarette smoking and disease. The press, responding to industry urgings for fairness and balance, dealt with the issue as it would a political debate and willingly provided "both sides" of the science.

As a judge concluded in 2006 in a suit against the industry, "over the course of 50 years, defendants lied, misrepresented, and deceived the American public – including smokers and the young people they avidly sought as replacement smokers – about the devastating health effect of smoking and environmental tobacco smoke." Recognizing the role they inadvertently played in fanning the so-called controversy, many universities have banned the acceptance of tobacco money, historically used to gain status and legitimacy while influencing the scientific process.

2.4 Corporate power

Crucial to the rise of cigarettes in 20th century America was its promotion and use among soldiers during wartime (e.g., World Wars I, II, and Korea). The industry often provided the cigarettes, which were included as part of supply rations.

The tobacco lobby for decades was considered the most powerful lobby in Washington D.C. It avoided the regulation by the Federal Trade Commission (FTC), the Consumer Product Safety Commission, and the Food and Drug Administration (FDA). In the 1980s, for example, the FDA approved Nicorette chewing tobacco which was intended to help smokers quit. The FDA was in the strange position of regulating products to help individuals quit smoking, but having no jurisdiction over the cigarette itself.

The tobacco industry had more political power at the federal and state than at the local level. They thus wanted and were able to have most states pass "preemption laws" which forbade local authorities from passing more restrictive tobacco legislation than passed by the state.

Even when the industry appeared to have lost legislative battles it typically won by promoting its own interests. For example, a year after the 1964 Surgeon General's report concluding that smoking was hazardous to health, the Federal Cigarette Labeling and Advertising Act mandated warning labels on cigarette packages. But the law, in effect, rebuked the FTC for considering cigarette regulation. The label deterred few smokers but provided cover for the companies to defeat lawsuits brought against it. The New York Times called the warning label requirements "a shocking piece of special interest legislation." Similarly, in 1969, the industry acceded to the FCC and agreed to TV advertisements for cigarettes. But the ban meant that the effective anti-tobacco ads, which had been required by the FCC fairness doctrine, also disappeared; it also made it harder for new firms to enter the industry.

After industry duplicity was disclosed through internal documents, it appeared that the industry would be sued successfully by each state's attorney general for contributing to state medical costs. But the "Master Settlement" effectively imposed only a long term excise tax on the industry which made the state coffers dependent on the firms' survival. This meant the states were against lawsuits that might threaten the financial viability of the industry, with the respective attorney general protecting company cash flow from other litigants.

In more recent years, the industry has sought and received support from the U.S. government to help open markets, especially in developing nations. U.S. tobacco companies have successfully made major inroads, particularly in those nations where health regulations have yet to be firmly established. Public health observers compare U.S. international tobacco policy with the opium wars of the 19th century. While we are pleading with foreign governments to stop the export of their cocaine, we are pushing for the export of our tobacco. Former Surgeon General Koop asserted: "I think the most shameful thing this country did was to export disease, disability and death by selling our cigarettes to the world." It is now estimated that the 21st century worldwide death toll from tobacco will be 1 billion people.

Allan Brandt wrote the history that calls cigarettes a "rogue industry". Economists, I believe, would largely see the companies in this industry as simply acting to maximize their profits, as companies tend to do in all industries. For example, I would suspect that if all the internal documents were available for the soft drink industry, we would see some of the same types of activities. The companies successfully sell flavored sugar water to youth, in large part by promoting lifestyle choices, and for many years managed to promote and sell their product in public schools. It is not an industry focused on improving the public's health.

146

3 Discussion

Microeconomic textbooks typically do a good job teaching about many important basic concepts, such as opportunity cost, marginal analysis, moral hazard, externalities, and the prisoners' dilemma. However, I believe these textbooks tend to leave out, or de-emphasize, five basic economic issues. I picked the cigarette story to illustrate these five ideas in large part because so much is known about this industry. But that many other retail markets – whether for luxuries or necessities – could be used to illustrate many of these concepts. For example, what one wears is largely determined by what others wear. Few people today would feel socially comfortable wearing what was fashionable a century ago. What one wears to conferences, to the beach, indeed anyplace, is largely a "coordination game" where participants do not want to be too far out of style. Tastes are quite malleable. For example, the 'acceptable necktie width has changed back and forth in my lifetime. And most consumers actually know little about many important aspects of their clothing, such as who actually made it (e.g., children in sweat shops?) or how flammable it is.

While I believe that much of what is currently emphasized in microeconomic textbooks is useful, in their entirety, I find that microeconomic texts are skewed and somewhat misleading. I am sure that other economists will have different issues they would like to see receive more or emphasis in microeconomic texts, but these are mine. I am not arguing that economists have paid no attention to my five issues. Indeed, economists and other scholars have often written widely about these topics (see References for a very small sample of the literature on each issue), but these ideas have not yet found a home in most microeconomic texts.

To conduct good policy analysis, and even to vote wisely, people need to be knowledgeable about the world in which they live. I believe if economic students come to understand these five ideas, along with all the others they have learned from microeconomic textbooks, they will become better economists and better citizens.

References (by subject)

i) General

Brandt, Allan, M. (2007) *The Cigarette Century: The Rise, Fall, and Deadly Persistence of the Product that Defined America*. New York: Basic Books.

Diekman, C. and Malcolm, K. (2009) 'Consumer perception and insights on fats and fatty acids: knowledge on the quality of diet fat'. *Annals of Nutrition and Metabolism*, 54: 25-31, suppl. 1.

Gawande, A. (2009) 'Hellhole'. *New Yorker*, March 30, http://www.newyorker.com/reporting/2009/03/30/090330fa_fact_gawande#ixzz1Ec3h nxKB

Hemenway, D. (1975) *Industrywide Voluntary Product Standards*. Cambridge, MA: Ballinger.

Lusardi, A. (2008) *Financial literacy: an essential tool for informed consumer choice*. NBER Research Paper 14084.

ii) People are social animals

Chamley, C. P. (2004) *Rational Herds: Economic Models of Social Learning*. Cambridge, UK: Cambridge University Press.

Dijksterhuis, A. (2005) 'Why we are social animals: the high road to imitation as social glue'. In: Hurley, S.L. and Chater, N. (eds.) (2005) *Perspectives on Imitation: From Neuroscience to Social Science*. Cambridge, MA: MIT Press.

Kahneman, D. (2003) 'A psychological perspective on economics'. *American Economic Review*, 93: 162-68.

Marmot, M. (2004) *The Status Syndrome: How Social Standing Affects Our Health and Longevity*. New York: Henry Holt & Company.

iii) Tastes are malleable

Frank, R. H. (1987) 'If homo oeconomicus could choose his own utility function'. *American Economic Review*. 77: 593-604.

Harsanyi, J. C. (1953) 'Welfare economics of variable tastes'. *Review of Economic Studies*, 21: 204-13.

Karni, E. and Schmeidler, D. (1990) 'Fixed preferences and changing tastes'. *American Economic Review*, 80: 262-67.

Von Weizsacker, V. (1971) 'Notes on endogenous change of tastes'. *Journal of Economic Theory*, 3: 345-72.

iv) Children in society

Goldberg, M. E., Gorn, G.J. and Gibson, W. (1978) 'The effects of TV messages for high and low nutritional foods on children's snack and breakfast food choices', *Advances in Consumer Research*, 5: 540-45.

Gunter, B, and Furnham, A. (1998) *Children as Consumers: a Psychological Analysis of the Young People's Market.* New York: Routledge.

Schor, J. B. (2004) *Born to Buy: the Commercialized Child and the New Consumer Culture.* New York: Scribner.

v) Consumer knowledge

Nelson, P. (1970) 'Information and consumer behavior', *Journal of Political Economy,* 78: 311-29.

Ratchford, B. T. (2001) 'The economics of consumer knowledge'. *Journal of Consumer Research,* 27: 397-411.

vi) Social and political power

Holden, C. and Kelley L. (2009) 'Corporate power and social responsibility: the political economy of transnational tobacco companies'. *Global Social Policy,* 9: 328-54.

Lindblom, C. E. (1977*) Politics and Markets: the World's Political Economic Systems.* New York: Basic Books.

Nestle, M. (2007) *Food Politics: How the Food Industry Influences Nutrition and Health.* Berkeley, CA: University of California Press.

Zingales L. (2012) *A Capitalism for the People: Recapturing the Lost Genius of American Prosperity.* New York: Basic Books.

CHAPTER 9

Market, human mind and social change: a pluralistic and interdisciplinary perspective

Arturo Hermann

1 Introduction

In this period of economic and social distress, a thorough re-appraisal of the foundations of our economic and social systems has emerged in virtually all the most developed countries. This chapter addresses some elements of such issues by analysing how, within a pluralistic and interdisciplinary perspective, a number of heterodox theories can help us to identify significant aspects of market, human mind and social change. These concepts convey complex meanings which are interpreted differently according to the different theories, interests, values of the subjects involved. Furthermore, these interpretations often acquire an implicit character, since, to each person, they are ingrained in deep seated habits of thought in which the unconscious component is likely to play a relevant role.

Also for this reason, the social and political conflicts related to these issues often assume an emotional and intransigent character, which does not help to clarify the real issues at stake. For instance, a strong conflict exists between the advocates and the detractors of the market. But what is the meaning of the market? Is it, as held by classical and neoclassical economists, a kind of "exogenous" mechanism strictly associated with capitalism? Or is it an institution created and maintained by public intervention and which, for this reason, can be present also in a socialist economy?

In this chapter we employ this pluralistic and interdisciplinary perspective for analyzing some controversial elements of the (i) the institutional and legal foundation of the market; (ii) the manifold character of the market, with the presence of various and often contradictory features; (iii) the growing complexity of the system and the emergence of "concerted" capitalism;

(iv) the international dimension of market relations; and (v) the importance of a better collaboration between economic and psychological sciences for reaching out to the manifold aspects of these concepts and, on this basis, to identify suitable policies for our most urgent economic and social problems.

2 The institutional analysis of the market

As is known, the analysis of the market constitutes perhaps one of the most controversial aspects in the study of the various forms of economic organization. For instance, the long-standing debate on "market socialism" has triggered diametrically opposed positions concerning the role played by the market in economic and social development: on the one hand, advocates of this system[1] posit that the market existed before capitalism and, consequently can also be present in a socialist society. On the other hand, opponents maintain that the market constitutes an economic device for the exploitation of workers and, as such, can exist in its most developed form only in a capitalistic economy. Even non-socialist economists differ widely regarding the role of the market in many structural, and related, issues–for instance, scientific and technological progress, economic development, unemployment, environmental protection.

As a matter of fact, the analysis of the market lies at the juncture of many important aspects of economic and social structure and the corresponding

---

[1] For an analysis of the various opinions on market socialism refer, for instance, to Ollman (1998). A comprehensive analysis of socialist thought is contained in Cole (2003). We note that these issues can receive a better insight also by employing the concepts of institutional economics. A good example is Commons' account of the evolution of the concept of ownership, from simple possession of goods to one of relationships, rights, and opportunities referred to as incorporeal and intangible property. Commons showed how the evolution of the concepts of ownership and freedom has accompanied the birth and evolution of capitalism that saw (and sees) the rise and development of new social classes in respect to which has arisen the need of building a body of norms, transactions and institutions in order to increase their participation in economic and social life. Regarding the worker, this implies a significant shift from a physical concept of ownership, tending to consider labour force as mere goods, to a notion of rights and relationships extending the opportunities to participate in productive life. It is from this basis that, through a wide scrutiny of legislation and court rulings, Commons investigated the evolution of labour rights, union rights, and social legislation.

policy action: in particular, public action and private initiative, forms of competition, and the related concepts of capitalism, socialism, sustainable development, participation and democracy.

The main problem in this debate is that the concepts involved are extremely complex and intertwined and can be interpreted differently according to the experiences and values of the different subjects. In fact, as we are trying to show, the market does not constitute an "exogenous mechanism" in relation to the goals and values of the subjects involved. But, rather, it is an institution that, in J.R. Commons' terminology, with its relationships of "conflict", "dependence", and "order" – which are expressed, as noted above, in a complex system of juridical relations of rights, duties, liberties and exposures – evolves along with other institutions, thus contributing to identify the distinctive features of economic, social and cultural evolution[2] in any given context.

In this respect, if we consider the alleged more free market-oriented productive sectors, we realize that, even here, consumer demand rarely constitutes the sole criterion for the existence and development of these sectors. Indeed, in the related policy action there often comes into play other goals which tend to be latched onto numerous policies and institutions: for example, scientific and technological development, increasing employment, industrial restructuring, social and environmental impact. Moreover, these policies tend to carry multifarious influences on consumers' demand. This complexity tends also to be reflected in the increasing articulation of the ownership structures of companies, which tend to mirror the presence of the various – "public" and "private" – interest groups involved.[3]

It is also worth noting that changes occurring in the market system directly impinge upon the forms of competition. In this sense, we can observe that

---

[2] We can define culture in a broad meaning as the systems of knowledge, values, beliefs, rituals and code of conducts typical of a given context. As we will see later on, cultural factors interact in a complex way both with the economic mode of production (the so-called "material" basis of society) and with the psychological orientations and conflicts of the persons involved.

[3] It is important to note that the notions of "public" and "private" are not absolute concepts but are created by, and evolve with, the set of norms, institutions and policies of any given context.

competition[4] does not constitute a static concept but evolves along with the transformations of economic and social organization.

3 The market as a manifold entity

Now, we can employ these concepts for the analysis of some controversial aspects of the market. Here it is useful to look more closely into its definition. The market, in its simplest and broadest meaning, can be defined as the possibility for persons to exchange their goods and services, either directly or through the medium of any socially accepted definition of "money". As can be seen, this definition includes a countless range of economic situations: for instance, isolated, bartered-based, exchanges in primitive economies, or more articulated exchanges in well developed markets – which can be more or less "capitalistic" or "socialistic". In the related debate, and also in psychological perception, the market appears as a manifold entity, which embodies various and often contradictory features. In this sense, the market can appear, on the positive side, as:

- an instrument for attaining more liberty and better economic co-ordination, in that it allows the unfolding of personal initiative and creativity through a system of decentralized actions.
- a means for comparing and revealing information about the characteristics of goods and services.

On the negative side, the market can appear as:

- a device, under the appearance of equal opportunities in the labour market, for exploitation of workers.

---

[4] It is important to note that competition arises not only in economic action. As widely investigated in psychology, psychoanalysis and sociology, forms of rivalry and competition, often associated with emotional problems, are likely to play a pivotal role in childhood during family and school experiences. Relatedly, social environment can also embody forms of competition among persons, groups, classes, institutions and nations based on values not directly economic-driven, such as influence, power and prestige. In this regard, competition assumes a distinct "institutional" character. As effectively expressed by Commons, "Competition is not Nature's "struggle for existence" but is an artificial arrangement supported by the moral, economic, and physical sanctions of collective action" (Commons, 1934 [1990]: 713).

- a way for devising, within the reality of pronounced market imperfections, unfair deals in the marketplace, through reduction in the quality of products and shrewd manipulation of information realized also by means of well-organized advertisement strategies.
- a consequence of these negative characteristics, the market is likely to constitute an ineffective system for resource allocation. Also for this reason, the market is likely to entail alienation, frustration and distorted social value process for all the participants, also through its effects on increased economic inequalities, the uncertainty and disorder of the economic system, and environmental decay.

What is the relevance of these aspects? In our view, they are all potentially significant for social life and mutually interact in a dialectic and conflicting way. The prevalence of one or the other depends on the social, economic and psychological relations underpinning market structures and the related typologies of transactions occurring therein. If these relations engender an increasingly unequal distribution of power and income – in short, if they rest on a kind of more or less sublimated "predatory attitude" rooted in the structure of the social, cultural and institutional framework – then it follows that the market can reinforce the negative effects outlined before. But, supposing that the predatory aspects are not so predominant, the positive effects of market can, at varying degrees, outweigh the negative.

In our view, the real problems do not lie in the market – e.g., in the exchange activity *per se* – but in the complexity and often conflicting character of our motivations which are reflected in, and at the same time blurred by, the complexity and ambiguity of the market in any given context. A complex reciprocal interaction occurs between the "individual" and "holistic" aspects of the market, where, in the former, individual action influences market structure and, in the latter, market structure influences individual behaviour. For instance, a professional can sell her services in the market chiefly out of creative and altruistic motivations – for instance, out of Veblen's workmanship and parental bent propensities – but even chiefly out of predatory and aggressive propensities aimed at increasing without limits the quest for money and power. And, in turn, market structure impinges more or less heavily on the shaping of these propensities and the related "freedom" of individual action within the market.

The economics curriculum: towards a radical reformulation

Thus, different propensities, both among different individuals and within the orientations and motivations of each individual, are likely to be always present in the market and therefore constitute one of the most intricate aspects of the socio-economic dynamics. By adopting this approach, the market cannot realistically be appraised as an abstract mechanism amenable automatically – provided only that it be perfect enough – to individual and social utility maximization.

In fact, the market constitutes an institution which has been created and maintained by public policies and therefore is heavily embedded in the economic, social and cultural domain. This happens not only when market transactions clearly acquire the nature of a social and cultural phenomenon, as in the cases, widely investigated in social sciences, of the numerous economic relations framed within a well-established family and social network of customs, trust, kinship, friendship and citizenship. As a matter of fact, even the (seemingly) most atomistic and impersonal transaction occurring between individuals unknown to each other is rooted within a dense framework of collective action, with all its rights, duties, values and cultural orientations.

In this sense, the "market" implies, on the part of the actors involved, a process of social valuing[5] which, however, can be seriously impaired in

---

[5] As is known, the theory of social value has a long tradition in economic theory. It was introduced by Commons mainly through the elaboration of the concept of reasonable value. The complexity and evolutionary meaning of reasonable value emerges from the following passage, "The preceding sections of this book brought us to the problems of Public Policy and Social Utility. These are the same as the problems of Reasonable Value and Due Process of Law. The problem arises out of the three principles underlying all transactions: conflict, dependence and order. Each economic transaction is a process of joint valuation by participants, wherein each is moved by diversity of interests, by dependence upon the others, and by the working rules which, for the time being, require conformity of transactions to collective action. Hence, reasonable values are reasonable transactions, reasonable practices, and social utility, equivalent to public purpose... Reasonable Value is the evolutionary collective determination of what is reasonable in view of all changing political, moral, and economic circumstances and the personalities that arise there from to the Supreme bench", written by Commons (1934 [1990]: 681, 683-684). Following these insights, the theory of social value has become one of the core concepts of institutional economics, as evidenced in the following passage, "To conceive of a problem requires the perception of a difference between 'what is going on' and 'what ought to go on'. Social value theory is logically and inescapably required to

situations where the negative aspects of market prevail. Furthermore, it is important to remember that market relations certainly constitute one important way for expressing predatory attitude but by no means the only one. Predatory behaviour can be present also in non-market relations and, in this regard, human history is full of such instances. Thus, the fundamental problem becomes to understand the psychological reasons and problems underlying predatory relations in their connections with the economic, social and cultural structure.

Likewise, the market does not constitute the sole instance for expressing personal initiative. In fact, the market can be compatible with a socialist society, while personal initiative can unfold very well in public administration providing that the related organization is flexible enough for allowing a real involvement of the workers in its activities. As emerges from Commons' analysis and, within a different context, from the literature on quasi-markets, forms of transactions and competition can exist in any kind of public institution.

4 The growing complexity of the system and the emergence of concerted capitalism

As noted by many authors, the complexity of markets has increased with the development of economic systems. We can mention, as crucial elements of the modern economic evolution, (i) the growing importance of public intervention in the economy – underscored by various authors in the tradition of democratic socialism, institutionalism and Keynesian economics – in order to provide a host of important public goods and also an adequate level of effective demand, and hence of profit, for the private sector. (ii) The

---

distinguish what ought to be from what is....In the real world, the provisioning process in all societies is organized through prescriptive and proscriptive institutional arrangements that correlate behaviour in the many facets and dimensions of the economic process. Fashioning, choosing among and assessing such institutional structure is the 'stuff and substance' of continuing discussions in deliberative bodies and in the community generally. The role of social value theory is to provide analyses of criteria in terms of which such choices are made." written by Hodgson, Samuels and Tool (1994: 406-407).

relevance of "market imperfections"[6] which are also interlinked with the emergence of big and articulated corporations. (iii) In this regard, it is possible to identify two important, and related, groups of imperfections: (a) microeconomic-based imperfections; for instance, market power associated with monopoly and oligopoly situations, informational asymmetries, externalities of various kind, public goods; (b) macroeconomic-based imperfections, for instance imbalances between aggregate demand and aggregate supply, environmental decay, growing disparities in income and opportunities between persons, economic classes and groups and, at geographical level, between districts, regions, nations and wider economic and geographical areas. (iv) Also in order to cope with these "imperfections", there is an increasing importance of collective action involving every level of economic and social life. This process has seen the emergence of a number of "mixed institutions" such as unions, associations, "authorities", which have been accompanied to a growing complexity of the pure public and private institutions. (v) And, last but not least, this situation has been accompanied by a growing articulation of economic activities and of social classes and groups, that tends to increase the diversity of objectives and values of the subject involved. (vi) All these aspects are framed within the economic and social crisis of today and the related profound transformations of economic and social system.

All this implies that the forms of inequalities, exploitation and marginalization are as dramatic as before but they are much more complex and diversified. There are still, of course, the classic proletarians, but there are also the unemployed, precarious workers, immigrants, elderly, women, etc. Furthermore, all these groups are characterized by many internal differences, identities and stratifications. The same applies to economic activities, which are marked by a growing differentiation regarding market power, rate of profits, scale economies, technological trajectories, social and cultural identities, evolutionary patterns.

---

[6] As emerges from the institutional analysis of the market (cf. above) this does not imply that such imperfections cannot be in some way reduced, but that all these relations are heavily embedded in the complexity of economic, social and institutional structure. For this reason, any change in the market system is likely to interact with all these dimensions.

As emerges from the institutional analysis of the market, these situations do not evolve out of an "impersonal and necessary" mechanism but interact in complex way with the institutional and legal framework and with the policy strategies which combine to shape societal evolution. Hence, capitalistic societies tend to become more and more dependent for their development on the "agency of collective action". To understand these processes, it is useful to employ the conceptual framework elaborated by Commons (one of the main founders of institutional economics) which identifies three stages in the development of capitalism: (i) the period of scarcity, in which there was "the minimum of individual liberty and the maximum of communistic, feudalistic or governmental control through physical coercion"; (ii) the period of abundance, characterised by "a maximum of individual liberty, the minimum of coercive control through government, and individual bargaining takes the place of rationing"; (iii) a third period of "stabilization" whose main features are "a diminution of individual liberty, enforced in part by governmental sanctions, but mainly by economic sanctions through concerted action, whether secret, semi-open, open, or arbitrational, of associations, corporations, unions, and other collective movements of manufacturers, merchants, labourers, farmers, and bankers" (Commons, 1934 [1990]): 334-335).

5 The international dimension of market relations

It is worth noting that the more harmful effects of market relations tend to be more pronounced in the international domain. In fact, as investigated in particular by the literature on economic development and on "unequal exchange", it is through the internationalization of production involving the developing and emerging countries that the worst forms of exploitation are likely. There are several reasons for this. Firstly, as highlighted in particular by Veblenian contributions, the formation of modern nation-states has its economic and cultural ancestors in ceremonial institutions chiefly rooted on emulative and predatory habits of thought and life.

In this respect, contemporary capitalistic institutions, including the juridical form of nation-state, continue to express these predatory attitudes, even though, as we have seen, in Veblen's analysis such situations could be overcome by the rationalizing role of technology. But, this being the case, it follows that competition associated with market process occurs not only between individuals and firms but also, and perhaps even more, between nations and larger supranational agglomerations, and in the latter cases economic competition is likely to be more intense. Not only because cultural and political rivalry is most often injected in such competition, but also because such competition – unlike national situations where in most cases economic competition is regulated and "concerted" in many respects through legislative and contractual provisions – tends to be almost completely unregulated in the "globalized" world.

True, there are important initiatives for promoting fair trade but they have not yet taken a strong foothold in developing and emerging economies. In these situations, social and psychological factors are likely to reinforce each other in a kind of vicious circle. In fact, where the only faith in economic progress rests on a kind of a wild and unregulated competition, the market tends to be psychologically perceived as an inflexible and punitive *superego*. In that vision, the only possible thing we should do is to comply with the "needs of the market", without any further enquiry on the adequacy of the system to respond to the profound needs of economy and society.

6 Psychoanalysis and social change

In order to better understand these complex phenomena, an enquiry into how people tend to perceive market phenomena becomes paramount: for instance, if, as just noted, the market is perceived as an inflexible and punitive *superego* this implies that persons try to repress their neurotic aggressiveness, which, however, can find expression in the marketplace in a more or less disguised way.

Let us now focus attention, within our interdisciplinary[7] approach, on a number of psychoanalytic contributions on the issue of social change. In this

---

[7] Needless to say, other interesting theories in social and psychological sciences can offer valuable contributions. We believe that, owing to the complexity of these issues, no discipline (or field or school within a discipline) is self-sufficient and perfect. The insulation process typical of many scientific approaches can really impair a far

regard, Freud and subsequent psychoanalysts have provided relevant insights into the conflicts of individual and collective life and the possibility of social change. However, notwithstanding these contributions, among social scientists Freud is rarely regarded as a social reformer. Rather, social scientists – owing, perhaps, to a rather pessimistic vein arising from his theory[8] of death instinct – tend to regard his theory as essentially "conservative", since it implies that little can be done to abate human aggressiveness and the social relations resting upon it. Certainly, such a vein exists in Freud's theory; but, at the same time, his theory is more far-reaching than this interpretation suggests, as it contains aspects which clearly point to the possibility of social change. For instance, in discussing the October Revolution, he is not against such transformation but underlines the importance for social reformers – in order to build a truly better society – to acquire a deeper understanding of human nature.

In this regard, individual self-understanding is not without consequences for social self-understanding, since psychoanalysis is (cf. Freud, in particular 1921) at the same time an individual and a collective psychology. Therefore, the application of psychoanalysis to the comprehension of social phenomena, although not entailing a direct ethical impact as such (cf. Freud, in particular 1926), can have important consequences in this respect. Freud thinks that psychoanalysis, in collaboration with other social sciences, can find interesting applications in a host of social issues. As he points out, in a coloured discussion with an imaginary interlocutor:

---

reaching understanding of economic and social phenomena. As observed by the famous sociologist Karl Mannheim, a landscape can be seen only from a determined perspective and without perspective there is no landscape. In this sense, observing a landscape (or phenomenon) from different angles (or disciplines) can help acquire a much clearer insight into the features of the various perspectives. Therefore, an interdisciplinary perspective does not imply that each discipline would lose its distinctive features. Quite the contrary, such a more comprehensive approach, by broadening the horizon of the observer, can contribute to a better appraisal also of the specific characteristics of his/her main fields of specialization.

[8] As we have shown in another work (Hermann, 2009a), this theory is now dismissed by the vast majority of psychoanalysts. However, even within such a framework, Freud clearly pinpoints the role of psychoanalysis in furthering the processes of social change (cf.below).

"[Psychoanalysis]....as a 'depth-psychology', a theory of the mental unconscious, it can become indispensable to all the sciences which are concerned with the evolution of human civilization and its major institutions such as art, religion and the social order. It has already, in my opinion, afforded these sciences considerable help in solving their problems. But these are only small contributions compared with what might be achieved if historians of civilization, psychologists of religion, philologists, and so on would agree themselves to handle the new instrument of research which is at their service. The use of analysis for the treatment of neuroses is only one of its applications; the future will perhaps show that it is not the most important one.....Then let me advise you that psycho-analysis has yet another sphere of application....Its application, I mean, to the bringing-up of children. If a child begins to show signs of an undesirable development, if it grows moody, refractory, and inattentive, the paediatrician and even the school doctor can do nothing for it, even if the child produces clear neurotic symptoms, such as nervousness, loss of appetite, vomiting, or insomnia....Our recognition of the importance of these unconspicuous neuroses of children as laying down the disposition for serious illnesses in later life points to these child analyses as an excellent method of prophylaxis.... Moreover, to return to our question of the analytic treatment of adult neurotics, even there we have not yet exhausted every line of approach. Our civilization imposes an almost intolerable pressure on us and it calls for a corrective. It is too fantastic to expect that psycho-analysis in spite of its difficulties may be destined to the task of preparing mankind for such a corrective? Perhaps once more an American may hit on the idea of spending a little money to get the 'social workers' of his country trained analytically and to turn them into a band of helpers for combating the neuroses of civilization." (Freud, (1926 [1989]): 83-86).

Subsequent contributions[9] have further developed these concepts, by highlighting the role of groups and institutions for expressing the needs and conflicts of the person. For instance, for the person, the group may represent an idealized *ego*; and, in this connection, its "morals" and "code of conduct" symbolize parental figures that, through a process of "internalization", play the role of *superego*. Thus, it is worth noting that the *superego* stems also from a normal human tendency to establish sound interpersonal relations; and, accordingly, to behave with affection and solicitude towards each other and continually improve the positive aspects of personality. However, whereas in non-neurotic situations the "code of conduct" emerging from such tendencies asserts itself as a genuine behaviour, in neurotic situations leading to the formation of *superego* things can be quite different: here, the tendency of improving personality tends to be, under an appearance of goodness and morality, subordinated to the expression of neurotic contents at cross-purposes with such tendencies.

In particular, quite often the severity of *superego* leads – through the so-called paranoid and narcissistic transformation of personality, extensively studied in psychoanalysis – single individuals, groups or societies to do nasty and persecutory actions towards other individuals, groups or societies into which their aggressiveness has been projected, and so to sabotage, in the meaning reviewed before, the possibility of establishing sound interpersonal relations. These psychological processes can help explain – and history is full of such instances – the neurotic roots of racism, xenophobia and other phenomena of exclusion and marginalization. As already noted, these phenomena tend to be reinforced by economic and social crises.

7 Conclusions: how can heterodox economics and psychoanalysis contribute to social change?

Let us now address how heterodox economics and psychoanalysis can interact in promoting, at the national and supranational levels, a roadmap of

---

[9] Cf. among others, Ammon (1970), Bion (1971), Horney (1950), Kernberg (1998), Klein (1964; 1975), Sullivan (1964).

policy action specifically targeted at the solution of the most urgent economic and social problems.

The reason why we attribute much importance to psychoanalysis rests on the circumstance that such a discipline, by providing a thorough understanding of the complex motivations and orientations of persons in their individual and collective unfolding, can contribute to answer, among others, the following questions: (i) What are the profound meanings of the various aspects of economic action – in particular, work, consumption, saving, investment – considered in their psychological, social and cultural dimensions? (ii) Is, for instance, the quest for money the sole target, or else it covers other motivations of the person? (iii) For example, the (partly unconscious) need for affection and consideration, which the person tries to pursue through a perceived socially accepted behaviour? (iv) Is the quest for money a primary or secondary goal to the person? (v) And what are the psychological, social and cultural factors (including the role of mass media) leading the person to a given consumption (or work, investment and saving) pattern? (vi) In particular, what is the role of any given context in orienting, fostering or frustrating the various propensities, values and conflicts of the person?

In this regard, a more systematic interaction between heterodox economics and psychoanalysis can help attain a deeper insight into the main factors underlying the emergence of the recent economic and financial crisis, and into the multiple links between the various spheres of policy action. We can mention, in particular:

- The economic and psychological significance of economic and social crisis;
- The main features and transformations of the economic, social and institutional system that – together with the role played by predatory behaviour, inadequate response of many policies, individual and social conflicts – can have facilitated the emergence of these imbalances;
- The systemic character of the crisis, with particular attention to the factors, highlighted in particular by Keynes and Galbraith, that drive

163

the system towards a society less based on the classic "economic motive" and more on social and cooperative relations.

- How a pluralistic interpretation of key concepts like market, socialism, social justice can improve our understanding of these phenomena;
- The most suitable macroeconomic policies and their interaction with structural policies;
- How these policies are perceived, appraised and influenced by citizens.

The significance of this approach for policy action is shown by a simple example: if we wish to further personal initiative at the economic and social level, a narrow conception of the *homo oeconomicus* suggest policies centred only on pecuniary incentives. Conversely, a proper acknowledgement of the significance for the person of establishing sound interpersonal relations will help devise more effective and far reaching policies, as they would be more tailored to the real needs and orientations of the person. The usefulness of this approach springs from the fact that, if it is true that the processes of social valuing perform a key role in the dynamics of policy action, this role very often acquires an implicit and partly unconscious nature. This happens especially when such processes take place, at least in part, on the basis of "consolidated habits of thought and action" that mirror the economic, social, and cultural features and conflicts of the given reality.

Thus, it can be created the basis – in particular, in the more disadvantaged countries which tend to be stuck in a vicious circle of (i) insufficient level of economic, social, scientific and technological development and (ii) inadequate institutional structure and policy action – for the definition of a policy strategy more able to comprehend and promote the experiences and capabilities of the subjects involved.

References

Ammon, G. (1971) *Gruppendynamik Der Aggression*, Berlin: Pynel-Publicationen.

Bion, W. R. (1970) *Attention and Interpretation: a Scientific Approach to Insights in Psycho-analysis and Groups*, London: Tavistock Publications.

Cole, G. D. H. (ed.) (2003) *A History of Socialist Thought* (7 volumes), London: Palgrave Macmillan, latest edition.

Commons, J. R. (1924 [1995]) *Legal Foundations of Capitalism*, New Jersey, U.S.A.: Transaction Publishers.

Commons, J. R. (1934 [1990]) *Institutional Economics: Its Place in Political Economy*, New Brunswick, New Jersey, U.S.A.: Transaction Publishers.

Dewey, J. (1939 [1989]) *Freedom and Culture*, New York: Prometheus Books.

Freud, S. (1912-13) *Totem und Tabu*, Lipsia, Vienna and Zurich, Internationaler Psychoanalytischer Verlag. [Trans.: *Totem and Taboo*, London, 1950; New York, 1932; Standard Ed., 13, 1.]

Freud, S. (1921) *Massenpsychologie undlich-Analyse*, Lipsia, Vienna and Zurich, Internationaler Psychoanalytischer Verlag; [Trans.: *Group Psychology and the Analysis of the Ego*, London and New York, 1959; Standard Ed., 18, 69)

Freud, S. (1924) "Vorlesungen zur Einführung in die Psychoanalise", *Gesammelte Schriften*, vol.7; (Trans.: *Introductory Lectures on Psycho-Analysis*, London, 1929 (*A General Introduction to Psychoanalysis*, New York, 1935); Standard Ed., 15-16)

Freud, S. (1926) *Die Frage der Laienanalyse. Unterredungen mit einen Unparteiischen*, Lipsia, Vienna and Zurich, Internationaler Psychoanalytischer Verlag; (Trans.: *The Question of Lay Analysis*, London, 1947; New York, 1989; Standard Ed., 20, 179)

Freud, S. (1930) *Das Unbehagen in der Kultur*, Lipsia, Vienna and Zurich, Internationaler Psychoanalytischer Verlag; (Trans.: *Civilization and Its Discontents*, London, 1930; New York, 1962; Standard Ed., 21, 59)

Freud, S. (1933) *Neue Folge der Vorlesungen zur Einführung in die Psychoanalise*, Lipsia, Vienna and Zurich, Internationaler Psychoanalytischer Verlag; [Trans.: *New Introductory Lectures on Psycho-Analysis*, London and New York, 1933; Standard Ed., 22)

Galbraith, J. K. (1958 [1998]) *The Affluent Society*, New York: Mariner Books.

Hermann, A. (2008) 'The Institutional Analysis of the Market', *International Journal of Green Economics*, 2, 4: 379-391, http://www.inderscience.com/search/index.php?action=record&rec_id=22448

Hermann, A. (2012) 'Policy Responses to Economic and Financial Crises: Insights from Heterodox Economics and Psychoanalysis', *International Journal of Pluralism and Economics Education*, 3, 1: 8-22, http://www.inderscience.com/info/inarticle.php?artid=47477

Hermann, A. (2012) *Towards a Sustainable and Equitable Society: Insights from Heterodox economics and Psychoanalysis*, Rome, Italy: Aracne Editrice.

Hermann, A. (2014) 'The Essays in Persuasion of John Maynard Keynes and Their Relevance for the Economic Problems of Today', In: Hölscher, J. and Klaes, M. (eds), *Keynes's Economic Consequences of Peace: A Reappraisal*, London, Pickering and Chatto.

Hodgson, G. M., Samuels, W. J. and Tool, M. R. (eds) (1994) *The Elgar Companion to Institutional and Evolutionary Economics*, Aldershot (UK): Elgar.

Horney, K. (1950) *Neurosis and Human Growth: The Struggle Toward Self-Realization*, New York: Norton.

Kernberg, O. F. (1998) *Ideology, Conflict and Leadership in Groups and Organizations*, New Haven: Yale University Press.

Keynes, J. M. (1931 [1963]) *Essays in Persuasion*, London and New York: Norton.

Keynes, J. M. (1936) *The General Theory of Employment, Interest and Money*, Cambridge, Macmillan: Cambridge University Press.

Klein, M. (1964) *Contributions to Psychoanalysis 1921-1945*, New York: Mac Graw-Hill.

Klein, M. (1975) *Envy and Gratitude and Other Works 1946-1963*, New York: Delacorte Press.

Mannheim, K. and Wolff, K. H. (1993) *From Karl Mannheim: Second Expanded Edition*, NJ, USA: Transaction Publishers.

Ollman, B. (ed.) (1998) *Market Socialism*, London and New York: Routledge.

Sullivan, H. S. (1964) *The Fusion of Psychiatry and Social Science*, New York: Norton.

Veblen, T. (1914 [1990]) *The Instinct of Workmanship and the State of the Industrial Arts*, New Brunswick, New Jersey, U.S.A.: Transaction Publishers.

Veblen, T. (1919 [1990]) *The Place of Science in Modern Civilization*, New Brunswick, New Jersey, U.S.A.: Transaction Publishers.

Veblen, T. (1934 [1998]) *Essays In Our Changing Order*, edited by Ardzrooni, Leon, New Brunswick, New Jersey, U.S.A.: Transaction Publishers.

CHAPTER 10
Notes on a real world economics curriculum
Paul Ormerod

1 Introduction

John Sutton is a mainstream economist, but one who is very thoughtful and reflective about the subject. In his excellent little book *Marshall's Tendencies: What Can Economists Know?* he describes the process of socialisation which occurs with students of economics. The core model of the discipline remains the so-called rational agent, operating autonomously, with fixed tastes and preferences, gathering information about alternatives, and making the optimal choice. Gradually, students who doubt the validity of these assumptions fall by the wayside and abandon economics. By the post-graduate stage, only the true believers remain.

This by itself would not necessarily be a problem. Like any scientific theory, the model of economic rationality makes assumptions which are approximations to reality. It is ultimately an empirical question as to whether, in any given situation, the assumptions offer a reasonable approximation. But, somewhere along the line, a transmutation occurs, and the believers come to imagine that the model *is* reality. If the real world appears different, it is the world which must be changed and not the theory. Preposterous though this may sound, it is reflected in practice in, for example, the advice given by teams of economists who proliferate in regulatory bodies.

Mainstream economics is not a completely empty box, and it does contain some powerful insights. However, it cannot be stressed too strongly that it is a way of thinking about the world rather than a series of scientifically validated propositions. Much of the material in, say, engineering textbooks has been shown to be a very close approximation to reality. In general, for example, bridges tend to stay up. But the same cannot be said for many of the 'theorems' in economics textbooks, especially in the case of macroeconomics.

167

Mastering the intricacies of economic theory and the demanding statistical techniques of econometrics is hard, and so it is perhaps not surprising that students who succeed in these tasks begin to confuse the models with reality. But we need to teach them that we are providing them with a set of tools to apply to real world problems, and the tools need to be selected according to the particular set of circumstances. This means that the curriculum needs to become much broader. For example, it should draw on behavioural models developed in other social sciences. The economic definition of rational behaviour is by no means the only one. In many contexts, the assumptions lying behind other theories of agent behaviour may be more realistic.

Above all, we should be inspired by the phrase from Hayek which was cited in the presentation speech at his Nobel ceremony, "Nobody can be a great economist who is only an economist – and I am even tempted to add that the economist who is only an economist is likely to become a nuisance if not a positive danger."

There are many potential changes and developments to the curriculum as it presently stands. But the four main changes which I propose are:

- Teaching the use of modern simulation software which enables behaviour out of equilibrium to be explored.
- Teaching alternative models of agent decision making, which again can be examined using simulation.
- Teaching network theory, and using this to relax the assumptions that agents operate independently with fixed tastes and preferences.
- Teaching macro through the perspective of important episodes in economic history.

I address these issues in turn.

2 Agent behaviour and simulation techniques

Economics at the moment is in a schizophrenia: On the one hand, behavioural economics is very fashionable; on the other, the 'rational' agent continues to be the bedrock of the curriculum. The contrast is perhaps not as great as it first seems. Much of behavioural economics consists of identifying empirical situations in which the behaviour of agents deviates systematically from that of the rational choice model. Increasingly, regulatory policy is directed towards measures which either try to restrain what are assumed to be rational, profit-maximising firms from exploiting irrational consumers, or try to 'educate' consumers into behaving closer to the rational model of economics. The paper by Azar (2006) is a seminal one in this respect. An alternative view, that there are frequent deviations from rationality by firms as well, is given by Ellison (2006).

By far the single most important paper in behavioural economics is Simon's 1955 paper, 'Behavioral Model of Rational Choice'. In this paper, Simon introduced the concept of 'satisficing'. Modern economics has adopted this phrase, but in doing so has effectively neutered it. In mainstream economics, it means the following: Faced with a large number of alternatives, an agent begins to search through them until he or she discovers one which, although it may not be optimal, matches the agent's preferences reasonably closely. It is a 'satisfactory' choice. The agent takes the view that the additional costs involved in further search will not be offset by potential gain from discovering a slightly better alternative.

However, this is not how Simon described satisficing. He argued that in general, it was simply not possible to discover the optimal decision, even *ex post*. Simon wrote "the task is to replace the global rationality of economic man with a kind of rational behaviour which is compatible with the access to information and computational capacities that are actually possessed by organisms, including man, in the kinds of environments in which such organisms exist". He meant by 'satisficing' that agents use rules of thumb to guide their behaviour, and rejected in general the optimising model of behavioural choice in mainstream economics.

A similar view was taken by Alchian (1950), who attempted to modify economic analysis in order to incorporate incomplete information and uncertain foresight as axioms. He argued, which is now familiar, that "uncertainty arises from at least two sources: imperfect foresight and human inability to solve complex problems containing a host of variables even when an optimum is definable". Alchian argued that agents – not just consumers but firms – in general use rules of thumb. Specifically, he believed that imitation, or copying, offered the most sensible decision making situation.

I suggest that all students of economics read these two papers. Despite their power, clarity and insight, behavioural economics has struggled to enter the theoretical mainstream. Papers on applied economics, discovering empirical deviations from rationality are published, with little impact on theory. The *Journal of Economic Literature* in 2013 published a forum on bounded rationality, in which it was concluded, "Simon and his followers produced many interesting results. But what is still lacking is a body of systematic theory that is as orderly and teachable as the neoclassical theory of the firm" (Harstad and Selten, 2013).

One of the great intellectual attractions of the mainstream theory of agent behaviour is its ability to obtain analytical results. It is undoubtedly satisfying to be able to wade through thickets of calculus and establish a 'theorem'. This can then be used to compare the outcomes in two equilibria when, for example, a tax rate if changed. For all the power of the arguments, Alchian and Simon essentially lacked the technical tools to meet the challenge posed by Harstad and Selten decades later.

Simulation modelling offers a way forward. Think of this as numerical rather than analytical approaches to obtaining solutions. In the harder sciences, numerical techniques are frequently used to obtain solutions of systems of partial differential equations. Analytical results may be desirable, but they may not always be possible to obtain; and even when they are, they may require large amounts of intellectual effort. It makes sense to use instead the well-established numerical solution techniques. The obsession of economists with analytical solutions to models is a 20th, or even a 19th century one. Despite its attractions, this places serious constraints on the type of models which can be examined.

Simulation has two advantages:
- it enables exploration of a wider range of agent rules of behavior; we are no longer constrained to choose rules which facilitate the use of calculus in order to obtain analytical results;

- it enables us to examine the paths along which a system moves between two equilibria (assuming for the moment that equilibria exist); in other words, we can examine the behaviour of the system when it is out of equilibrium.

So we can readily model agent behaviour using empirical insights from behavioural economics, or draw on models from other social sciences.

Such models are straightforward to program in packages such as Matlab or Mathematica. Even better from a teaching perspective, programs such as Netlogo are easier to use and contain excellent graphics. A wide range of models developed by the Netlogo community can be downloaded. These are, admittedly, of varying scientific quality, but an important model such as the Schelling segregation model can be downloaded and explored (http://ccl.northwestern.edu/netlogo/models/Segregation) as an introduction to the methodology. A very useful book which takes the student further in understanding agent-based models and the simulation approach is Squazzoni (2012). Most of the examples are from sociology rather than economics, but following the work of Gary Becker in expanding economics into traditional sociological areas, this is by no means a bad thing.

Analytical results are always desirable when they can be readily obtained; but it is a great mistake to remain fixated by them. We should embrace technological developments and introduce students to simulation models at the earliest possible opportunity.

3 Networks

Two key assumptions of the neoclassical paradigm of agent behaviour are that agents make decisions independently and that their tastes and preferences are fixed. All scientific theories must make assumptions; a great deal therefore depends upon how close to reality such assumptions are. Our world is rendering the assumptions of independence and time invariant tastes less reasonable descriptions of reality.

This does not mean that incentives no longer operate. This is a very powerful insight from economics. But, increasingly, agent behaviour is influenced directly by the behaviour of others. In the standard model, the decision of any given agent can influence the decisions of others, but this influence operates only indirectly via the price mechanism. In many real world situations, the tastes and preferences of an agent are affected directly by the behaviour of others. We see this most clearly in web-based activities such as YouTube or Flickr. Even the most casual knowledge of these sites is enough to reveal that, in general, the attributes of the most viewed/downloaded are indistinguishable from very large numbers of alternatives which receive very few viewings or downloadings. Copying is the decisive motivations in these 'markets'.

Neoclassical economics acknowledges such phenomena, but essentially regards them as a special case. The general model of agent behaviour remains the one with independent agents and fixed preferences. But reality has inverted this relationship. It is the standard model which has become the special case.

Influence spreads across networks. This has been acknowledged in the work on financial institutions by Andy Haldane and his team at the Bank of England. Recently, the European Central Bank has recognised the importance of the propagation of shocks and cascades across networks for banking stability (e.g., Castren and Rancan, 2013). Incredibly, prior to the financial crisis, regulators did not envisage the possibility of such systemic risks. The criteria for bank solvency related to banks as individual agents, not to the network connections between them and the possibility of a cascade of failures.

There is a massive literature outside economics on networks in general and how the inclusion of networks into the rules describing agent behaviour produces outcomes which significantly differ from those of the rational agent model of standard theory. A very good introduction, and one which as the book progresses can satisfy the taste for hard-line maths of the most addicted economist, is Newman (2010). The maths which underlies network models – graph theory to mathematicians – is just as hard as calculus, so economists who relish the abstract intellectual challenge of maths will find more than enough to keep them occupied.

But we should teach students the basics of network theory as well as calculus. This is essential. Many of the examples of alternative models of choice are based upon the principle of copying or imitation. In such models, tastes and preferences are no longer fixed but evolve, and agents are able to influence each other's behaviour directly, rather than simply indirectly via the price level, as is the case with mainstream economic theory. Examples include Schelling (1973), Watts (2002) and Bentley et al. (2011; 2014).

4 Teaching macro through economic history

Macroeconomics is in most need of thorough change. The mainstream models, despite their mathematical sophistication, have been shown by the crisis to be sadly lacking. We need to remember the claims made for them. For example Robert Lucas in his Presidential Address to the American Economic Association in 2003 said: "the central problem of depression prevention [has] been solved for all practical purposes". In August 2008, just three week before the collapse of Lehman Brothers, Olivier Blanchard, Chief Economist at the IMF, concluded in an MIT Discussion paper entitled 'The State of Macro' that "the state of macro is good".

One of the problems with macro, indeed with almost all mainstream theory, is that it is essentially timeless, that is, that the theory is taught without reference to historical events. It is this which must be changed.

All students of economics would benefit from studying certain key episodes in economic history. The idea is to make history a key part of the macro theory which students are taught. It is not economic history *per se*, but using events in economic history to illustrate theory. This has the added advantage of emphasizing that theory needs to be able to explain empirical reality; it is not an abstract intellectual exercise.

The Great Depression of the 1930s, for example, is one of only two truly global financial crises since the late 19th century (the other of course the most recent one). A wide range of topics can be discussed in the context not just of the Great Depression, but of the inter-war period as a whole. For example:

- Unemployment. Was this a supply-side phenomenon caused by the level of benefits relative to wages? To what extent was demand deficiency a reason? And heterodox macro ideas such as the role of the profit share (Goodwin's work, for example (1960) can also be introduced.
- The impact of fiscal policy. Under what conditions is this expansionary? What role did it actually play in the recovery of the 1930s? How might wealth affect behaviour?
- Monetary policy. Does this only affect the price level or does it also affect real output?

These are not meant to be an exhaustive list of topics which can be dealt with under each heading, nor is the list of headings necessarily complete. For example, under the topic 'unemployment', students can be introduced to mainstream models such as real business cycle and dynamic stochastic general equilibrium.

In terms of topics, a novel one for almost all economists is 'networks', though it is one which is beginning to get much more traction in the context of the transmission of shocks across the banking system. There is a massive literature on the mathematics of networks and their property of being 'robust yet fragile'. In other words, whilst most shocks to a system do not spread very far across a network, occasionally one of identical size generates a cascade across the entire network.

The empirical evaluation of evidence can also be introduced with respect to themes such as the above in the context of the inter-war period. Econometrics would form the core of this teaching, but the wider evaluation of evidence and understanding the reliability of data used in statistical analysis would be part of these modules. For example, different authors arrive at quite different estimates of the replacement ratio. How can this be? In addition to the inter-war period as a whole and the Great Depression specifically, the oil shock crisis of the 1970s and the contrasting transitions to peacetime after the two world wars are examples that spring readily to mind. The period after the First World War was characterized by deep recessions in some countries. Serious problems with both international trade and the world monetary system persisted throughout the interwar period. In contrast, output after the Second World War recovered very rapidly, even in the defeated countries, and a long period of unparalleled growth followed.

Again, whilst by no means being exhaustive, the themes raised by these periods of economic history include:

- The role of institutions. Is theory independent of institutions, or can these play a key role in outcomes?
- Trade theory. What are the benefits of trade? What exceptions might there be?
- Growth theory. Just why did the West have a prolonged period of sustained growth after World War Two?

During the 1950s and 1960s, inflation rates in the West were similar. However, in the middle 1970s there was a rapid and dramatic widening of the differences between them. In 1975, for example, the inflation rate in Germany was only 4%, but it was above 20% in both Italy and the United Kingdom. The analysis of such formative periods raises many important questions in economic theory; in this context, an obvious topic is the cause(s) of inflation.

Again, with both the transitions to peace-time after the two world wars, and the inflationary experience of the 1970s, empirical evidence and its evaluation would be a key part of the curriculum.

5 What is left?

The above is a fairly fundamental reform of the curriculum. But it is not meant to be a detailed manifesto. For example, the core model of agent behaviour in mainstream economics should still be taught. It is not completely irrelevant to the real world. But it should be just one of a number of ways in which agents behave rather than *the* way. Inevitably, quite a lot of elements from the standard curriculum would have to give. In their place, material should be introduced which highlights the interrelations between human behaviour, economics and history. New models and techniques can help in the process of teaching economics as real world economics.

Finally, and once again, the main reforms which I would make are in summary:

- Teaching macro through the perspective of important episodes in economic history.
- Teaching the use of modern simulation software which enables behaviour out of equilibrium to be explored.
- Teaching alternative models of agent decision making, which again can be examined using simulation.
- Teaching network theory, and using this to relax the assumptions that agents operate independently with fixed tastes and preferences.

References

Alchian, A. A. (1950) 'Uncertainty, Evolution and Economic Theory', *Journal of Political Economy*, 58: 211-221

Azar, O. H. (2006) 'Behavioral industrial organization, firm strategy, and consumer economics', http://mpra.ub.uni-muenchen.de/4484/

Bentley, R. A., O'Brien, M. J. and Ormerod, P. (2011) 'Quality versus Mere Popularity: A Conceptual Map for Understanding Human Behaviour', *Mind and Society*, 10: 181-191.

Bentley, R. A., Caiado, C.C.S and Ormerod, P. (2014) 'Effects of Memory on Spatial Heterogeneity in Neutrally Transmitted Cultures', *Evolution and Human Behavior*, 35, 4: 257-263, July.

Blanchard, O. J. (2009) 'The State of Macro', *Annual Review of Economics*, Annual Reviews, 1, 1: 209-228.

Castren, O. and Rancan, M. (2013) 'Macro Networks: an Application to the Euro Area Financial Accounts', *ECB Working Paper 1510*, February.

Ellison, G. (2006) 'Bounded rationality in industrial organisation', Blundell, Newey and Persson (eds.), *Advances in Economics and Econometrics: Theory and Applications*, Ninth World Congress, Cambridge University Press.

Lucas, R. E. (2003) 'Macroeconomic Priorities', *American Economic Review*, 93, 1: 1-14.

Newman, M. E. J. (2010) *Networks: An Introduction*, OUP.

Schelling, T. C. (1973) 'Hockey Helmets, Concealed Weapons and Daylight Saving Time', *The Journal of Conflict Resolution*, 17, 3: 381-428.

Simon, H. A. (1955) 'A Behavioral Model of Rational Choice', *The Quarterly Journal of Economics*, 69: 99-118.

Squazzoni, F. (2012) *Agent Based Computational Sociology*, Wiley.

Watts, D. J. (2002) 'A Simple Model of Global Cascades on Random Networks', *Proceedings of the National Academy of Sciences*, 99, 9: 5766–5771.

CHAPTER 11

A new economics curriculum for a new century and a new economy

Constantine E. Passaris

1 Introduction

The 21st century ushered in two defining and apocalyptic events on the economic landscape. One was foundational and the other was cataclysmic. Both have revealed the pedagogical fault lines for the contemporary economics curriculum. These defining milestones are the emergence of the new global economy and the devastating consequences of the 2008 financial crisis.

The new global economy has transformed the economic, social, educational and political landscape in a profound and indelible manner. Never before in human history has the pace of structural change been more pervasive, rapid and global in context. The new economy is composed of a trilogy of interactive forces that include globalization, trade liberalization and the information technology and communications revolution. Globalization has melted national borders and redefined economic policy. Free trade has enhanced economic integration and revealed the vulnerability of the economic governance architecture. The information and communications revolution has made geography and time irrelevant and extended the reach of economic parameters (Passaris, 2006).

The cataclysmic event was the massive global economic consequences in the aftermath of the 2008 financial crisis. There is no denying that the financial crisis developed with record speed into a devastating economic, social and political crisis of global proportions. The global financial meltdown of 2008 took most economists by surprise. Furthermore, the financial crisis had a more devastating effect than simply creating the most significant global economic crisis since the Great Depression of the 1930s: it rocked the epicentre of the economics profession; more specifically it revealed the fault lines and significant deficiencies in the training and pedagogy of contemporary economists.

Indeed, its economic tremors continue to be felt several years later. Its outcome was the Great Recession which took the form of a protracted economic stagnation, persistent high levels of unemployment and financial instability. There was also a more devastating reputational outcome. Contemporary economics has extended its reputation as the 'dismal science' to being perceived by the general public as perfunctory and incompetent.

It is evident that the contemporary preparation and training for future economists has significant deficiencies. The current economics curriculum contains errors of commission and omission. Consequently, academic training of contemporary economists is myopic and lacking in breadth, depth and diversity. In particular, there is a need for a new and more comprehensive curriculum for economic training is congruent with the challenges and opportunities of the new global economy of the 21st century.

In Chinese, the word crisis is composed of two characters- one represents danger and the other opportunity. Indeed, a Chinese proverb reads "a crisis is an opportunity riding the dangerous wind." There is no denying that the global financial crisis of 2008 has precipitated a wake-up call for addressing the deficiencies in the economics curriculum. It also requires realigning the academic mission and the instructional tool set for the teaching of economics. Indeed, the recent financial and economic crisis may turn out to be the catalyst for redesigning our pedagogical philosophy, reinventing the economics curriculum and renovating our modus operandi.

2 Internationalizing the economics curriculum

In the future, the redesign of the economics curriculum must reflect the lessons of our collective economic historiography. Our disciplinary memory must serve as a compass in order to realign the academic mission and the teaching of economics with the new global economic landscape. A modern economics curriculum must also embrace innovative pedagogical directions such as academic mentorship. Furthermore, a revised economics curriculum requires building intellectual bridges with the new global economy, acknowledging the academic value of interdisciplinarity, internationalizing the curriculum and redefining the role of quantitative economics. In order to teach economics effectively in the context of the 21st century, instructors should familiarize their students with the changing structural realities of the new global economy. Their pedagogical mission should instill a global mindset in economic thinking.

The recent global financial crisis confirmed that economic pedagogy has not evolved in step with the structural and foundational changes on the economic landscape. The advent of the new global economy requires the introduction of a global contextual appreciation to contemporary economic issues and policies. The domestic insularity of economics is no longer appropriate or relevant for the 21st century. The internationalization of economics will empower the discipline with an enhanced global awareness and engagement.

At the outset, we should start with internationalizing the economics curriculum. More precisely, the economics curriculum should become an exciting adventure of intellectual discovery in a global context, since internationalizing the economics curriculum will provide the contextual narrative and build intellectual bridges between economic pedagogy and the new global economy of the 21st century. In this manner we can develop an integrated sense of global cultures and international awareness. Indeed, we should be cognizant that modern economists are required to be globally mobile. They should also possess personal and professional attributes such as intellectual agility, an operational comfort level in a multicultural work environment as well as highly trained professional skills.

Internationalizing the economics curriculum is not simply a matter of adding a few additional courses to the existing array taught under the guise of international economics. Rather it should incorporate and weave an international focus and dimension to the current curriculum including those courses dedicated to economic theory, mathematical economics and econometrics, thus ensuring that future generations of economists have a global mindset.

The internationalization of instruction and the curriculum can forge the contextual linkages with the new structural foundations and the evolving economic parameters of the new global economy. In this regard, internationalization will modernize and enhance the pedagogical efficacy and the academic mission of economics. Internationalizing the economics curriculum will enhance the students' learning and academic experience and empower future generations of economists with the tools and skills to successfully navigate the new global economy.

3 Interdisciplinary origins

The new global economy has many facets, numerous dimensions and intricate linkages. In order to achieve a compelling presence economics must abandon its disciplinary isolation and insularity. It must discard its maxim of professional and intellectual silos. Indeed, it must revisit the roots of its academic heritage and develop a contemporary web of interdisciplinary outreach.

Economics is the brain child of interdisciplinarity. It is worth noting that the discipline of political economy which was born in the 18th century had three intellectual fathers, Adam Smith, David Ricardo and John Stuart Mill. It subsequently evolved in the 20th century into three separate disciplines: economics, political science and sociology.

Interdisciplinarity in economics has a long and distinguished provenance. It is only during the latter part of the 20th century, that economics has embraced a more discipline specific and academically insular specialization. In part, this is the result of the evolution of the scientific method in the Newtonian tradition. This has developed an economic pedagogy that is void of an appreciation of related disciplines. This course of action has failed in empowering future economists with a broader intellectual perspective and a global framework for the contemporary economic issues.

The 21st century requires a turnaround in the defiantly discipline specific direction of neoclassical economics. Indeed, economics requires a rediscovery of interdisciplinarity which acknowledges the importance of interdependent variables and the intellectual interface of academic enquiry. The contemporary requirement for interdisciplinarity is a response to societal pressures in defining the new parameters for academic mutation and intellectual discourse. Interdisciplinarity provides contemporary relevance and a pragmatic approach. Society has become more complex and multifaceted and it is not possible to understand it from within the boundaries of one discipline.

As countries grapple with the economic problems of the 21st century such as sovereign debt, economic stagnation, persistent unemployment and business ethics, the need for the discipline of economics to lower the drawbridge and connect with its traditional and as well as more modern disciplinary affiliates has never been more acute. In particular, the disciplines of political science, sociology, law and philosophy can make a significant contribution towards the interdisciplinary transfusion that contemporary economics manifestly requires.

In consequence, social, economic, political, demographic and cultural dimensions, to name but a few, are interdependent intellectual disciplines. One of the tasks of interdisciplinary applied research is to build intellectual bridges and close academic gaps. Interdisciplinary research broadens one's intellectual horizons, challenges one's perceptions, promotes constant new learning and has pragmatic appeal and practical usefulness.

An interdisciplinary approach facilitates thinking outside the box and can provide historical depth, cultural sensitivity, social context, policy direction, ethical implications, statistical relevance and much more. The *sine qua non* of the interdisciplinary approach is the acknowledgement of disciplinary complementarity.

4 Interdisciplinary research

Contemporary economists are not equipped with the requisite skills and tools to confront the challenging economic issues of modern society. The new global economy has created new economic issues that are more complex and intricate and whose resolution requires a more holistic and multifaceted approach.

The hot button contemporary topics include climate change, averting future financial crises, sustainable economic prosperity, demographic challenges, inadequate financial resources to provide for sustainable health care and gender pay inequality to name but a few. One perennial issue that stands out is that of economic development. The insularity of our academic resources and discipline specific tools in economic development has prevented economists from producing any significant results in eradicating global poverty.

There is an urgent need for an expansion of applied interdisciplinary studies and research which will move decidedly away from discipline concentrated specialization and create new disciplinary boundaries as well as crossing old disciplinary borders. The contemporary requirement for interdisciplinarity is a response to societal pressures in defining the new parameters for academic mutation and intellectual discourse. Interdisciplinarity provides contemporary relevance and a pragmatic approach. Civil society has become more complex and multifaceted and it is not possible to understand it from within the boundaries of one discipline. In short, social, economic, political, demographic and cultural dimensions, to name but a few, are part of the contemporary setting of most academic issues. Interdisciplinary work can be as far reaching as to encompass the humanities, social, educational, natural and health sciences or as narrow and focused as history and demography, and anything in between.

Solving our contemporary challenges requires a different set of tools, a more holistic approach and a multidisciplinary focus. The use of methodological pluralism, currently not part of the economics curriculum can help resolve the present stalemate. New and modern analytical strategies should be applied to confront contemporary economic issues. In this context a more pronounced interdisciplinary approach is required: our economic problems should be examined from a plurality of disciplinary angles and prisms.

An interdisciplinary approach requires economists to be fully cognizant of diverse schools of thought within their own discipline as well as developments in other related disciplines. This in addition to the emergence of new research frontiers and new academic disciplines requiring collaborative research, multidisciplinary and interdisciplinary research teams and path breaking pedagogical techniques in response to advances in computer science and information technology. In short, the economics curriculum of the 21st century must reflect an appreciation and an intellectual comfort zone with related disciplines.

Increasingly during the 21st century, economists will be called upon to play a leading role in interdisciplinary research and studies. Economics has a central role and a pivotal function in the multifaceted, multidimensional and over-arching reach between the humanities and the social sciences. It is therefore a matter of ensuring that the discipline of economics has the contextual predisposition to make a significant contribution to this modern academic mission encompassing a shared vision, a plurality of disciplinary prisms and the complementarity of ideas.

5 Interdisciplinary curriculum and pedagogy

Our contemporary challenges expose us to a multifaceted, multidimensional and an over- arching reach between economics, the social sciences, the humanities and the natural sciences. In fact, solving social challenges will lead to mutations, linkages and variations within disciplines and between disciplines. All of this leading to a redefinition of interdisciplinary boundaries for the purpose of building intellectual bridges, closing academic gaps and providing evidence based public policy. This is of particular importance in addressing the interdisciplinary nature of contemporary economic challenges, social problems and environmental sustainability. An interdisciplinary approach will translate into improved public policies contributing to sustained wealth creation and multidimensional efficiencies.

Our pedagogical mission and the scope and substance of our economics curriculum should reflect the importance and strategic deployment of an interdisciplinary approach in the training of future economists. In my opinion the value of an interdisciplinary approach to contemporary economic pedagogy is irrefutable. I therefore suggest an innovative Pedagogical template for achieving the desired interdisciplinarity in the teaching of economics. No single economics instructor can be adequately well versed in all relevant interdisciplinary subjects. Instead, I purpose that economics departments experiment with interdisciplinary team teaching. This will require assigning several instructors from different disciplines to teach the same economics course. For example, an economics instructor, a political scientist, a sociologist, a scientist, a mathematican and a biologist may be assigned to teach a course in environmental economics. In this manner, future generations of economists will acquire the interdisciplinary tools, the intellectual agility and multidisciplinary perspective that will serve them well in exercising their professional responsibilities as economists in the 21st century.

6 Historical vacuum

The contemporary economics curriculum suffers from a historical vacuum. It lacks an appreciation of our collective economic history, thus presenting a compelling need to rediscover the value of economic history and the history of economic thought.

There are two foundational tenets defining the historical context in economics. First, an appreciation of the history of economic thought and second, the historical context for economic events. It should be emphasized that the history of economic thought and economic history are two different fields of study and contain distinctive subject matter. It is a sad commentary that on both counts the historical potency of the discipline of economics is found lacking. The historical back drop has become an increasingly neglected dimension in economics and in the teaching of the economics curriculum.

There is an urgent need to rediscover the value of economic history for future generations of economists. History and economics are in many respects complementary and inter-dependent with strong structural linkages. Furthermore, the history of economic thought introduces a critical and contextual appreciation to modern economic theory. In effect, the history of economic thought provides us with the genetic topography and the DNA composition for the modern discipline of economics.

To correct this historical amnesia, contemporary economics instructors have a potent pedagogical role to play. For example, when defining and explaining theoretical concepts and constructs, they should also identify the name of the economist associated with that theoretical innovation, their overall contributions to the economic discipline and the significance of this theoretical parenthesis to the evolution of economic science.

7 Historical antecedents

The emphasis on quantitative economics in the latter half of the twentieth century cast a long shadow over the sub-discipline of economic history. The infatuation with mathematical elegance relegated the value of economic history to the academic dustbin.

It should be noted that economic history is not simply about the past, it is important for the present and the future. History is a continuum from the past to the present and into the future. It preserves the past, explains the present and shapes the future. In many respects economic history illustrates the lessons of hindsight and prevents us from repeating the errors of the past. It also sheds light on the present and helps us chart an enlightened course for the future.

Economic history is the record of the collective memory for *homo economicus*. It is the context for contemporary economic issues and events. It is also a valuable tool for predicting the future evolution of economic events. Indeed, economic history can be a valuable analytical tool for a proactive approach that averts crises and identifies new opportunities.

In this regard, economics instruction should explain the historical context of contemporary economic events. These historical flashbacks provide a time line and a historical narrative that enhances the analytical pedagogical role of modern economic events and contributes a historical continuum that would otherwise be absent. Indeed, the guiding principle should be that the more economists know about the past, the better prepared for the future.

The most penetrating observation regarding the value of economic history was offered by Joseph A. Schumpeter. In his last book, *History of Economic Analysis,* he emphasized that the proper study of economics requires three elements: theory, statistics and history. He concludes that: "If, starting my work in economics afresh, I were told that I could study only one of the three but could have my choice, it would be economic history" (Schumpeter, 1954: 12).

The intrinsic pedagogical role of economic history was most recently confirmed in the awarding of the 2011 Nobel Prize in Economics to Professors Thomas Sargent and Christopher Sims for their lifetime contributions in statistical history which explored clues in past economic events in order to forecast what will transpire in the future.

A modern economics curriculum should proceed with repatriating the few economic history courses that are currently being taught in history departments to the economics department. There is a pedagogical disparity between an historian teaching a course in economic history compared to an economist. Economists, more than historians, are grounded in economic theory and analysis and are, therefore, best able to explain and interpret the economic underpinnings of historical events. Economic instructors are best able to articulate the intrinsic subtleties of the lessons of economic history to enhance the overall pedagogical mission for training the next generation of economists with the most efficacious tools. Furthermore, the pedagogical value of the history of economic thought must be weaved into the modern curriculum. More specifically, the dormant history of economic thought courses should be re-introduced in the economics curriculum. Furthermore, all economics courses currently being taught should be realigned so that they are integrated with a grounding of the contextual value of the history of economic thought.

Lastly, the economics curriculum should position economic history courses so that they serve as a tool of economic research and analysis for contemporary economic issues. Economic history enables us to analyse and explain the contemporary and historical specific dimensions of economic life. In short, the redesign of the economics curriculum for the 21st century must reflect that history is not simply about the past, it is perhaps more important in analyzing and explaining the present and predicting the future.

Rediscovering the value of economic history and the history of economic ideas will correct a glaring omission in the economics curriculum. Indeed, it will eradicate the diagnosis of historical amnesia in our arsenal of economic pedagogy.

8 Quantitative dilemma

The academic mission of economic pedagogy and the economics curriculum of the 21st century will have to resolve the contemporary quagmire regarding the focus of economics predominantly on the quantitative rather than the qualitative. The emergence of the new global economy and the financial crisis of 2008 have accentuated the disciplinary limitations of the quantitative approach. Indeed, they have underlined the constraints associated with the extensive use of the mathematical approach in the study and application of contemporary economics. In addition, economics is susceptible to being influenced by collateral forces such as social, political, cultural and demographic variables that are not amenable to quantitative modelling.

The latter part of the 20th century witnessed a concerted effort to make the study of economics more of a science in an effort to upgrade its academic respectability. This was achieved by promoting the Newtonian approach developed for the 19th century natural sciences and embracing a rigid quantitative focus and application. Newton invented a scientific method which became the universal gold standard for scientific reasoning. In this respect, economics has attempted to mimic the 19th century sciences of physics, chemistry and biology.

Kenneth J. Arrow who shared the Nobel Prize in Economics in 1972 is widely regarded as one of the principal architects of the mathematical approach in modern economics. The quantitative approach meant restating economic theories on the basis of assumptions and techniques developed by the University of Chicago school of economics and its founder Milton Friedman. These efforts produced grand theories of economics supported by elegant mathematical models and empirical analysis of *prima facie* scientific rigour.

At the same time, the quantitative focus has been criticized as being falsely scientific with no role for human intentionality or choice, understating the economic narrative, assumptions and theory. It has also been suggested that quantification has resulted in simplistic models of individual human behaviour in the genre of rational, self-interested, utility maximizing *homo oeconomicus*. Indeed, Arrow emphasizes that the extensive reach of modern neoclassical economics has transformed basic economic concepts such as rational choice and profit maximization among others into parameters with different mutations and more diverse interpretations. Furthermore, mathematics (at least the mathematics used by neoclassical economics) is not conducive to incorporating the social, cultural and political dimension of economic issues (Arrow, 2009).

The quantitative approach has made economics more model driven and hence less responsive to variables that have an implicit qualitative focus. Mathematical formulation requires a degree of abstraction and technical rigidity that consequently has contributed to the observation that contemporary economic models bear little resemblance to the real world and do not adequately reflect the economic passion for developing a road map towards achieving the eternal human ambition for economic prosperity, improving the quality of life and personal fulfillment. In short, neoclassical economists have become so fixated with the mathematical application that they have lost sight of the fundamental mission and mandate of economics.

In many respects the founding fathers of modern economics had a visionary insight into the role and mandate of economics. Indeed it was an intellectual vision that has stood the test of time and placed the use of mathematics within the appropriate boundaries. It is worth quoting from Alfred Marshall, "I know I had a growing feeling in the later years of my work at the subject that a good mathematical theorem dealing with economic hypotheses was very unlikely to be good economics" (Pigou, 1925: 427).

The quantitative progression of economics has emphasized the abstract to the detriment of the pragmatic, adversely impacting the intellectual discourse regarding the global economy of the 21st century. It is worth noting that it is not entirely coincidental that the founding father of modern day macroeconomics, John Maynard Keynes, well versed in mathematics hardly used it. And Nobel laureate Milton Friedman was not a forceful proponent of the quantitative approach, either. He captured the essence of the quantitative dimension in economics:

"A similar criticism applies to the extensive use of mathematics, which again has greatly extended the power of economic analysis, but is often used to impress rather than inform. Results that might have been attainable only by sophisticated mathematics can nonetheless be explained in understandable English. Again and again, I have read articles written primarily in mathematics, in which the central conclusions and reasoning could readily have been restated in English, and the mathematics relegated to an appendix, making the article far more accessible to the reader" (Friedman, 1991: 36).

In his seminal article entitled "Toward a Newer Economics", William Baumol argues:

"There can hardly be any argument with the proposition that the use of mathematical methods has not solved all problems in economic analysis, and that some problems lend themselves more readily to statistical, experimental, historical or other lines of attack. While formal mathematical theory has made invaluable contributions in fields where its success might have caused considerable surprise in an earlier day – fields such as public finance and industrial organisation – each of these areas surely still leaves considerable scope for other research procedures. And there are still other areas, for example, labour economics, in which this is probably even truer. The trouble is that if individuals are not respected for the pursuit of alternative

190

approaches, if only those whose writings are pockmarked by algebraic symbols receive kudos, one can expect a misallocation of resources like that which always results from a distortion of relative prices" (Baumol, 1991: 2).

9 Quantitative limitations

Sadly, despite the complicated mathematical modelling of contemporary economics it fails to take a holistic approach that would include the elements of the political, social, psychological, moral and historical parameters. In short, two-dimensional models that attempt to be scientific and rigorous often end up trading off the real world and a dose of realism and pragmatism. This questions the degree to which abstraction necessitated by mathematical rigour has resulted in a marked decline in the pertinence of contemporary economics. There is an urgent need for a broader vision from econometric technicians (the economic version of statistics known as econometrics) to become more inclusive of the qualitative variables that embrace the economic issues that confront us in the 21st century.

There is no denying that the enhanced processing power of computers has captured and promoted the quantitative focus of economics. In this scenario, the social and political dimensions have been excluded from enabling an analysis of the real world. In fact, these altered realities are adversely impacting on the intellectual discourse regarding the new global economy of the 21st century.

10 Methodological compromise

The quagmire between contemporary relevance and scientific rigour should be resolved by adopting an intellectual compromise. Mathematical sophistication and rigidity must be tempered in order to embrace the qualitative dimension of contemporary economic issues. This will undoubtedly enhance the role that economists will play in the 21st century by becoming more relevant and responsive to economic, social, political and cultural public policy issues.

This balance between quantitative rigour and qualitative realism must become a central feature of economic pedagogy in the 21st century. In consequence, economics instructors should alert their students to the limitations of the quantitative approach and at the same time open the door to the qualitative interpretation of contemporary economic models.

The pluralist requirement in contemporary economic pedagogy must find expression in selecting the appropriate mathematical formulas that will assist us in understanding, explaining and predicting the contemporary economy. Indeed, we need to balance our economic pedagogy between the analytical potency of our mathematical models and their ability to reflect the complex and intricate reality of our modern economic system.

A central issue regarding the quantitative approach is not how much mathematics to use and how often but rather what kind in order to avert coming to conclusions that do not reflect the contemporary and pragmatic nature of our economy and society. In doing so, a determined effort must be applied to avoid constructing a boxed in model that ultimately bears little resemblance to the real world. This can easily be resolved by first of all concentrating on defining the economic parameters of an issue and then proceeding to incorporate that form of mathematics that may be applied to solve it.

The modern economics curriculum should recognise that mathematics and econometrics provides the tools for testing economic variables and avoiding conjecture. However, economic pedagogy must select the appropriate mathematical formulas that will assist us in understanding, explaining and predicting the contemporary economy.

11 Economics curriculum

Education is a public trust, an intellectual legacy and a collective inheritance to be passed from one generation to the next. The intellectual mission of education, in its most ambitious form, instills knowledge, human capital, personal skills and tools that permit broad based learning; discipline specific specialized competencies; promotes critical thinking, good judgment and incisive reasoning; provides for clarity of writing and numerical application; empowers human resources to achieve a global competitive edge; enables a smarter population to enhance productivity and create economic growth and, last but certainly not least, can unleash the innovative, entrepreneurial and creative potential of our students.

The contemporary landscape offers an opportunity to launch a new and innovative economics curriculum that values new breadth and new ideas in order to equip economics students with the knowledge and skills to resolve the problems of the real world. The principal objective of a revised curriculum is to provide future generations of economists with an education that is well-rounded, not simply well-trained. In short, to elevate our pedagogical ambitions from grooming narrowly focused specialists towards a broader and more versatile intellectual capacity, by avoiding focused specialization and empowering a broader education. In this manner, we can acquire an appreciation of the intellectual connection for how the micro components create the macro framework.

Given that the technical knowledge one learns today will become obsolete in a relative short time; thus, the most empowering form of education is one that embraces values about how to learn than what to learn. Furthermore, the prerequisite for a commitment to life-long learning has never been more necessary or pertinent.

The acid test of the pedagogical efficacy of the economics curriculum is the workplace. In this regard, the contemporary economics curriculum develops deep technical knowledge but not the intellectual agility and nimbleness to put this knowledge to full and practical use. Furthermore, it lacks a commitment to continuously update its fluency and effectiveness. Indeed, it is a common observance in the contemporary workplace that young economics graduates have trouble communicating their ideas, working in multi-disciplinary teams and are lacking in the skills to analyze a problem from diverse perspectives. All of this can be easily remedied by renewing the foundational tenets of the economics curriculum to include social awareness, an interdisciplinary approach and increased community engagement.

12 New directions

The reshaping of the economic landscape has been defined by a complex structural realignment of the investment streams, the clustering of business enterprises, the transformation of the production process and the need to invent a new institutional economic architecture. Furthermore, it has necessitated the effective integration of state-of-the-art technologies in information and communications in order to enhance competitive advantage. All of this has resulted in the fundamental restructuring of economic society (Passaris, 2008).

The role of innovation as a catalyst of economic growth needs to be acknowledged as a fundamental postulate of the new global economy. Furthermore, the pivotal role of a country's human resources and the unique economic value of its human capital endowment which is reflected in the educational attainment and technical skills of its population is an essential prerequisite for empowering the new economy and facilitating the integration of labour in the knowledge-based industries.

13 Institutional economics

The advent of the new global economy has opened the door for a rediscovery of the merits of institutional economics and created a unique opportunity to redefine the scope and substance of economic pedagogy. The time has come for a new model of economic pedagogy and for the academic training and the professional preparation of future generations of economists. In the process empowering a new generation of economists with the required knowledge, skills and tools to successfully navigate the new global economy of the 21st century. In particular, we need to confront the errors of commission and omission in the academic training of contemporary economists and propose specific remedies and solutions towards enhancing the efficacy of the economics curriculum.

The process of modernizing the economics curriculum will require building intellectual bridges with the new global economy, enhancing historical content, acknowledging the academic value of the interdisciplinary approach, embracing academic mentorship, internationalizing the curriculum and redefining the role of quantitative economics. All of this in a holistic and integrated approach.

14 Neoclassical retrospective

The prevalence of neoclassical economics in the 20th century was perceived as an appeal to a coherent articulation and a rigorous scientific approach to address current economic issues. Its principal disposition was that economies necessarily gravitate towards equilibrium. The incapacity of mainstream theory to address some of the contemporary economic and social issues has forced the development of sub-disciplines such as gender economics, environmental economics, transition economics, multicultural economics and the economics of jurisprudence to name but a few. It has also spawned the emergence of a splinter school of economics. In this regard, heterodox economics which encompasses the Austrian school, post-Keynesians, Marxist economics and institutional economics has emerged to challenge the dominance of neoclassical economics.

It is increasingly evident of a disconnect between neoclassical economics and the hot button issues of the new global economy of the 21st century. As a result, the efficacy of the discipline of economics has been compromised. Goodwin articulates very succinctly:

> "...the major problems with mainstream economic theory begin with its assumption of final ends – most notably, maximizing GDP – that are not appropriate to a resource-constrained world. It views the economy as separate from its social and ecological contexts, understanding neither its dependence on these contexts nor the impacts of meta-externalities from the economic system upon them. It only counts things that go through the market, and it has a bias against the public sector and in favor of the status quo" (Goodwin, 2010: 2).

The most resounding repudiation of neoclassical economics and its adverse effect on financial stability was pronounced by the former chairman of the USA Federal Reserve System, Alan Greenspan. In testimony before the Committee of Government Oversight and Reform of the U.S. Congress, he stated very bluntly, "those of us who have looked to the self-interest of lending institutions to protect shareholder's equity, myself included, are in a state of shocked disbelief" (Greenspan, 2008: 1).

15 Institutional relevance

In its contemporary phase, neoclassical economics proved impotent in predicting the financial meltdown, in mustering an arsenal of economic tools to combat the crisis and in renovating the institutional architecture to bring about good economic governance. Furthermore, the theoretical parameters of neoclassical economics have proved inadequate to deal with the operational constructs of the new economy. In consequence, in order to avoid a repeat of the economic depression of the 1930s, governments resorted to a Keynesian economic stimulus and public regulation in order to limit the excesses of the free market, swinging the pendulum away from neoclassical economics (Passaris, 2011b).

In short, the economic crisis revealed that neoclassical economics was hampered by unrealistic assumptions, model failings, errors of judgement and a very narrow and filtered focus. In consequence, it was ineffective in addressing structural change in the new global economy and analyzing the qualitative issues of relevance on the economic landscape. Paul Krugman summarized the current state of economics:

> "...the economics profession went astray because economists, as a group, mistook beauty, clad in impressive-looking mathematics, for truth[...] the central cause of the profession's failure was the desire for an all-encompassing, intellectually elegant approach that also gave economists a chance to show off their mathematical prowess" (Krugman, 2009: 36).

The economics curriculum: towards a radical reformulation

The recent financial crisis has opened the door for the rediscovery of institutional economics and a reorientation of the discipline of economics. Economics' new frontiers will be determined by more appropriate theoretical parameters for confronting the contemporary challenges of structural change in the new global economy. In this regard, institutional economics can make a positive and constructive contribution towards building the scaffolding for a more potent approach to economic theory (Passaris, 2011a).

Rutherford goes beyond defining institutionalism as simply a rejection of neoclassical theory and lists five tenets that encompass the institutional approach:

> "(1) a clear recognition of the *central* analytical importance of institutions and institutional change, with institutions acting not merely as constraints on the behavior of individuals and concerns but as factors shaping the beliefs, values, and preferences of individuals; (2) a desire to base economics on a social psychology consistent with this emphasis on the role of institutions, and a related rejection of hedonistic psychology and of the idea of the individual as a perfect utility maximizer; (3) the adoption of a view of correct scientific method in social science as empirical and 'investigational' (including but not limited to quantitative and statistical work), and a related rejection of the highly abstract and 'speculative' nature of much orthodox theory; (4) emphasis of the *critical* examination of the functioning of existing economic institutions (including issues such as bargaining power, standards of living and working conditions, corporate finance and control, market failures of various types, business cycles, unemployment, and so on), and a related belief in the need for new forms of 'social control' involving greater government regulation *of* the market and other interventions; and (5) the adoption of a pragmatic and humanistic approach to social value (from John Dewey), and a related rejection of the standard theories of value and of market efficiency as adequate tools for policy appraisal" (Rutherford, 2009: 311).

The contemporary institutional landscape for economic governance was designed for the old economy and is no longer potent in meeting the challenges and opportunities of the new economy. Indeed the next generation of economists should be trained in adapting the tools of architecture and engineering in terms of designing and building the new institutional economic landscape that is more congruent with the new global economy and reflective of the hazards of the 2008 financial crisis.

In short, the contemporary economic landscape requires the introduction of new models and the design of a new institutional architecture that is congruent with the new global economy. There is an urgent need for a new economic template, innovative theoretical parameters and a rediscovery of the moderating and regulatory role of government. The predisposition of institutional economics which addresses structural change and the role of economic institutions make it better equipped than mainstream economics to produce a road map for sustained economic recovery and a blueprint for economic development that is more congruent with the structural framework of the new global economy of the 21st century. More specifically, institutional economics offers a broader study of economic society for analyzing structural change that takes into account the role of institutions in determining the course of economic events. At the end of the day, institutional economics has the potential to chart an alternative road map towards achieving a revitalized discipline of economics that is more congruent with its mission in the 21st century.

16 Embracing mentorship

A new economics curriculum must embrace new pedagogical directions, discard obsolete methods and enhance the tools for empowering future generation of economists with the required skills and expertise. In this regard, mentorship is one of those new directions that should be incorporated in the new curriculum.

Mentorship has a long and distinguished provenance and pedigree. Its roots and practice can be traced to Greek antiquity. Indeed, the word mentorship is inspired from the character of Mentor who was featured by the prominent

The economics curriculum: towards a radical reformulation

Greek poet Homer in his classic book *The Odyssey*. In that epic poem, Odysseus, King of Ithaca fought in the Trojan War and entrusted the care of his kingdom to Mentor, who served as the teacher of Odysseus' son, Telemachus. Mentor, through the intervention of the goddess Athena was able to guide the young Telemachus during a challenging period of his life. Mentorship was also the educational tool of choice for the Greek philosopher Socrates who invented the Socratic method of teaching.

More recently, mentorship became an operational axiom for several faiths and religions. For example, Hinduism and Buddhism model their transference mechanism on the guru-disciple tradition. Furthermore, Rabbinical Judaism and the Christian religions have relied on elders in order to serve as the fountain of religious knowledge for the younger generation. On the labour front, the origins of the mentorship model can be found in the apprenticeship system that prevailed in the medieval guild system.

An operational definition for mentorship is:

> "Mentoring is a process for the informal transmission of knowledge, social capital, and the psychosocial support perceived by the recipient as relevant to work, career, or professional development; mentoring entails informal communication, usually face-to-face and during a sustained period of time, between a person who is perceived to have greater relevant knowledge, wisdom, or experience (the mentor) and a person who is perceived to have less (the protégé)" (Bozeman and Feeney, 2007: 731).

The relationship between mentorship and education is direct and complementary. In my opinion, education is a transformative process that is empowering, enabling, enriching and enlightening. It is a multifaceted and multidimensional human endeavor in order to reach a higher plateau for civil society. Education adds value and quality to our daily lives and enhances our workplace productivity through specialized skills. It contributes to economic growth, good governance and democratic empowerment. In this regard, mentorship should be perceived as an extension of the educational process. On the contemporary landscape, education has been facilitated and enhanced by the information technology and communication revolution.

In the modern pedagogical context, mentorship is a form of customized and individualized learning. It serves as an intellectual and professional life-line with the added benefit of task specific guidance. It has the potential of facilitating the process of lifelong learning.

Unfortunately the prevailing academic contacts outside of a classroom setting between teacher and students is primarily limited to assistance in transitioning to post graduate education or the workforce. This takes the form of writing letters of personal reference in support of applications to graduate schools or for posted jobs. Other forms include the supervision of graduate theses, advice towards program completion and academic confidence building. In some rare instances, faculty members will mentor younger economists as they take their first steps in academia or in their early careers in the public sector or the business world.

A renewal of the economics curriculum should embrace mentorship for a longer term. Indeed, there is a compelling and persuasive argument for integrating a more formal mentorship program in a more pragmatic economics curriculum. There are several reasons for both the practicality and the contemporary pertinence of an eclectic form of mentorship in a more visionary economics curriculum, including emphasis on life-long learning, the structural transformation of the economic landscape, the rapidity of change, the emphasis on customized learning and the need for a professional life-line that extends beyond the traditional and the conventional four year teaching cycle or longer in the case of doctoral studies. In short, I am proposing extending the pedagogical milepost and building intellectual bridges between different generations of economists with a longer-term time frame and does not abruptly terminate upon graduation.

In a more practical format economics mentorship takes the form of intellectual guidance, serving as a sounding board, acting as a resource for literature up-dates, facilitating an informed dialogue and providing a forum for intellectual regeneration, which form an innovative and transformative dimension for the 21st century economics curriculum.

I envisage economics mentorship as an operational medium that permits an institution of higher learning to change with the times and provide an intellectual outreach that serves its alumni after graduation. This innovative direction requires some academic re-engineering and intellectual bridge-building that comports with a more visionary role for economic education in the 21st century.

17 Conclusion

The structural changes that accompanied the emergence of the new global economy and the cataclysmic consequences of the global financial crisis of 2008 have magnified the pedagogical fault lines on the contemporary economic landscape. In particular, they have underlined the limitations of the contemporary economic theory in dealing effectively with current economic issues. They have also underlined the need for a modernized economics curriculum and new directions in the pedagogy and training of future generations of economists.

In the future, the design of the economics curriculum must reflect the lessons of our collective economic history. Our collective institutional and disciplinary memory must serve as a compass to correlate the academic mission and the teaching of economics with the new global economic landscape. It must also reflect the structural changes and evolutionary directions that have occurred in the recent past. In this context, modern economic pedagogy must serve as a catalyst for transformational change.

New economic frontiers are emerging and a significant transformation of the discipline of economics is required. Contemporary economists should rediscover the value of critical thinking and apply the prism of real world relevance to their ideas, assumptions and models rather than adopt theories simply on the basis of mathematical elegance. Pluralism and diversity in theoretical approaches within economics is a strength and not a weakness. It is the foundation for innovative ideas that are tested by rigorous examination and informed debate. All of this for the purpose of ensuring that the discipline of economics is defined in terms of the application of a potent academic approach to understand and explain economic events and challenges rather than be confined to a set of narrowly defined and predetermined assumptions and techniques. Economic instructors should embrace this mandate and use the pedagogical tools at their disposal to instill these values in their students in order to best equip them to successfully navigate the new global economy.

The transformation of economics during the 21st century will require the rediscovery of the value of economic history. It should resolve the confrontation between the quantitative school and the qualitative approach. It should also highlight the distinctive role that institutional economics should play in the resurgence of an interdisciplinary approach and the emergence of new disciplinary synergies. All of this by way of emphasizing the urgency for a new pedagogical vision for future economists and an innovative economics curriculum that will empower economists in the 21st century to higher standards of academic efficacy. In this regard, economics instruction will have to embrace transformational change in order to affect these changes and renew the economics curriculum.

In conclusion, the recent financial crisis has revealed the fault lines on the economic landscape. Correcting those fault lines will require redesigning the pedagogical mission and revising the economics curriculum. The process of modernizing the economics curriculum requires building intellectual bridges with the new global economy, repatriating economic history, acknowledging the academic value of interdisciplinarity, internationalizing the curriculum and fine tuning the role of quantitative economics. In this regard, institutional economics has the potential to make a significant contribution towards redefining the scope and substance of economic pedagogy.

References

Arrow, K. J. (2009) 'Some Developments in Economic Theory Since 1940: An Eyewitness Account', *Annual Review of Economics*, 1, 1: 1-16.

Bozeman, B. and Feeney, M. (2007) 'Toward a Useful Theory of Mentoring: A Conceptual Analysis and Critique', *Administration and Society*, 39, 6: 719-739.

Friedman, M. (1991) 'Old Wine in New Bottles', *The Economic Journal*, 101, 404: 33-40.

Goodwin, N. (2010) 'A New Economics for the Twenty-first Century', *World Future Review*,
http://www.ase.tufts.edu/gdae/Pubs/te/Goodwin_WorldFutureReviewOct2010.pdf
(accessed January 5, 2012).

Greenspan, A. (2008) *Testimony before the Committee of Government Oversight and Reform*, US Congress, October 23, 2008,
http://web.archive.org/web/20081030220043/http://oversight.house.gov/documents/2
0081023100438.pdf (accessed June 6, 2011).

Krugman, P. (2009) 'How Did Economists Get It So Wrong?', *The New York Times Magazine*, September 6,
http://www.nytimes.com/2009/09/06/magazine/06Economic-t.html?pagewanted=all
(accessed October 17, 2011).

Passaris, C. (2006) 'The Business of Globalization and the Globalization of Business', *Journal of Comparative International Management*, 9, 1: 3-18.

Passaris, C. (2008), 'Macroeconomic Policy in the New Global Economy of the Twenty first Century', *Proceedings of the Society of Heterodox Economists Conference on Contemporary Issues for Heterodox Economics*, Sydney, Australia, 8–9 December, pp. 109–137.

Passaris, C. (2011a) 'The 2008 financial crisis and economic pedagogy', *International Journal of Pluralism and Economics Education*, 2, 3: 318–324.

Passaris, C. (2011b) 'Redesigning Financial Governance for the New Global Economy of the 21st Century', *Journal of Comparative International Management*, 14, 1: 1-15.

Pigou, A. C. (ed.) (1925) *Memorials of Alfred Marshall*. London: Macmillan.

Rutherford, M. (2009) 'Towards a History of American Institutional Economics' *Journal of Economic Issues*, 43, 2: 308-318.

Schumpeter, J.A. (1954) *History of Economic Analysis*, London: Allen and Unwin.

William J. (1991) 'Toward a Newer Economics: The Future Lies Ahead!', *The Economic Journal*, 101, 404: 1-8.

CHAPTER 12

A radical reformation of economics education

Jack Reardon

1 Introduction[1]

Alfred Marshall, in the eighth edition of his *Principles of Economics,* wrote that "economic conditions are constantly changing, and each generation looks at its own problems in its own way" (Marshall, 1920 [1946]: v). Our generation is beset with many problems including climate change, a global financial crisis, a palpable disparity in income and wealth, and a health care crisis. These problems are mutually reinforcing and will only worsen. At the center, however, is the discipline of economics itself and economics education, which obfuscates the interrelationship of our problems, inures its students to human suffering and abnegates thoughtful discussion of the human predicament.

To date, calls for reform of economics education within the neoclassical paradigm have been tepid, content with tinkering around the edges, adding less chalk to more talk, while leaving the bulk of the curriculum intact. Despite the persistence of one of the worst recessions in recent history, and the collective failure of neoclassical economics to predict or understand it, "the generals of [the] mainstream status quo, along with middle ranks, show no signs of giving ground or even of feeling the need for appeasement" (Fullbrook, 2010: 94). The crisis "doesn't seem to have any decisive impact on the way economics is taught and the trends in economic research" (Otsch and Kapeller, 2010: 22). The emphasis is overwhelmingly on 'more of the same.'

---

[1] An earlier version of this paper was presented at a plenary session of the Joint Conference of the AHE, IIPPE and the FAPE, held at the Sorbonne, Paris, July 6, 2012. A revised version was presented at the Rethinking Economics Conference, Kings College, London, July 2, 2014. The author thanks conference participants for helpful comments.

The economics curriculum: towards a radical reformulation

There is no better example than Gregory Mankiw, author of one of the best-selling economics textbooks, writing during the depths of the financial crisis, "We still have to teach the bread and butter issues, the gains from trade, supply and demand, the efficient properties of markets and so on. These topics will remain the bread and butter of introductory courses" (Mankiw, 2009). But "it is hubris run amuck that assumes we only need minor adjustments" (Reardon, 2010: 182).

What is wrong with neoclassical economics that precludes an honest re-assessment? Where is the humility? Where is the umbrage? Where is the *mea culpa* of university professors, textbook authors and publishers? Where is the willingness to go back to the drawing board? Where is the public shock that despite the prodigious change in our economy, "...students at the beginning of the 21st century are receiving much the same instruction about how firms set prices as did their counterparts at the end of the 19th century [and] that any scientist from the 19th century would be bewildered by what is commonplace today in his [sic] discipline - save an economist" (Keen, 2011: 168-169).

Imagine "if universities continued to use for nuclear engineering a textbook by an engineer who had headed a team managing a nuclear power plant that without external causes exploded creating a huge devastation, there would be a public outcry" (Fullbrook, 2009: 22). Or imagine the outbreak of a disease, an epidemic, that caught the medical profession unaware, with most of the profession (and textbooks) fastidiously denying the epidemic's possibility. Wouldn't there be public outrage? An enraged demand to hold the profession accountable?

Why is such a similar situation tolerated in economics? Why isn't there a public effort to disbar economists who continue to teach such failed policies? Why isn't there an effort to de-commission the universities that grant such degrees? Why isn't there a detailed public hearing to ascertain what is taught in economics courses and published in economics textbooks?

Imagine a book written for economics students that describes in detail what is missing and wrong in their textbooks so that they "can begin to think critically about what they read in their textbooks, to defend themselves against the unconscious acceptance of ideology" (Hill and Myatt, 2010: 2).

Unfortunately we don't have to imagine- such a book has been written (Hill and Myatt, 2010). The book's title, *The Economics Anti-Textbook – A Critical Thinker's Guide to Microeconomics* acutely underscores the problem: students need a book not as a helpful guide in learning complex material but to unlearn what is written in their texts.[2]

Several reasons explain the collective failure of neoclassical economics to reform and its steadfast refusal of an honest re-assessment. One, a proclivity (I am not sure if it is natural or not) for individuals and academics to become comfortably immersed in the old ways of doing things, while viscerally impugning anything new that might disturb the accepted way. Indeed Francis Bacon noted almost four centuries ago that:

> "In the manners and customs of the schools, universities, colleges and similar institutions, which are intended to house scholars and cultivate learning, everything is found to be inimical to the progress of the sciences... For the readings and men's (sic) writings are confined and imprisoned in the writings of certain authors; anyone who disagrees with them is instantly attacked as a troublemaker and revolutionary" (Bacon, 1620 [2000], Book I, XC: 75-76).

Two, and closely related, a reluctance exists to admit that one's work has been in vain. Ironically, for a discipline that claims rationality, it is hard for established practitioners to jettison their life-long beliefs in favour of a new paradigm. And sadly the myopic and fundamentalist limitations of their education preclude understanding of the manifold alternatives. It is this "irrational tenacity [to] hold its core beliefs in the face of either contrary factual evidence or theoretical critiques" (Keen, 2011: 168) that keeps

---

[2] While this book only tackles one subject in economics – microeconomics, the malaise and disconnect described by Hill and Myatt unfortunately affects all subjects within the discipline of economics. Expect more such books to be written.

neoclassical economics "a pre-science, rather like astronomy before Copernicus, Brahe and Galileo" (Keen, 2011: 158).

Three, the basic institutions of neoclassical economics: university departments, associations, journals, classification systems, economics 101 textbooks, and its basic narrative, collectively and interactively block any effort at meaningful reform (Fullbrook, 2010: 95). Fullbrook notes that "this intransigence and insuperability stems from the fact that as institutions, although independently constituted, they are interlocking and their characteristics inter-determined" (Fullbrook, 2010: 95).

Four, uniting each of the above factors and, important in its own right, is economics education, which in my opinion best explains why neoclassical economists could not predict the recent crisis; why they are ignorant of alternative paradigms; why they obdurately cling to failed policies; and why they chastise and bully dissenters. Indeed, "economics [and economics education] as currently constituted and practiced, acts as a most effective barrier against the understanding of [our] problems" (Schumacher, 1989: 50); and as Keen noted:

> "...economists may be the main force preventing the introduction of countervailing measures to any future economics slump. Economics may make our recessions deeper, longer and intractable, when the public is entitled to expect economics to have precisely the opposite effect" (Keen, 2011: 1).

We need economics and we need economists to help fix our problems but more importantly we need educated (and not proselytized) real world economists. And we don't need an economics or economics education that insists on proselytization rather than education; an education that is monist rather than pluralist; that produces students unable and unwilling to understand the myriad diversity of human behavior and unable to work with other social scientists in solving our generation's problems. Economics education is a problem of our generation and must be radically reformed[3].

2 The problem with economics education

One of my students wrote on a recent exam, "I took two economics classes before yours, and I had a hard time finding a relationship between the study of economics, firms and the entire society." Given that the overall objective of economics is the study of the economy (isn't it?) and given that the economy is comprised of firms and individuals, isn't this a damming criticism?

If this was an isolated comment, I could cavalierly dismiss it, but I hear it time and time again. My heart stops when students tell me that they were excited to begin their study of economics only to be turned off by an onslaught of deductive logic and abstract models with little resemblance to the world in which they live. Indeed, "in the business, government and other non-academic communities, the perception is widespread and growing of economics as a technical and rarefied discipline, of questionable relevance and limited practical use" (Hodgson, 2001: 9).

Imagine a physicist being told that her lectures had nothing to do with the physical world; or an anatomy professor being told that his lectures had nothing to do with the human body. Wouldn't there be umbrage; a humbled admission of fault and a dedicated desire to amend the pedagogy?

---

[3] Although Marshall is most responsible for the neoclassical synthesis, Marshall along with other founding fathers of neoclassical economics, would "be surprised to find that a manner of thinking they thought would be transitional has instead become ossified as the only way one can do economics and be respectable" (Keen, 2011: 35). A constant theme of Marshall's work is the exhortation that "the study of local circumstances as the only way to bring general economic principles to bear on the solution of factual problems [which presupposes that the economic principles themselves are given an inherently flexible formulation and conceived as evolutionary instruments by means of which human societies can learn how to deal with changes either of the endogenous sort or those deriving from external sources" (Raffaelli et al., 2010: xvi). And not surprisingly "some of Marshall's economic ideas had an indirect and almost underground diffusion on political science, urban planning, sociology, demography, rural studies, and so on" (Raffaelli et al., 2010: xi)

Not so with neoclassical economics, which claims that "economics isn't defined by its subject matter but by its way of thinking" (Coyle, 2007: 231-232). No wonder students are disappointed and perplexed when they open up a textbook and expect to learn about the economy in which they live and (will) work, only to be told that economics is about allocating scarce resources among unlimited wants and then hit with an abstract production possibilities curve to drive home the point.

The problem with neoclassical pedagogy isn't too much math – actually quite the opposite: it uses the wrong math (simple calculus) to study the wrong problem – optimization. And even worse, it is bad math – a distorted and misunderstanding of the limitations of mathematics (Keen, 2011: 402-411). Mathematics can elucidate, especially the laws of nature, "natural inquiry succeeds best when the physical ends in the mathematical" (Bacon, 1620 [2000], Book II, VIII: 108).

Nor is neoclassical economics too complex: as a former physics major who switched to economics, I found it deceptively simple; and perhaps this is its appeal as Keynes wrote on the completeness of the Ricardian victory:

> "That it reached conclusions quite different from what the ordinary uninstructed person would expect, added... to its intellectual prestige. That its teaching, translated into practice, was austere and often unpalatable, lent it virtue. That it was adapted to carry a vast and consistent logical superstructure, gave it beauty" (Keynes, 1936: 33).

The problem with neoclassical pedagogy is threefold:

First, a disconnect between what is taught as subject matter and how the world works. Consider a flyer sent by Hugo Radice in 1969, a Cambridge University postgraduate student in economics.[4] Many of us who study or

---

[4] The flyer led to a Conference held in London, January 1970, which developed the Conference of Socialist Economics an important institution in developing heterodox economics in the UK; and the *Bulletin of the Conference of Socialist Economists* which in 1976 was superseded by *Capital and Class* (Lee, 2009: 127-130)

teach economics feel that much of our subject matter is irrelevant and meaningless in the face of the intense social and economic problems of the world. For the most part, economics takes the existing capitalist system for granted, and is concerned solely with making it work more efficiently, or with making marginal adjustments which are totally inadequate. Furthermore, economists persistently deny that economic problems are inevitably social and political problems as well (quoted in Lee, 2009: 127).

Simply put, neoclassical economics has failed to construct a workable model that reflects the world in which we live, while "critical thought is pushed aside to make room for apocryphal stories of how human selfishness in an unfettered market environment leads to social progress" Magnuson (2012: 13). Rather than teach students how real firms operate in real industries, students are 'bullied' (Fullbook, 2009, passim) into accepting basic axioms as true, which is anathema to science (Fullbrook, 2009).

Students are then asked to use these axioms in order to analyze hypothetical firms in idealized industries, with "ficticious values invented at the desk of the textbook author in order to fit the courageous assumptions necessary for developing the respective economics model" (Otsch and Kappeller 2010: 17).

Second, the wilful ignorance of the social sciences and the physical sciences, particularly physics and mathematics:

> "In other sciences, chaos theory, complexity analysis and their close cousin evolutionary theory have had profound impacts. It shows how isolated economics has become from the scientific mainstream of the late 20th and early twenty-first century that such ignorant views could be commonplace" (Keen, 2012: 410).

Third, neoclassical pedagogy is anti-pluralist. Instead of enabling students to grasp the complexity of our problems with a multi-faceted emphasis on different theoretical and empirical approaches, neoclassical economists train students to think like economists – as if all economists think alike – and that only one perspective exists, while denying the legitimacy of all others. Partly this is due to the "incestuous relationship between capitalism and economics" (Dowd, 2004: xiii) whereby neoclassical economists are ideological apologists for the business community and capitalism" (Lee, 2009: 49).

So anyone who crticizes the established orthodoxy or thinks beyond the conventional boundaries is instantly attacked as a 'troublemaker and revolutionary' and/or bullied, vilified, black-listed, or worse. Take Diane Coyle's chastisement of John Kenneth Galbraith, as one example among many, the reason many economists think Galbraith wasn't one of us lies in his methodology. His work covers the terrain of economics... but it uses the methods of sociology and history... many of us spurn Galbraith because he wasn't a modeler (Coyle, 2007: 232). This is notwithstanding Galbraith's presidency of the American Economic Association and his authorship of numerous books explaining in lucid prose how the economy works.[5]

And needless to say only one conceptualization of a modeler is taught, tolerated and accepted for publication in the leading neoclassical journals. Economists who challenge the accepted dogma and/or develop alternative model conceptualizations are ostracized, as Lee writes:

> "it is not just that [heterodoxy] represented *no* research but that they represented (to use a phrase that is becoming popular with mainstream economists) anti-economists and being the enemy of economics such research and researchers should be cleansed from the profession" (Lee, 2009: 175-176).

In this sense neoclassical pedagogy is no different from fundamentalism marked by "intolerant zealots presenting themselves as the true guardians of

---

[5] The invidious term 'one of us' comports with the ubiquitous statement found in neoclassical textbooks that the goal is to teach students to think like an economist-as if we all think alike -- its constricting and conformist overtones send shivers down the spine of anyone with an open mind. Shouldn't our goal be to educate students so that they understand history, sociology, psychology, etc., and can work with other social scientists to address the many problems of our generation? No wonder neoclassical economists cannot understand power and the historical evolution of institutions.

orthodoxy" (Bruce, 2008: 2, 100). If we don't tolerate fundamentalism in our universities why should we tolerate the teaching of neoclassical economics?

We have abnegated the lofty goal of educating our students in lieu of the easier (yet ethically questionable) goal of prosyletization.

3 Solutions

I am inspired by William Lloyd Garrison, who began publishing *The Liberator* in 1831 and vowed to continue until the abominable injustice of slavery was outlawed. Our generation is also enslaved by an outdated and unrealistic neoclassical economics that ignores pressing environmental realities and inures its practitioners to our generation's many problems. As Keynes wrote on the Ricardian victory, "That it could explain much social injustice and apparent cruelty as an inevitable incident in the scheme of progress, and the attempt to change such things as likely on the whole to do more harm than good, commended it to authority" (Keynes 1936: 33). Reforming and reconceptualization of economics education is our most important task.

As founding editor of *the International Journal of Pluralism and Economics Education,* it is assumed that I fully endorse pluralism as a ubiquitous solution.[6] On the contrary I feel that pluralism is a necessary but not sufficient condition for the reconceptulization of economics education.

While different definitions of pluralism exist (is this surprising?) a simple definition that conveys its essence is, "a mutual respect for the legitimacy of competing views." Perhaps one reason for the different definitions of pluralism is that it exists on several levels – ontological, epistemological, methodological and pedagogical (Negru, 2009).

Pluralism is necessary (but not sufficient) for the following reasons. One, pluralism ensures vitality and innovation since, "in ideas, as in nature, *variety*

---

[6] For an introduction to the historical evolution of pluralism please see (Negru, 2009; 2010). The objective of the IJPEE is to reconceptualize and reform economics education and to foster and encourage inquisitive cooperation between the many disciplines in economics and among the social sciences.

is the evolutionary fuel. When pluralism and variety disappear, innovation and progress may slow to a halt... Pluralism is necessary for innovation and scientific advance" (Hodgson, 1999: 13, emphasis in original). Variety gives competition and competition in the realm of ideas is necessary for economics to advance, and can only do so if "it is genuinely pluralist, stimulating full competition in the market place of ideas" (van Staveren, 2011: 123) The antithesis of pluralism is monism, and neoclassical economics as currently practiced is monist with fundamentalist zealots protecting against any encroachment on orthodoxy. Accordingly Lee, the "intolerant and anti-pluralist" attitude *modus operandi* of neoclassical economics has degenerated into an 'intellectual insularity' in which disciples are unaware of economic theory beyond neoclassical economics (Lee, 2009: 48).

Two, only pluralism is consistent with democracy and only a democracy in ideas is consistent with the ideals of a university, "Intellectual diversity, free inquiry, and the principle that there is no humanely accessible truth that is not in principle open to challenge are indispensable to the achievement of the central purposes of a university" (Lee, 2009: 185). And hence:

> "an intellectual faction that has a monopoly on truths and wisdom and utilizes state and/or organizational power (such as control over research and testing funding or university budgets) to maintain and enhance this monopoly, that rejects the unsettled character of all human knowledge, and that rejects a diversity of approaches to unsettled questions is not compatible with the idea and nature of a university" (Lee, 2010: 185-186).

Three, pluralism exposes students to different viewpoints, "so they can debate their relative merits and develop an awareness about the weaknesses and strengths of competing theories" (Ostch and Kapeela, 2010: 23). Not only is pluralism consistent with a democracy of ideas and a democratic society, but democratic interaction can lead to a 'transformative dialogue,' which can help move economics forward (Soderbaum and Brown, 2011).

Four, pluralism is useful because:

> "no paradigm or theoretical perspective can claim universal applicability, i.e., usefulness for all kinds of all problems. Each paradigm or theoretical perspective may have something to offer and preference for one theoretical perspective over another is... partly a matter of ideology" (Soderbaum, 2008: 10).

In other words, given "the presence of values and ideology in social science research...a complementary relationship between theoretical perspectives or paradigms, each reflecting a specific ideological viewpoint is relevant" (Soderbaum, 2008: 41). For we "cannot understand contemporary societies very well unless politics, economics, psychology, and the other social science disciplines are all brought together to study the complexities of modern life" (Bowles et al., 2005: 51).

Five, pluralism enhances student-based learning. Developing the ability to ask probing questions is empowering. It draws upon the students' analytic, global perspective taking, and valuing abilities. The assumption inherent in this approach is that students are entitled to inquire and to explore and that economic phenomena are subject to continual investigation (Davis and Emami, 2009).

Six, only pluralism can instill passion into economics; and passion is necessary to "identify redressable injustice" (Sen, 2009: vii). Passion in turn is necessary to give us the intellectual courage to help solve the problems of our generation. As Joan Robinson exhorted, "independent economists ought to be speaking up on the side of humanity" (1980: xiii). In addition, we should be ashamed to hide behind the ideological cloak of positive science, long ago jettisoned by other social scientists. Neoclassical economists, still stuck in the 19th century, have inured their students to "redressable injustice" while fastidiously extirpating passion.

And finally, if a reformed economics is to help make the world a better place – and it must – then economics must be concerned with justice, which in turn is interconnected at many levels with pluralist dialogue since:

"not only are dialogue and communication part of the subject matter of the theory of justice... it is also the case that the nature, robustness and reach of the theories proposed themselves depend on contributions from discussion and discourse" (Sen, 2009: 88-89).

To be passionate about economics requires being able to recognize injustice, which in turn requires an understanding of power and how institutions evolve, which in turn requires an open mind and a willingness to learn from other disciplines. Passion and justice are incommensurate with monism – the current modus operandi of neoclassical economics, especially at the pedagogical level.[7]

Despite the above-mentioned virtues of pluralism, it is a necessary but not sufficient element in the reformation of economics education for two reasons. First, as Fullbrook writes:

"Pluralism, both its ethos and epistemology, is extremely important, but no matter how robust it may become among economists it will never be a sufficient basis for breaking the hegemony of neoclassical economics. That will require a new cohesion of underlying economic ideas other than the neoclassical ones and which heterodox schools will in the main accept and, even more importantly, which their members will become in the practice of relating to their particular school of thought as they currently do with neoclassical ideas" (Fullbrook, 2010: 101).

Second, pluralism is currently a one-way street, "[although] heterodox economists are willing to engage in pluralism the mainstream economists generally do not reciprocate" (Lee, 2009: 283, note #26). While neoclassical economists claim to be pluralist and perhaps they are to a very limited extent

---

[7] Even Coyle admits, after almost ebullient about the advances made on the frontiers of economics, the disconnect between practice and pedagogy, "I accept that critics of mainstream economics have a point until we economists teach what we preach" (Coyle, 2007: 250) But alas, keep in mind her strict requisite of an economist!

at the methodological level (Coyle, 2007: 239-254) they are certainly not at any other level, which explains their fundamentalist 'bullying, cajoling, threatening, expelling, disparaging, etc., (Lee, 2009, passim) and their 'irrational tenacity' to hold onto cherished beliefs.

Given this intransigence, real world economists have three options. One, do nothing and to continue letting neoclassical economics dominate and influence the intellectual baggage of all citizens. But as Fred Lee emphatically writes "to do nothing is not an option" (Lee, 2009: 206). At the same time, "Economics cannot be trusted to reform its own house" (Keen, 2011: 23-4) suggesting a concerted action from real world economists.

Third, renounce any attempt at dialogue with neoclassical economics while continuing to develop a robust agenda and a vibrant real world economics research community. Fred Lee delineates what must be done to establish a robust agenda:

> "Heterodox economics [must] be taught to more students, more doctoral students be produced, and heterodox economists [must] become more professionally and theoretically engaged through joining multiple heterodox associations, subscribing to multiple heterodox journals, attending multiple heterodox conferences and engaging in open pluralistic theoretical dialogue with other heterodox economists [and must] challenge the research assessment exercises, subject benchmark statements, and the mainstream ranking of journals and departments" (Lee, 2009: 206).

Fourth, while not necessarily engaging in dialogue – which given the anti-pluralist nature of neoclassical economics is an oxymoron – to actively lessen the tenacious grip of neoclassical economics, with its almost exclusive western thinking and its self-absorption in the scientific methods of the 19th century, such is the explicit goal of the World Economics Association (Fullbrook, 2010).

The economics curriculum: towards a radical reformulation

Fifth, while not denying the efficacy of building a robust real world economics agenda and attenuating the grip of the current institutions, it is also important to reform neoclassical education head-on. If we don't, they will continue to bully, exclude, disparage and discredit, while using the powers of the state to cement their ascendancy, dominate and influence public policy, and to infect the baggage of the intellectual elite; while we will be relegated to the status of second class citizens, regardless of how vigorous and robust our research agenda.

It is in the best interest of real world economics, economics in general, our students, and the future well-being of our planet to add the reconceptualizion of neoclassical economics and pedagogy to our agenda. To rest content with building our own research program is self-defeating, as echoed by Zola's Charvet in the *The Belly of Paris*, "Class self-interest is one of the most powerful allies of tyranny" (2007: 139). In other words, minding your own business – literally – gives a carte blanche to the continuation of the status quo and allows the "ruling elites to continue to control the discourse" (Leech, 2012: 96). Thus, in my view, attacking the provenance of the lack of pluralism in neoclassical economics – education – is paramount.

Before we address specific solutions, it is perhaps necessary to briefly address the question – as real world economists, should we continue teaching neoclassical economics in one form or another? Several reasons are usually given to do so. One, if we are to change neoclassical economics we must understand it. Two, neoclassical economics is, for better or worse, the *lingua franca*, so one must understand it. Three, it is often the foundation upon which policy is built. Four, knowledge of neoclassical economics can chip away at the edifice and establish ports of entry in order to establish a pluralist dialogue. Five, exposure to neoclassical economics is necessary In order to understand multiple viewpoints.

Although I see merit in the above arguments, I respectfully disagree with my colleagues that we should continue to teach neoclassical economics. I don't know of any other science that insists on teaching failed, out-dated thinking, particularly since "neoclassical economics is not really about the economy, so how can it be useful for the analysis of institutional structures such as markets" (Hodgson, 1999: 44).

And as Keen writes:

> "Neoclassical economics, far from being the font of economic wisdom, is actually the biggest impediment to understanding how the economy actually works – and why, periodically, it has serious breakdowns. If we are ever to have an economic theory that actually describes the economy, let alone help us manage it, neoclassical economics has to go" (Keen, 2011: 15).

A discipline should move on; there should be no reason why the rest of the profession feels obliged to continue to teach this stuff. Perhaps in a history of thought course; or in a course on logic; or as part of a course that introduces multiple viewpoints, but never alone, and not in a course on the economy, since "neoclassical theory... does not show how real markets work" (Otsch and Kapeller, 2010: 21).

It is time for a radical break with orthodoxy:

> "it is futile to expect a great advancement in the sciences from overlaying and implanting new things on the old; a new beginning has to be made from the lowest foundations, unless one is content to go round in circles for ever, with meagre, almost negligible results" (Bacon, 1620 [2000], Book I, CXXIV: 96).

The opportunity cost is too high to continue teaching neoclassical economics, especially if we are to develop sufficient knowledge to help solve our generation's problems, which can only come from a vigorous real world economics research agenda which is first and foremost concerned with the social provisioning process (Lee, 2009: 8). And conversely, the opportunity cost is too high to acquiesce to the continued teaching of neoclassical economics.

But in the spirit of pluralism, isn't neoclassical economics necessary, especially in light of the virtues mentioned earlier? Yes of course, but only if neoclassical economics can reciprocate and practice pluralism – as of now it cannot. Thus, our goal is to reconceptualize neoclassical economics so its practitioners are no longer obdurate and unwilling to notice, discuss and accept alternatives. Only then can the "universal mindset of the neoclassical project" (Fullbrook, 2010) be broken. Easier said than done! And, like William Lloyd Garrison, we are in this for the long haul; but nevertheless, this is a necessary and important battle.

But how to teach open-mindedness and tolerance? That such a question must be asked is testimony to the sorry state of economics education; I don't know of any other discipline where this is an issue. While much attention has been devoted to 'how to' for individual courses and 'how to' redesign the curriculum the remainder of this paper will focus on a neglected issue: that given the contested nature of economics (Lee, 2010, passim) and the highly ideological content and anti-pluralism of neoclassical economics, it is necessary for a set of prerequisite courses to be incorporated into the economics curriculum.[8] This comports with the necessity of an integrative and multi-faceted attack on the citadel of neoclassical economics, which in turn requires numerous ports of entry, including students, university officials, and the public (Reardon, 2004). Offering a set of prerequisites targets students by enabling them to withstand (and hopefully parry) the inevitable ideological neoclassical onslaught from later courses. Thus, this suggestion will help chip away at the neoclassical edifice from within.

Hill and Myatt hope "to help stoke the fires of revolution" (2010: 2) from below by peppering their text with '71 Questions for Your Professor'. While many professors welcome the give-and-take in a college classroom and relish the opportunity to learn from their students, these questions go far beyond prepping students with thoughtful questions. They are designed to reveal the ignorance of neoclassical economics professors of their own discipline, their lack of understanding of alternative theories and their willful neglect of conflicting evidence. That Hill and Myatt's book was written in the first place suggests the seriousness of this problem.

So when a neoclassical professor bullies students into assuming that all consumers are rational or when a textbook claims that markets, left

---

[8] See various issues of the *International Journal of Pluralism and Economics Education* for helpful articles.

uninhibited, arrive at a beneficent equilibrium for all students rather than absorbing this like a sponge, can think for themselves, develop their own minds, and challenge their professors.[9]

4 Establishing prerequisites for the economics major

Otsch and Kapeller suggest reforming the economics curriculum with, "additional courses in related areas such as economic history, sociology, political science or philosophy in order to provide students with some context knowledge on economic systems (What is the history of an economy? Where do its institutions come from? What's the relation between economy and society?" (Otsch and Kapeller, 2010: 23). Once it is decided that pluralism is to be adopted at the department level, it then becomes necessary to actively work with faculty and administrators to develop a curriculum. The following is an extreme version which requires a complete and fundamental overhaul, which might be unpalatable to many departments. Nevertheless, it is possible to implement some of the reforms piecemeal.

The first issue to discuss is whether a set of prerequisite courses is warranted, for either students or teachers? How can they be expected to jump right into the program? Within this second stage it is important to devise a set of prerequisites for every student majoring in economics before they begin their actual study. Offering prerequisites targets students by enabling them to withstand (and hopefully parry) the inevitable ideological neoclassical onslaught from later courses, and can provide a fruitful foundation from which pluralism can flourish. That we even need prereqs is testimony to how fundamentally flawed economics education has become.

---

[9] While numerous examples abound, one in particular struck me for its insidious ignorance, "Economists often personify market forces by saying that the market works with an invisible hand. RIDDLE: How many economists does it take to change a light bulb? ANSWER: None. The market will do it" (Froeb and McCann, 2010: 99). Left unanswered, of course, is ignorance over what constitutes the market, who makes the light bulb and the power relationship between the decision makers and the workers who actually install them, and a myriad of other questions.

The economics curriculum: towards a radical reformulation

Is it enough to assume that pluralism learned elsewhere in the university curriculum is sufficient for the economic major? John Siegfried argues that within the overall university setting the algorithmic thinking typically emphasized in neoclassical economics (involving deduction) is in short supply, and thus economics departments, at least neoclassical ones augment a much needed supply (Siegfried, 2009: 219). The prerequisites discussed below can help students themselves decide on the usefulness of the algorithmic knowledge. I have thought a lot about such courses; here is an outline of my suggestions:

a. *World Literature* – There is no better primer on the diversity of the human condition than fiction. Properly taught, fiction can explain the myriad forms of behavior and human predicaments as good as, or even better, than any individual academic discipline. As Johann Goethe's main character explains in *The Sorrows of Young Werther*, "things in this world seldom come down to an either-or-down decision, and possible courses of action, and feelings, are as infinitely various as kinds of noses on the gamut from hooked to snubbed" (Goethe, 1774 [1989]: 58). And to parry the highly gratuitous claim that all people are rational, here is Goethe's Werther again, "Human kind is merely human, and that jot of rational sense a man may possess is of little or no avail once passion is raging and the bounds of human nature are hemming him in" (Goethe, 1774 [1989]: 64). And the poet Imlac in Samuel Johnson's *The History of Rasselas, Prince of Abissina*:

> "The truth is, that no mind is much employed upon the present: recollection and anticipation fill up almost all our moments. Our passions are joy and grief, love and hatred, hope and fear. Of joy and grief the past is the object, and the future of hope and fear; even love and hatred respect the past, for the cause must have been before the effect" (Johnson, 1759 [1976]).

Fiction can also efficaciously describe injustice and can be a powerful call to action. And there are no better examples than Zola's *Germinal* and Upton Sinclair's *The Jungle*. If the goal of economics is to understand the provisioning process and help the world become a better place, then fiction and pluralism are natural allies. As Sen writes, "we have to be able to react

221

spontaneously and resist inhumanity whenever it occurs. If this is to happen, the individual and social opportunities for developing and exercising moral imagination have to be expanded" (Sen, 2005: 278). While fiction is obviously not history, quite often the apt descriptions and careful dialogue are more evocative and stick in one's memory far longer than any historical description, and thus are instrumentally more efficacious. And for me, one of the most powerful images in Dickens' *Tale of Two Cities* is Madame Defarge's vigilant knitting of names of the condemned once the French Revolution begins. This captures the patient vengeance of the long-oppressed peasants far better than any historical narrative.

This is not the place to debate what type of fiction works best – poetry, novels or drama or even which of the works are best; rather just to place the argument that prerequisites are necessary bulwark against future intimidation and bullying, and fiction is most apt.

While much has been written on necessity of reinstating history of economic thought into the curriculum (Dow, 2009) the prerequisites discussed here will prepare students well for such an important course.

b. *History of Capitalist Systems* – It is essential for economics majors to understand how the present system of capitalism has evolved, the role of government and how people respond to contemporary problems by constructing appropriate institutions. There is nothing natural or inevitable about capitalism or any economic system. Neoclassical economics, which is taught from a historical vacuum, tries to prove that capitalism, albeit with less government intervention, can ideally allocate resources.

A course in the History of Capitalist Systems will discuss how and why capitalism developed, who loses and who benefits, as well as the necessary institutions to construct a better society. Such a course is also beneficial since:

> "History by giving context and examples, helps when it comes to thinking about the present world. It aids in formulating questions, and without good questions it is difficult to begin to think in a coherent way at all. Knowledge

of history suggests what sort of information might be needed to answer those questions" (MacMillan, 2008: 167).

c. *History of Intellectual Thought* – A course in the history of intellectual thought will elucidate how ideas developed in response to certain problems; and students will understand how and why neoclassical economic theory was developed. And history, within the liberal arts tradition is a natural ally of pluralism: "History can help us to make sense of a complicated world, but it also warns of the dangers of assuming that there is only one possible way of looking at things or only one course of action" (MacMillan, 2008: 168). And what better introduction to the excitement of college learning than a course in the intellectual development of ideas?

And as the poet Imlac speaks in Samuel Johnson's *The History of Rasselas, Prince of Abissina:*

> "there is no part of history so generally useful as that which relates the progress of the human mind, the gradual improvement of reason, the successive advances of science, the vicissitudes of learning and ignorance, which are the light and darkness of thinking beings, the extinction and resuscitation of arts, and all the revolutions of the intellectual world" (Johnson, 1759 [1976]: 104-105).

d. *Quantum Physics* – not only are many of the accoutrements of today's economy such as the CD, laser, computer, MRIs and traffic lights the result of the intellectual achievements of quantum physics, but no better example exists of the scientific willingness to test and experiment and the openness to reform theory if necessary than quantum physics. In addition, "the rise of quantum theory is... an outstanding example of the revisionism imposed by physical reality upon the thinking of the scientist" (Polkinghorne, 2002: 85). This is because, "every interpretation of nature which has a chance to be true is achieved by instances, and suitable and relevant experiments, in which sense only gives a judgement on the experiment, while the experiment gives a judgement on nature and the thing itself" (Bacon, 1620 [2000], Book I, L: 45). Compare this to the dismal record of neoclassical economics (Keen, 2011, passim) and economics textbooks which "often present hypotheses and policy prescriptions with surprisingly little or no supporting evidence, or (worse) ignoring inconvenient contrary evidence" (Hill and Myatt, 2010: 6).

No better example exists of how physics progresses as a science than the discovery of the Higgs boson. In a paean to the discipline of physics, *The Economist* wrote that it was the crowning achievement of one of history's most successful scientific theories. It is also certainly the beginning of that theory's undoing, and its replacement by something better. In science, with its constant search for the truth, this is something to celebrate (The Economist, 2012).

e. *Philosophy* – An introductory course, perhaps with a focus on ethics, aptly illustrates the tradition of philosophy for debating ideas within a pluralist context and the vanity of human understanding. As Bacon writes, 'The human understanding from its own peculiar nature willingly supposes a greater order and regularity in things it finds, and though there are many things in nature which are unique and full of disparities, it invents parallels and non-existent connection" (Bacon, 1620 [2000], Book I, XLV: 42).

While agreement exists for a need for ethical standards within economics (DeMartino, 2010), today's students of neoclassical economics are taught that not only will the market correctly allocate resources, but there is no need to worry about ethics, since the market, will correctly make such decisions. Consider, for example, a popular managerial economics textbook claiming that the most important lesson of business is, "identifying assets in low-valued uses and devising ways to profitably move them to higher-valued ones" (Freob and McCann, 2010: 16). But what is meant by value and how do we conceptualize it? Whose perspective do we use? What ethical standards should help us to decide which assets to move and how to move them? Philosophy can also help attach meaning to deliberately vague words like "efficiency, rationality, choice, freedom often found in economics textbooks but seldom discussed" (Fullbrook, 2009: 19).

5 Objections to the prerequisites

There are two objections to this proposal. First, these courses will constrict the course offerings for the economics major. But economics education is not working – it is not educating our students; so, if one of the end results is either a diminution in the traditional number of courses or the content of existing courses, so be it. And besides, these suggested prerequisites are fundamental to a university education and will produce better educated (rather than trained) economists, able to converse intelligently with all social scientists. Such prerequisites will also enable students to parry the inevitable ideological onslaught in later neoclassical courses.

Second, who can teach such courses? Certainly not neoclassical economists – who underscore that this proposal must be part and parcel of a long term planning strategy.

While we can debate whether these prerequisites are too little or not enough and or whether they are the right ones, the basic point is that in order for pluralism to become effective, not only must the future educators be educated in how to teach a revised economics, but students must be prepared to be receptive to pluralism. And students must be intellectually prepared to parry the inevitable ideological onslaught from future courses in the program. Starting immediately with the traditional macro/micro courses is a recipe for failure. Of course the main obstacle is such attention to prerequisites will attenuate the ability of the department to offer more in-depth courses.

It is incumbent to design the exact course sequence. Once again it is not imperative that every course share equally in the development of pluralism but that overall the courses integrate and that traditional silos disappear. It is also imperative to remember that we are on a novel pathway, where we know the destination, but where we still need to dialogue and deliberate about the most efficacious way to get there.

While much talk has been made in light of the financial crisis to revise the curriculum, for the most part the emphasis is to tinker along the edges, with the traditional format of introductory macro/micro courses, followed by intermediate macro/micro courses, then statistics, econometrics with a heavy dose of calculus in order to understand the optimization problem, followed by the traditional upper level courses such as trade, development, labor and monetary economics, to remain intact. After all, this is the quintessence of neoclassical economics:

> "the essence of what is taught in most applied field courses is the same, regardless of the specific questions and institutional context of the subject matter... Economists teach the basic principles of economics—opportunity costs, marginal analysis, the role of prices as signals, incentives, specialization, unintended consequences—regardless of the [course]. These ideas are the same whether the applied field course focuses on factor markets or product markets" (Seigfried, 2009: 219).

If economics is to become useful once again, it must identify our generation's problems and actively tailor its curriculum to help solve them. I suggest reworking the curriculum along major themes – one for each year. Of course, these are subjective, with no pretense to be definitive. In my opinion the biggest problems of our generation are: (1) poverty and the inability of existing economics systems to allow individuals to provision for basic goods and services; (2) the crushing and debilitating burden of credit and debt; and (3) looming environmental catastrophe. These problems obviously are not set in stone, but if economics is to become useful again, than the curriculum must be redesigned to enable our students to eventually solve them.

I propose to restructure the economics curriculum along the following themes for each of the four years of the degree program. Within a given year individual modules should be offered ranging from one to four credits. My objective is merely suggestive; and I hope that readers can help flesh out a specific course offering. Also, these are overall themes, specific analysis and inter-relationship to specific units such as the firm, and the consumer can be integrated as demand requires.

6 Description of the proposal

6.1 Year One: exclusively devoted to prereqs; no economics course taken.

6.2 Year Two: Political Economy, Money and Credit

6.2.1 Five Modules

Module 1: Introduction to Economics: Part One. What is economics? What is political economy and how has the discipline evolved? How does economics relate to other social sciences? (Suggestion: 1 credit.)

Module 2: The different schools of thought within economics. I suggest a specific three credit module delineating the specific attributes of each ideology that will be used during the four years: Marxist, classical, post-Keynesian, Austrian, feminist, etc. This module will be team-taught by the faculty using them. The emphasis should be on points of contact- how students relate and segue into other views once they know one view. What are the similarities and differences? Note that this is the opposite of neoclassical economics which ignores and delegitimizes other views. I suggest to make the views come alive discuss each ideology within the context of unemployment, which most students understand, even without any economics background, as a problem central to any economic system. Keep in mind that this is novel territory, that there is a natural reluctance among social sciences to extend beyond the narrow interests in which they feel most comfortable. (Suggestion: 2 credits.)

Module 3: Modeling the Economy. Understanding economic dynamics, feedbacks, system dynamics and how to develop simple dynamic models of the economy using the right maths. How does this system work? How does the system influence individual behavior and how vice versa? (Suggestion: 2 credits.)

Module 4: Understanding finance, credit and money. How credit is established and its role in a market economy. Understanding the role of debt and what money is. The endogenous nature of money. What is the role of finance in capitalism? (Suggestion: 3 credits.)

Module 5: Communication. Graduates of economic programs are notorious for their poor communications skills. Perhaps this course can be taught by a journalist. How can we understand contemporary events and communicate them to others?

6.3 Year Three: Focus on Poverty

6.3.1 Five Modules

Module 1: Power. What is power and how it is used. Introduction to colonialism, neocolonialism, development and underdevelopment (Suggestion: 2 credits).

Module 2: Poverty. Definition, measurement, conception and solutions for poverty (Suggestion: 2 credits.)

Module 3: The firm and the evolution of industry structure. Emphasis on heterodox microeconomics, combining especially post-Keynesianism, Sraffian and evolutionary economics in order to understand the firm (Suggestion: 4 credits.)

Module 4: Trade and global institutions (Suggestion: 2 credits.)

Module 5: Role of government at all levels (Suggestion: 2 credits.)

6.4 Year Four: Focus on Environmental Sustainability and Global Warming

6.4.1 Five Modules

Module 1: What is sustainability? What does it mean and how can it be implemented? (Suggestion: 2 credits.)

Module 2: What is growth, can growth be sustainable? How do we measure and conceptualize growth? (Suggestion: 2 credits.)

Module 3: What are resources and what is the environment? Focus on externalities/public goods (Suggestion: 2 credits.)

Module 4: How can economics be used to understand climate change and global warming? (Suggestion: 2 credits.)

Module 5: A capstone course in which the existing ideologies are used within a pluralist context in order to solve an existing problem (Suggestion: 5 credits.)

6.5 Emphasis of Years Two, Three and Four

6.5.1 Emphasis of Year Two
Team teaching with history, anthropology and sociology. All different ideologies to be used during the four years should be introduced. Students should be taught the various ideologies to be used within a pluralist context to help understand how economic systems work. Student should be exposed in all modules to the contributions made by earlier economists; that this, they should receive a heavy dosage of both economic history and history of economic thought. It is important to emphasize the necessary coordination amongst all the courses and faculty involved. Nothing during the four years should be done ad hoc or without consideration of the larger overall objective. This remains preponderant and interested stakeholders should engage in constant dialogue.

6.5.2 Emphasis of Years Three and Four
Given the diverse courses and the diverse expected faculty expected to teach the above course, it is important to integrate the modules and the years along several themes:

- Excise the artificial and misleading divider between macro and micro.
- Resuscitate and emphasize the richness of history of thought; history proffers lots of lessons to be learned (Dow, 2009).
- Emphasis on pluralism throughout with humble consideration of what we don't know which can act as *a segue* into to other disciplines. It is the arrogance of economics and economists that has precluded any effort at pluralism.
- Given the paucity of alternative ideologies understood by most neoclassical economists, team teaching is essential, along with

alternative pedagogies such as student-learning, service learning and problem-based learning.

- Emphasize in all modules the dynamic nature of the economy and how dynamic modules can be constructed. What is the best way to combine/unite the different models constructed?

If existing faculty are not capable of teaching such modules then perhaps some courses can be contracted out to those who can – perhaps only on a limited basis – since doing so can be quite contentious.

Speaking of contention, another contentious issue, but well-deserving of discussion is: when should pluralism be introduced within the curriculum? Immediately or only after a foundation is well-established? If the latter, what should this foundation be and who should determine it? If we wait until a good foundation in neoclassical economics is established than unfortunately there could be a visceral reaction against any suggested alternative:

> "Once a man's (sic) understanding has settled on something (either because it is an accepted belief or because it pleases him), it draws everything else also to support and agree with it. And if it encounters a larger number of more powerful countervailing examples, it either fails to notice them, or disregards them, or makes fine distinctions to dismiss and reject them, and all this with much dangerous prejudice, to preserve the authority of its first conceptions" (Bacon, 2000 [1620], Book I, XLVI: 42).

This recalcitrance is reinforced by the deliberate attitude of neoclassical economics to inculcate monism along with a hegemonic superiority of economics and the economic approach.

A final contentious issue is whether to even teach neoclassical economics at all; or if to teach it, how much and what specific courses. Most pluralists agree that within the spirit of pluralism, it should be taught, not the very least because it is the lingua franca, and that in order to understand the myriad criticisms of neoclassical economics, it is necessary to understand neoclassical economics. I respectfully disagree: what other social science (or science) continues to teach failed, out-dated material? And this failed thinking is part of the problem:

> "Neoclassical economics, far from being the font of economic wisdom, is actually the biggest impediment to understanding how the economy actually works – and why, periodically, it has serious breakdowns. If we are ever to have an economic theory that actually describes the economy, let alone help us manage it, neoclassical economics has to go" (Keen 2011: 15).

If we are to help solve the problems of our generation, than our students must be educated – and not proselytized – so why should we teach what is part of the problem? A discipline should move on and discard the stuff that is no longer useful Sure, students should learn the neoclassical model as one way of understanding reality but it should not become the focal point of all courses and of all textbooks as it does now.

7 Notes on assessment of pluralism

While it might be assumed that this can wait, it is advised to have this done before implementation for several reasons. One, the specific assessment clearly establishes the overall goals and objectives of pluralism and allows its structure to be amenable to assessment. Based on our earlier discussion, it is important to properly align the objectives of pluralism with what and how it will be assessed. The objectives of implementing pluralism must be clearly articulated during stage one, and then carefully thought out and implemented during stage two. Both stages must be carefully coordinated which is both the lynchpin to making the system work and providing effective feedback so we can progress.

An additional point to be discussed: are we asking every professor in every course to be pluralist, or just the overall department? If the former, then assessment must be devised accordingly: the individual course with results differing according to the individual instructor. If the latter, then individual courses do not matter in terms of assessment, but only how they integrate into the whole; thus assessment on the adequacy of the department in teaching pluralism, becomes the focus, rather than on the competency of the individual. Does the department do an adequate job of teaching pluralism?

Within the pluralist literature assessment is in need of research and I would encourage pluralists to develop and conceptualize an assessment procedure that rewards and encourages pluralism. It is also likely that the assessment results will not meet expectations; thus requiring a redoing of the initial objectives, to close the loop so to speak, which is of course, the purpose of assessment. This process might require several iterations, but in the meantime, the underlying conditions might change as well, thus requiring flexibility in the construction of the assessment procedure.

Since pluralism is a respect for understanding other views and that one of our objectives in teaching pluralism is for our students to eventually work with other social scientists within a context of mutual respect and openness, any assessment should focus on the willingness and ability to understand and conceptualize alternative views. The most successful ingredient in teaching pluralism is not to teach every view within the curriculum, but to teach a respect for differences and to teach a willingness to learn from others and to cooperate. So implementing pluralism is teaching an attitude, or an outlook about how to get along with others – albeit an attitude consistent with the objectives of a university. Easier said than done!

But this suggests increased focus on assessment within a pluralism framework, which is very different from the current assessment, dominated by neoclassical ideology (Lee, 2009). And given the testing procedure, a student educated in a pluralist course would tend to score lower than a non-pluralist student, since the former is capable of questioning the faulty logic or sloppy deductive reasoning. As Fred Lee advocates, if heterodox economics is to succeed, (by success he terms an equal standing with neoclassical economics) then it is crucial to reform the assessment procedure:

> "But what is really necessary to do is for heterodox economics [to] challenge the research assessment exercises, subject benchmark statements, and the mainstream ranking of journals and departments through,

perhaps, developing their own methods of research assessments and ranking of journals and departments" (Lee, 2009: 206).

I agree and would also extend Lee's argument to pluralism – it cannot succeed within the neoclassical dominated assessment procedure. So in order for pluralism to succeed at the department level, we must (or at least some of us) as Fred Lee suggests, diligently work to change the assessment procedure.

Bacon's insight is apropos in deciding how to assess pluralism, "it is better to know as much as we need to know, and yet think we do not know everything, than to think that we know everything, and yet know none of the things we need to know" (Bacon, 1620 [2000], CXXVI: 97). Add to this a willingness to admit ignorance, a humble recognition of what we don't know and a humble willingness to work with other social scientists and we have the recipe for a successful conceptualization, implementation and assessment of pluralism.

8 Criticisms and shortcomings of implementation

An obvious criticism beyond the vested interests opposed to pluralism is that if we are to teach our students pluralism then who is going to teach the teachers? How can we ask our professors to commit to pluralism when most have never been exposed to it? This is a serious problem and suggests that pluralism can only successfully be implemented over the long-term.

A second problem is obtaining the resources to implement pluralism. Resources are needed to train, conduct workshops, and in some cases hire new faculty. In an age of ubiquitous budget cuts, obtaining any extra funds might be difficult, but nevertheless, an inability to do so will favor the status quo.

A third criticism is that no one recipe exists for implementing pluralism, although not necessarily a shortcoming it suggests the potential for conflict and disagreement. Pluralists should be pluralist in conceptualizing and implementing pluralism. Easier said than done!

9 Conclusion

Pluralism despite its potential shortcomings and potential liabilities in implementation is far better than any alternative and deserves serious contemplation:

> "Pluralism instills empathy, dialogue, humility, and understanding. Monism [its opposite], by filtering out different views, prevents one from knowing which view is better in certain situations. Monism is antithetical to pluralism and antithetical to education. It proselytizes rather than educates . . . pluralism enables student choice; monism constrains and disables" (Reardon, 2009b: 267).

It is the juxtaposition of different ideologies that provides the secret for solving the problems of our generation, as Graeber notes, "the one thing we can be confident of is that history is not over, and that surprising new ideas will certainly emerge" (2011: 384). We need a new way of thinking, but not just the inductive thinking proposed by Bacon at the dawn of the scientific revolution. We need new thinking that juxtaposes heretofore different ideologies and the social sciences and sciences. We need a holistic pluralism that goes beyond the traditional disciplines. Any new thinking will emanate and flourish within the context of pluralism.

As Minsky noted, "the economic theory that is taught in colleges and graduate schools – the equipment of students and practitioners of economics over the past thirty years and the intellectual basis of economic policy in capitalist democracies – is seriously flawed" (Minsky, 2008: 4). Rather than continue to teach the same topics, while continuing to ignore the same ones as well, we must devise and implement a new curriculum – a new world order it you will, one that is consistent with the overall goals of pluralism.

In this chapter I attempted to provide a *modus operandi* for the implementation of pluralism. I am under no pretense that this is the only effective method; far from it! We need a global dialogue from all interested pluralists.

References

Bacon, F. (1620 [2000]) *The New Organon*. Cambridge, UK: Cambridge University Press.

Bowles, S., Edwards, M. and Roosevelt, F. (2005) *Understanding Capitalism: Competition, Command and Change*, Oxford University Press: New York.

Bruce, S. (2008) *Fundamentalism*, Cambridge, UK: Polity Press, 2nd ed.

Coyle, D. (2007) *The Soulful Science – What Economists Really Do and Why it Matters*. Princeton, N.J: Princeton University Press.

DeMartino, G. (2010) *The Economist's Oath - On the Need for and Content of Professional Economic Ethics*. Oxford, UK: Oxford University Press.

Dickens, C. (1859 [2000]) *A Tale of Two Cities,* New York: Penguin.

Dow, S. C. (2009) 'History of Thought, Methodology and Pluralism', In: Reardon, J. (ed.), *The Handbook of Pluralist Economics Education,* London: Routledge, pp. 43-53.

Dowd, D. (2004) *Capitalism and its Economics – A Critical History*, London: Pluto.

Froeb, L. and McCann, B. (2010) *Managerial Economics- A Problem Solving Approach*, Mason, Ohio: Cengage Learning, 2nd ed.

Fullbrook, E. (2009) 'The Meltdown and Economics Textbooks', In: Reardon, J.(ed). *The Handbook of Pluralist Economics Education,* London: Routledge, pp. 17-23.

Fullbrook, E. (2010) 'How to Bring Economics into the 3rd millennium by 2020', *Real-world economics review*, 54, 27: 89-102, September, http://www.paecon.net/PAEReview/issue54/Kessler54.pdf

Goethe, J. (1774 [1989]) *The Sorrows of Young Werther,* London: Penguin.

Graeber, D. (2011) '*Debt - The First 5000 Years',* New York: Melville House.

Hill, R. and Myatt, T. (2010) *The Economics Anti-Textbook - A Critical Thinker's Guide to Microeconomics*. London: Zed Books.

Hodgson, G. (1999*) Evolution and Institutions – On Evolutionary Economics and the Evolution of Economics*. Cheltenham, UK: Edward Elgar.

Johnson, S. (1759 [1976]) *The History of Rasselas, Prince of Abissina*. New York: Penguin.

Keen, S. (2011) *Debunking Economics - The Naked Emperor Dethroned?* London: Zed Books. 2nd ed.

Keynes, J. M. (1936) *The General Theory of Employment Interest and Money*, New York, Harcourt: Brace and Company.

Lee, F. (2009) *A History of Heterodox Economics - Challenging the Mainstream in the Twentieth Century*, London: Routledge.

Leech, G. (2012) *Capitalism - A Structural Genocide*. London: Zed Books.

MacMillan, M. (2009) *Dangerous Games - The Uses and Abuses of History*. New York: Modern Library.

Magnuson, J. (2012) 'Economists and Education in A World without Oil' *Interconnections,* Issue 8: 7-15.

Mankiw, N. G. (2009) 'That Freshman Course Won't Be the Same', *New York Times*, http://www.nytimes.com/2009/05/24/business/economy/24view.html.   May   24, Accessed May 24, 2009.

Marshall, A. (1920 [1946]) *Principles of Economics*. London: MacMillan.

Minksy, H. (2008) *Stabilizing an Unstable Economy*, New York: McGraw Hill.

Negru, I. (2009) 'Reflections on Pluralism in Economics', *International Journal of Pluralism and Economics Education*, I, 1.2: 7- 21.

Negru, I. (2010) 'Plurality to Pluralism in Economics Pedagogy: the Role of Critical Thinking', *International Journal of Pluralism and Economics Education*, I, 3: 185-193.

Otsch, W. and Kapeller, J. (2010) 'Perpetuating the Failure: Economic Education and the Current Crisis', *Journal of Social Science Education,* 9, 2: 16-25.

Polkinghorne, J. (2002) *Quantum Theory- A Very Short Introduction*, Oxford: Oxford University Press.

Raffaelli, T.; Becattini, G.; Caldari, K. and Dardi, M. (2010) 'Introduction" In: Raffaelli, T.; Becattini, G.; Caldari, K. and Dardi, M. (eds.) *The Impact of Alfred Marshall's Ideas- The Global Diffusion of His Work*. Cheltenham, UK: Edward Elgar.

Reardon, J. (2004) 'Suggestions to Effectuate a Multi-paradigmatic Approach to the Teaching of Principles of Economics', *Journal of Economic Issues,* 38 (September): 839-841.

Reardon, J. (2009) 'Conclusion' In: Reardon, Jack (ed.) *The Handbook of Pluralist Economics Education*, London: Routledge, pp. 267-268.

Reardon, J. (2010) 'Foreword", *International Journal of Pluralism and Economics Education,* I, 3: 179-184.

Robinson, J. (1980) *What are the Questions and Other Essays*. Armonk, New York: M.E. Sharpe.

Schumacher, E. F. (1973 [1989]) *Small is Beautiful- Economics as if People Mattered* New York: Harper Perennial.

Seigfried, J. (2009) 'Really Thinking Like and Economist'', In: Colander, D. and McGoldrick, K.M. (eds.) *Educating Economists—The Teagle Discussion on Re-evaluating the Undergraduate Economics Major*, Cheltenham, UK: Edward Elgar, pp. 215- 224.

Sen, A. (2005) *The Argumentative Indian – Writings on Indian Culture, History and Identity.* London: Penguin.

Sen, A. (2010) *The Idea of Justice.* London: Penguin.

Söderbaum, P. (2008) *Understanding Sustainability in Economics- Towards Pluralism in Economics,* London: Earthscan.

Söderbaum, P. and Brown, J. (2011) 'Pluralism and democracy in political economics', *Int. J. Pluralism and Economics Education*, 2, 3: 240–243.

The Economist (2012) 'The Higgs-boson. Gotcha!', July 7th, pp. 67-68.

van Staveren, I. (2011) 'Mind and matter: developing pluralist development economics', *Int. J.Pluralism and Economics Education*, 2, 2: 120–144.

Zola, E. (2007) *The Belly of Paris.* Oxford, UK: Oxford University Press.

Part Five

Conclusions

Moving forward

Maria Alejandra Madi and Jack Reardon

1 Introduction

At the beginning of Dante's poem *Inferno*, the pilgrim despairs, "Midway on our life's journey, I found myself in dark woods, the right road lost" (1994, Canto 1, lines 1-2). Likewise today's economics students find themselves in a similar situation: in dark woods, the right road lost. Trying to understand complex and multi-faceted problems, students despair that economics is no longer helpful. Our students realize that problems like global warming are complex and multi-faceted, requiring multiple views, along with the ability to dialogue and communicate. In reformulating economics, isn't it best to equip our students with the best tools to enable them to solve our economic problems – problems which they did not create? Isn't it best to teach them to listen, to dialogue and to work with others? To continue to teach one view is to proselytize, but in order to solve the problems of our generation we need educated citizens, not proselytes. We need pluralism; we need to be rethinking economics, and we need a new curriculum.

Our book is certainly not the first to criticize economics or economics education by any means. Thorstein Veblen (1898) for example, wrote a blistering critique of neoclassical economics, with the self-explanatory title, "Why is Economics Not an Evolutionary Science." And a few years earlier Henry George wrote:

> "Political Economy has been called the dismal science, and as currently taught, is hopeless and despairing. But this is solely because she has been degraded and shackled; her truths dislocated; her harmonies ignored, the world she utter gagged in her mouth and her protest against wrong turned into an endorsement of injustice" (1879 [1948]).

We hope this volume will add to the current debate, will spark new ideas and lead directly to new curriculum design. Education is too important to be left

241

to economists; after all, education is "the most vital of all resources" (Schumacher, 1989: 84). Indeed "education is our most important function as human beings: it is an investment in ourselves, future generations and the planet" (Reardon, 2009: 267). Reforming economics education should be our top priority.

Perhaps we can take a lesson or two from William Lloyd Garrison, a strident abolitionist who founded the newspaper *The Liberator* in 1831, vowing to continue publishing until the abominable practice of slavery was abolished. In the inaugural edition he wrote, "I am aware that many object to the severity of my language; but is there not cause for severity? I will be as harsh as truth, and as uncompromising as justice. On this subject I do not wish to think, or speak, or write, with moderation. No! No!"

While we admire Garrison's uncompromising passion, we also need to remember his patience, his understanding that such a revolution takes time, and that one individual acting alone cannot change society. It is necessary for all of us interested in rethinking and reconceptualizing economics to work together, to disseminate new ideas, and to keep in mind the ultimate objective of rethinking economics.

2 Thoughts towards a reformulation

What is wrong with the existing economics education? This question is the axle of the contributions in Part Two – *Challenging the current economics curriculum.* Showing concern with the trajectory of the existing economics education, Lars Pålsson Syll highlights that when persuing today's more widely used economics textbooks, it turns out that the theories and models presented are imaginary worlds. He concludes that economics textbook writers ought to do some ontological reflection and heed Keynes's warnings on using laboratory thought-models in economics. Indeed, economic cannot be taught in a socio-economic vacuum. Following Pålsson Syll's concern on the current economics curriculum, Asad Zasman also emphasizes that the first step in curriculum change requires the creation of teachers who have a clear understanding of the epistemological, ethical, moral and social challenges that we face. He proposes that these teachers must de-program themselves to cleanse minds and hearts in order to change their ways of thinking and acquire new ways of looking at human beings and the world.

In Part Three – *Current gaps in economics curriculum*, Dow, Roncaglia, Ietto-Gillies, Madi and Acocella explore different methodological, theoretical and research topics that are missing in economics curriculum. Considering the methodology challenges, Sheila Dow argues that a methodologically aware approach, aimed to explain the different philosophical underpinnings of competing theories, can be taught implicitly by making it clear that economics is up for discussion. Remembering the challenges of the Scottish students in the eighteenth century, Dow proposes that the philosophical material could be made more accessible by pursuing it in terms of topical issues, especially debates in society at large on economic topics. Some suggestions are highlighted: for example different theoretical explanations for the 2007-09 financial crisis could be analysed in broad terms by exploring the assumptions made about the nature of the economy and which are the acceptable forms of argument. Similarly, the millennium generated a lot of reflection on the state of economics. However, she warns that more advanced economics would need to be taught to the students with this methodological awareness in mind. As a result, they will be better able to engage in argument and understand better the arguments in the literature and in society more widely.

Reinforcing the need to improve the openness to confrontation in with different points of view, Alessandro Roncaglia emphasises the importance of history of economic thought (HET) and the absence of definitive truths but consciousness of degrees of superior or inferior quality in economic analysis. In undergraduate education, HET has a crucial democratic role, confronting students with the idea that there are different approaches to economics, and providing them with some notion of the conceptual foundations of such approaches. This helps towards a better understanding and evaluation of formalised theories/models, thus constituting a prerequisite for serious study of economic theory. Roncaglia warns that current orthodox economics – a-historically interpreted as model building and applied analysis based on econometric exercises – is losing ground to business schools and to faculties of political and social sciences, and especially to sociology –

which, a century ago, was a sub-discipline internal to economics itself. He concludes that "Economics without HET is a body without soul".

Showing concern with the need to move forward a real-world curriculum, Grazia Ietto-Gillies argues for the inclusion of a study on transnational corporations (TNCs) for both the micro and macro curriculum. Her approach enphasises the strategic behaviour of companies and particularly strategies towartds labour. Moreover, TNCs derive specific advantages from strategic behaviour when used in the context of nation-states competing against each other for the attraction of foreign direct investment. She encourages collaboration with other disciplines as a way towards a better understanding of strategic behaviour.

Indeed, economics education needs to face the challenge to reshape hierarchies within the effort of searching for the nexus between economics, history, logic, political science and sociology. Taking into account the teaching of finance in a real world perspective, Maria Alejandra Madi proposes the study of the evolution and dynamics of the financial markets within a historical framework that is conditioned by social and political forces. Regarding the transformation of the economics curriculum, the consideration of a pluralist set of visions – Marx, Schumpeter, Keynes, Kalecki, Tobin, Friedman, Minsky among others – could be fruitful toward the challenge to comprehend the structure and dynamics of contemporary capitalism where financial issues play a relevant role. Madi concludes that the ability of a real world economist to deal with "mankind and the ordinary events business of life" should be preceded by the recognition of the boundaries of economics and of its political dimensions as a particular knowledge oriented to social and economic development issues.

The importance of the economist in public policy issues is addressed by Nicola Acocella who underlines the relevance of teaching economic policy as a consistent and autonomous discipline in economics curriculum. More recently the core of the discipline, which seemed to be defeated by the Lucas critique, has not only been shown to be exempt from this critique, when used in a strategic context, but also to be able to produce new interesting results in this context, in so far as existence, uniqueness or multiplicity of the game equilibrium is concerned. In the current setting,

244

The economics curriculum: towards a radical reformulation

Acocella identifies factors that would certainly run counter to some reaffirmation, at least in theoretical terms, of the power of the public institutions when endowed with a sufficient number of instruments and well managed to tame market forces and address them to desirable outcomes.

The recognition of the relevance of the social and political forces in a historical perspective in order to understand economics is an outstanding contribution of Part Four – *Laying the foundations for a future economics curriculum* – that emphasizes what economics major should know. David Hemenway underlines that the analysis of what is good policy (and even of how to vote wisely) presupposes that students know the main features of the world in which they live. In fact, his concern relies on the education of "better economists and better citizens" in order to face the growing economic power of the markets in shaping production and consumption patterns. As a result, issues related to social and political power need to be considered in any attempt to improve the understanding of microeconomics.

Arturo Hermann also emphasizes the need to promote a roadmap of policy action specifically targeted at the solution of the most urgent economic and social problems. Considering the fundamentals of social change, Hermann's interdisciplinary approach proposes a deep interaction between heterodox economics and psychoanalysis. In his view psychoanalysis provides a thorough understanding of the complex motivations, conflicts and orientations of persons in their individual and collective unfolding. Indeed, in his approach, a proper acknowledgement of the significance for the person of establishing sound interpersonal relations will help devise more effective and far reaching policy actions where the economic, social and cultural features and challenges should be taken into account.

Reinforcing the need of a *real world economics curriculum*, Paul Ormerod explores the importance of rethinking the teaching of macroeconomics. Ormerod highlights theories and methodologies that could enhance a more fruitful teaching of human behaviour and decision making. Besides, he emphasizes the importance of economic history. Also Constantine Passaris underlines that the design of the economics curriculum must reflect the lessons of our collective economic history. In his opinion, it is urgent to correlate the academic mission and the teaching of economics with the new global economic landscape where structural changes and evolutionary directions have occurred in the recent past. Passaris considers pluralism and diversity in theoretical approaches to economics as the foundations for innovative ideas towards rethinking the value of interdisciplinarity, the internationalization of the curriculum and the role of quantitative economics. In this context, modern economic pedagogy must serve as a catalyst for transformational change.

At the end of Part Four, Jack Reardon's proposal also emphasizes the relevant role of pluralism despite its potential shortcomings and potential liabilities in implementation of any change in economics curriculum. Reardon underlines that we need a new way of thinking that juxtaposes heretofore different ideologies and the social sciences and sciences. In other words, we need a holistic pluralism that goes beyond the traditional disciplines.

3 Being an economist in the 21st century

This book is written with current and future economics students in mind: they will be the economists of the future. One of the main ideas underlined throughout the book is that "being an economist" in the 21st century requires a radical change in the training of economists. A new economics curriculum is needed in order to improve the understanding of the deep interactions between economics and the political forces, the historical process of social change and the features of the human person in his or her integrity.

We hope the book will stimulate further debate by both students and professional economists – whether academics or not – on how to progress towards a new curriculum. The book makes suggestions for new areas to be included. Not all the relevant areas have been included here. Notably, there is no chapter on inequality.[1] We see as very relevant the inclusion of elements on measurement, determinants and effects of income and wealth inequality. It is an area neglected by orthodox economics. Robert Lucas (2004) has famously written that: 'Of the tendencies that are harmful to sound economics, the most seductive and in my opinion the most

---

[1] We are grateful to Grazia Ietto-Gillies for this suggestion.

poisonous, is to focus on the question of distribution' ....Its relevance has been acknowledged by unorthodox writers for some time (Galbraith, 1998; 2012). The recent phenomenal success of Piketty (2014) shows that the wider public is also interested in this issue. The wide commentary on Piketty's book including a whole issue of the *Real-World Economics Review* (2014: 69), one of the online, open-access journals of the World Economics Association is evidence of interest in the economics profession.[2]

If all of our desired reforms are actually implemented what will economics education look like? Will everyone be satisfied? Will there be vestiges of the old regime? Will the new education be a radical new revolution, or simply changing of the guard?

Although revolution is "a loose word with a wide range in popular usage and charged with emotional content" (Brinton, 1965: 3-4), we might look to a systematic study of revolutions in order to illuminate our path in rethinking economics. We believe that those of us engaged in rethinking or reconceptualizing economics are fomenting a revolution – a revolution of ideas – and understanding how and why they begin, how they unfold, how they sometimes unexpectedly veer off course, how and why they always generate strong counter-revolutions, and how they end, will elucidate a clear path to restoring our way, to help us find "the right road lost." It might be counter-intuitive and perhaps depressing to learn that:

> "our study of revolutions should confirm something that sensible men have always known and that exasperated reformers have occasionally come to admit, at least to themselves—that in some way very important ways the behavior of men changes with a slowness almost comparable to the kind of change the geologist studies" (Brinton, 1965: 244).

---

[2] All the comments published in the RWER, issue number 69, are also available in a separate book. See Fullbrook, E. and Morgan, J. (eds.) (2014) *Piketty's Capital in the Twenty-First Century,* UK: WEA/College Publications.

Maria Alejandra Madi and Jack Reardon

This of course does not mean that our revolution is pre-ordained to failure, that little substantive change will be accomplished. On the contrary it gives us optimism that with concerted help around the globe, our goals of reconceptualizing economics and designing a new economics curriculum can and will be accomplished. We hope this book contributes in one small way to this noble cause. As Sheila Dow notes that an excellent start is being made by the next generation of teachers: the students who are currently actively seeking and promoting curricular reform.

References

Brinton, C. (1965) *The Anatomy of Revolution*, Vintage Books: New York.

Dante (1313 [1994]) *Inferno,* New York: Noonday.

Galbraith, J. K. (2012) *Inequality and Instability: A Study of the World Economy Just Before the Great Crisis*, Oxford: Oxford University Press.

Galbraith, J. K. (1998) *Created Unequal. The Crisis in American Pay* USA: The University of Chicago Press.

George, H. (1879 [1948]) *Progress and Poverty,* New York: Robert Schalkenbach Foundation.

Lucas, R. (2004) 'The industrial revolution: past and future', *2003 Annual Report Essay, Federal Reserve Bank of Minnesota*, May.

Piketty, T. (2014) *Capital in the Twenty-First Century,* Harvard University Press, MA: Belknap Press.

Reardon, J. (ed.) (2009) *Handbook of Pluralist Economics Education*, London: Routledge.

Real-World Economics Review (2014) issue no. 69, http://www.paecon.net/PAEReview/issue69/Parker69.pdf

Schumacher, E.F. (1973 [1989]) *Small is Beautiful- Economics as if People Mattered,* New York: Harper Perennial.

Veblen, T. (1898) 'Why is economics not an evolutionary science?', *Quarterly Journal of Economics*, 12, 4: 373-397.

About the authors

Nicola Acoccela was Full Professor of Economic Policy at Sapienza University of Rome, 1984-2011 and is now retired. His fields of specialisation include: welfare economics, theory of economic policy, policy games, monetary and fiscal policy, European integration and institutions, globalisation, industrial organisation, labour markets and unions. He has intensively published in high-ranking journals and authored a number of books, notably: *Foundations of economic policy. Values and techniques*, Cambridge University Press, 1998, translated also into Chinese, Polish, Croatian; *Economic policy in the age of globalisation*, Cambridge University Press, 2005; (with G. Di Bartolomeo and A. Hughes Hallett), *The theory of economic policy in a strategic context*, Cambridge University Press, 2013. nicola.acocella@uniroma1.it.

Sheila Dow is Emeritus Professor of Economics at the University of Stirling in Scotland and Adjunct Professor of Economics at the University of Victoria in Canada. Her main research interests lie in the history and methodology of economic thought and the theory of money and banking. Recent books are *Economic Methodology: an inquiry*, Oxford University Press 2002, and *Foundations for New Economic Thinking: a collection of essays,* Palgrave Macmillan 2012. She is co-Editor of the WEA's online journal, *Economic Thought*, and co-Convenor of SCEME. Past roles include Chair of the International Network for Economic Method, co-Chair of the Post Keynesian Economics Study Group and special advisor on monetary policy to the UK Treasury Select Committee.
s.c.dow@stir.ac.uk

David Hemenway Ph.D., Professor of Health Policy, is Director of the Harvard Injury Control Research Center. He teaches classes on injury and on economics. He has won ten teaching awards at Harvard School of Public Health. He has written widely on injury prevention, including articles on firearms, violence, suicide, child abuse, motor vehicle crashes, fires, falls and fractures. He headed the pilot for the National Violent Death Reporting System, which provides detailed and comparable information on suicide and homicide. In 2012 he was recognized by the Centers for Disease Control &

Prevention as one of the "twenty most influential injury and violence professionals over the past twenty years".
hemenway@hsph.harvard.edu

Arturo Hermann is Senior Research Fellow at the Italian National Institute of Statistics (ISTAT) Rome, Italy. In his main research fields – Institutional and Keynesian Economics, Theories of Social Justice, Political Economy, Sustainable Development, also considered in their relations with psychology and psychoanalysis – he has authored four books and numerous articles in scholarly Journals. He is a member of important heterodox economics associations – in particular, AFIT, AHE, EAEPE, ICAPE, Green Economics Institute – and regularly participates in their conferences and activities.
ahermann@istat.it.

Grazia Ietto-Gillies is Emeritus Professor of Applied Economics, London South Bank University and visiting research Professor at Birkbeck University of London. Born in Calabria, southern Italy, she was educated at La Sapienza University, at the Massachusetts Institute of Technology. Research Officer at the Instituto Nazionale per lo Studio della Congiuntura (ISCO) in Rome; Lecturer at the University of Siena and at London South Bank University; Visiting Professorships at The Open University; King's College London. She is one of the founders of the World Economics Association. She has been Associate Editor of *Transnational Corporations*. She has contributed to several edited volumes and journals and made presentations at many international institutions. She has authored five books and many articles in academic journals. Her research interests include: economics of international business (theories of international production; globalization; effects of activities of transnational corporations; innovation and internationalization; a reinterpretation of Hymer's contribution; development of an index of the degree of internationalization; conceptual issues in the demarcation between services v manufactures; transnationals and the economics curriculum); Open Peer Review systems; economics and politics of the Third Way; methodological issues in economics; boundaries of the firm; innovation and absorptive capacity.
iettogg@lsbu.ac.uk

Maria Alejandra Madi PhD in Economics and MSc in Philosophy. Avocational Lecturer at Steinbes University Berlin, Co-editor of the Word Economics Association Pedagogy Blog, Assistant Editor of the *International Journal of Pluralism and Economics Education*. Currently, she is also Director of the Ordem dos Economistas do Brasil and Counselor of the Conselho Regional dos Economistas do Brasil-SP. Former Professor at the University of Campinas, Brazil (1983-2012) and coordinator of the undergraduate course in Economics (2004-2006). Her career includes visiting professorships at the University of Manitoba (2008) and the University of Kassel (2010). More recently, besides co-authoring chapter books edited by the Global Labor University, she has co-edited some of the Green Economic Institute books, including *The Greening of Global Finance* and *The Greening of Latin America*. Her research interests include finance, economic development and social justice.
alejandra_madi@yahoo.com.br

Lars Pålsson Syll received a PhD in economic history in 1991 and a PhD in economics in 1997. He is presently professor of social science at Malmö University. His primary research interests are in the philosophy and methodology of economics and critical realist social science. He is the author, among other works, of *Social Choice, Value and Exploitation: an Economic-Philosophical Critique* (in Swedish, 1991), *Utility Theory and Structural Analysis* (1997), *Economic Theory and Method: A Critical Realist Perspective* (in Swedish, 2001), *The Dismal Science* (in Swedish, 2001), *The History of Economic Theories* (in Swedish, fourth ed. 2007), *John Maynard Keynes* (in Swedish, 2007), *An Outline of the History of Economics* (in Swedish, 2011), as well as numerous articles in scientific journals.
lars.palsson-syll@mah.se

Constantine Passaris is Professor of Economics at the University of New Brunswick (Canada), an Onassis Foundation Fellow (Greece) and a Research Affiliate of the Prentice Institute for Global Population & Economy at the University of Lethbridge (Canada). He is listed in the International Who's Who in Education, the International Directory of Experts in Refugee Resettlement and Integration and the Canadian Who's Who. He has served as a member of the Economic Council of Canada, Chairman of the New

About the authors

Brunswick Human Rights Commission, President of the Atlantic Multicultural Council and President of the New Brunswick Multicultural Council. He has also served as President of the Canadian Association of Statutory Human Rights Agencies, Chairman of the New Brunswick Advisory Board on Population Growth and as an advisor to the Canadian Commission for UNESCO. In 2012, he was conferred the Queen Elizabeth II Diamond Jubilee Medal for his exceptional contributions to New Brunswick and Canada and in 2014 he received the academic title of Onassis Foundation Fellow for his contributions to international public policy.
passaris@unb.ca

Paul Ormerod is Visiting Professor in the Centre for Decision Making Uncertainty, University College, London and a partner in Volterra Partners LLP in London. He is the author of the best-selling books *Death of Economics* (1994), *Butterfly Economics* (1998), *Why Most Things Fail* (2005) and *Positive Linking* (2012). He studied economics at Cambridge and did the MPhil in economics at Oxford. He was elected a Fellow of the British Academy of Social Sciences in 2006 and was awarded a DSc honoris causa in 2009 by the University of Durham for 'the distinction of your contribution to the discipline of economics'.
p.ormerod@ucl.ac.uk.

Jack Reardon is a Professor in the School of Business at Hamline University. He is founding editor of the *International Journal of Pluralism and Economics Education*. His most recent book, *The Handbook of Pluralist Economics Education*, was published by Routledge in 2009. He is currently writing a principles of economics textbook with Maria Madi and Molly Scott Cato to be published by Pluto Press in 2015. His research interests include energy and the environment, economic education and labour economics. He also lectures at the Birla Institute of Management Technology in Bhubaneswar, India.
jackreardon864@gmail.com

Alessandro Roncaglia is Professor of Economics, Sapienza University of Rome; editor of Moneta e Credito and PSL Quarterly Review, member of the Accademia Nazionale dei Lincei. He has served (2010-2013) as President of Società Italiana degli Economisti. Among his books, translated in various

languages: *The Wealth of Ideas* (CUP, 2005), *Piero Sraffa* (Palgrave Macmillan, 2009). The Italian edition of his book *The wealth of ideas. A history of economic thought*, later published in an expanded edition in English with Cambridge University Press, has won the 2002 Jerome Blanqui Award of the European Society for the History of Economic Thought.
alessandro.roncaglia@uniroma1.it

Asad Zasman. BS Math from MIT (1974), MS Stat (1976), and Ph.D. Economics (1978) from Stanford. He has taught at leading universities including Columbia,U. Penn., Johns Hopkins, Cal. Tech. and Bilkent. Currently he is Vice Chancellor of Pakistan Institute of Development Economics. His textbook *Statistical Foundations of Econometric Techniques* (Academic Press, NY, 1996) is widely used as a reference in advanced graduate courses. He is managing editor *of International Econometric Review*. He has many publications in top ranked journals like Annals of Statistics, Journal of Econometrics, Econometric Theory, Journal of Labor Economics, etc. These have been widely cited, with more than 500 citations as per Google Scholar.
asadzaman@alum.mit.edu.

www.ingramcontent.com/pod-product-compliance
Lightning Source LLC
Chambersburg PA
CBHW070350200326
41518CB00012B/2190